MIRACLES AT THE JESUS OAK

HISTORIES OF THE SUPERNATURAL IN REFORMATION EUROPE

CRAIG HARLINE

Yale UNIVERSITY PRESS
New Haven & London

First published in paperback in 2011 by Yale University Press.
Originally published in hardcover in 2003 by Doubleday, a division of Random House, Inc.

Chapter 1 appeared in different form as "Miracles and This World:
The Battle for the Jesus Oak," in *The Archive for Reformation History* (2002).

Yale University Press books may be purchased in quantity for
educational, business, or promotional use. For information, please e-mail
sales.press@yale.edu (U.S. office) or sales@yaleup.co.uk (U.K. office).

Book design by Gretchen Achilles

Printed in the United States of America.

Library of Congress Cataloging-in-Publication Data
Harline, Craig.
Miracles at the Jesus Oak : histories of the supernatural in Reformation Europe / Craig Harline.
p. cm.
Originally published: New York : Doubleday, a division of Random House, 2003.
ISBN 978-0-300-16702-3 (pbk.)
1. Miracles—History—17th century. 2. Belgium—Religious life and customs.
3. Miracles—History of doctrines—17th century. 4. Catholic Church—Belgium—
History—17th century. I. Title. II. Title: Histories of the supernatural in Reformation Europe.
BX1524.H37 2011
231.7'30949309032—dc22 2010032321

A catalogue record for this book is available from the British Library.

This paper meets the requirements of ANSI/NISO Z39.48-1992 (Permanence of Paper).

10 9 8 7 6 5 4 3 2 1

CONTENTS

PREFACE TO THE PAPERBACK EDITION

The reprinting of this book in paperback will, I hope, make it more accessible than ever to those for whom it was always intended: college students and general readers.

Interest in miracles past and present seems as strong today as when the hardcover volume appeared nearly a decade ago—which isn't surprising. For though the body of this book is devoted to only one great century of miracles in Western history (the seventeenth), and though the epilogue suggests the continuing vitality of miracles in the present, I can hardly think of a time when miracles did *not* fire the Western imagination, or imaginations elsewhere, for that matter.

Hundreds, perhaps thousands, of miracle-working shrines were established in Europe during the seventeenth century, yet the industrializing nineteenth century, when the world was supposedly disenchanted, surely rivaled it and might have claimed even more heavenly visions (it's hard to count such things with precision). Nor did miracles cease during the Enlightened eighteenth century, as evident in the records of shrine after shrine around Europe, and in the costly elaboration of Rococo church after Rococo church frequented by alms-bearing pilgrims. Very recently, some health and mental health professionals report incorporating healing prayer into their treatment of the ill. And long ago were of course the miracles of the Middle Ages and of ancient Christianity, when the basic ways that Westerners came to think and feel about miracles largely took shape.

But if the allure of miracles has always been present, so has skepticism about them, even during what we might imagine to be the most unwaveringly devout centuries. Sixteen hundred years ago, Saint Augustine spent a great deal of energy trying to persuade his contemporaries that miracles were still occurring all around them, just as in "ancient times"—the more recent versions merely weren't as publicized, or recognized, he insisted, but they were certainly as wondrous. Indeed, there is a tendency in many societies to somehow imagine that miracles made more sense, or were more trustworthy, or more spectacular, in past times. But then the years pass and the smoke clears and a new string of miracles, some of a brand new variety, has emerged again for later generations to ponder.

This book treats only one age of miracles, and one place, but it is meant to provoke reflection about miracles in other ages and places, including our own—if not through absolute parallel, then through equally valuable absolute contrast. I have kept the original text intact for this edition, though were I starting to write it now I would of course incorporate insights from the latest studies, including a spate of them about Protestant forms of the miraculous. And I might add one small detail to the anecdote told in the epilogue, about the injury I suffered while walking to the shrine at the Sharp Hill.

Left out of the original story, which was already embarrassing enough, was the account of my visit to the doctor the next day. He sat down next to me, had a look at my swollen foot, and asked how I'd done it. I feared that if I told him I'd hurt it by walking seventeen miles to the Sharp Hill, along the old pilgrim route of the seventeenth century, he would think me an odd sort of religious fanatic. Who except a zealot would do that nowadays? What foreigner, except a zealot, had ever even heard of the place? What university professor would interrupt his precious weekend for such a thing, except a zealot? Thus I tried to affect a doctor-to-doctor tone, explaining in the doctor's native Dutch, with as much sophistication and fluency as I could muster, that as I was writing a book about miracles I had thought it might be instructive to engage in a sort of anthropological exercise of walking the road that pilgrims used to walk—but by no means was I a pilgrim myself: it was simply a long hike. He listened, reflected a few seconds, and then without another word put the cursor next to the prompt "Cause of Injury" and typed in, as I watched: "Pilgrimage to the Sharp Hill."

Though deflated, because reduced to just another simple-minded patient, I had to admit that his description was probably the truth after all.

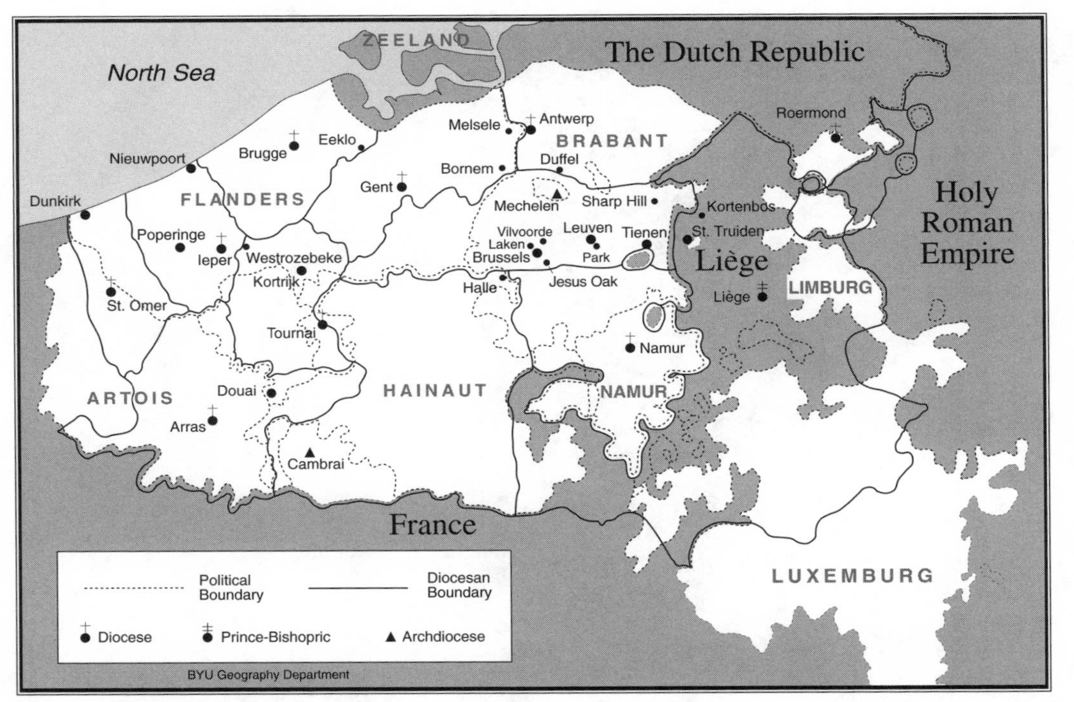

The Spanish Netherlands After 1629

PROLOGUE

An Abbey in Belgium, in Summer. The tall, kindly prior greets me in the parlor, where I have been instructed to wait, and where the walls are in eighteenth-century green. Because the prior is also the archivist, it is he who leads me through immense doors into the private domain of the monks, and toward the precious documents of his dying abbey.

Down the cloistered hallway, past the barren garden, past endless portraits of the abbey's distinguished superiors (over eight hundred years' worth in all), we at last reach the heavy double doors of the archive. The prior turns the key, pulls on the first door, then pushes in the second. It groans open, slowed by ancient hinges and the uneven settling of equally ancient floorboards. We walk through, into a world that is no more.

Beneath a towering, inefficient ceiling stand rows of yellowish calfskin registers, untidy heaps of vellum charters, and open chests containing human skulls and other once revered relics, all covered in everlasting layers of dust. The sense of another time is so overpowering that it renders invisible the room's steel bookshelves, iron radiators, electric bulbs, and any other hint that there had ever occurred on this earth such a thing as the Industrial Revolution. Awestruck, I walk slowly behind the prior, toward the single, large reading table, located under a southern window; unlike most archives, which herd researchers into bare, sterile reading areas, away from fragile documents, this one sets you down in the middle of them. Because I am the sole researcher today, and most days, I have my pick of the straw-bottomed, relentlessly straight-backed chairs around the table, all built for shorter people of less pampered centuries.

After helping me decipher the archive's old, handwritten inventory, and after bringing the documents I wish to see, the prior returns to his duties elsewhere in the abbey. Closing the doors behind him, he leaves me alone, in uncommon stillness. For the next several hours sounds are few and thus startling—a rooster crowing, the wind rustling towering trees, the anachronistic clicking of a computer keyboard. It is here in the archive of the abbey called Park, where the table's dim lamp is inferior to the window's natural light, where the view of the abbey's placid lakes and crumbling brick walls would make any of the Romantic poets feel quite at home, and where the very survival of monks and documents for so many centuries is itself dramatic and wondrous, that I find the Jesus Oak. And it is here, amid the papers of the Jesus Oak and the otherworldly aura of the abbey, that I not coincidentally begin to sense how people of an age long past might have understood their miracles.

I had long been interested in miracles past, largely because they seemed far more common than miracles present. But I decided to study them closely only a few weeks earlier, after laying eyes on a fat seventeenth-century manuscript located in another Belgian archive.

This manuscript overflowed with riveting testimony by hundreds of witnesses who claimed to have experienced miracles—from spectacular cures to the conquering of demons to outbursts of heavenly song. More and more such miracle books, also from the seventeenth century, soon came to my attention as well, full of two- and three-page stories by an endless string of enthusiastic witnesses. Yet the more such accounts I read, the more I wondered how to study them. What do you do with a thousand three-page stories?

I soon discovered that there were already plenty of models from which to choose, beginning with the four most venerable approaches to miracles over the centuries: (1) accept that the stories happened as told and simply recount them, for inspirational or commercial purposes, or both; (2) accept the stories as told but then explain away any supposedly miraculous causes as "natural" or "demonic," based on scientific or theological concepts from my own world; (3) dispute the stories as told on grounds that they are unbelievable, either in the events themselves or because all-too-fallible witnesses and scribes, deliberately and otherwise, distort things; and (4) use the stories to help establish the latest absolutely foolproof definition of "miracle," good for all times and places, forever and ever, amen. There were more recent models too: I might don a white lab coat and start organizing stories by time, place, or motif, then subject them to the most excruciating sorts of statistical manipulation. Or I could use the endless physical ailments reported in the stories to assess the age's medical understanding and problems.

Each of these influenced me in one way or another, but what influenced me most was yet another model, based on a seemingly simple question hardly original with me: namely, what did miracles mean to people of the time? This question did not concern itself with the inevitable laboring over whether an event was "truly" miraculous (by the questioner's implicitly objective standards), but with trying to understand how people in and around the event saw things.

It was harder than it looked. Beyond the built-in metaphysical challenges—that despite one's good intentions in trying to understand a past world on its own terms it is still quite possible to get things wrong, not to mention that sources are of course imperfect and incomplete—there was the rather practical matter of having to read many more documents than merely the miracle stories that first inspired me, for these stories were saturated with the beliefs, assumptions, settings, and practices of another age. In other words, these miracles, like all others, occurred in a specific context, not a timeless vacuum. If I wanted to write a living, breathing cultural history of miracles, grounded in earthly time and place, and viewed as much as possible through contemporary eyes, then I would have to learn not only about miracles but the world that produced them. And the world that interested me so deeply was seventeenth-century Europe, especially the tiny corner of Europe known as the Spanish Netherlands (roughly modern Belgium).

Among the golden ages and places of miracles in Christian history, here was one of the brightest. For although the Middle Ages are most often associated with miracles and saints and God, in fact more miracle-commemorating shrines were born in Europe's seventeenth century than in any other. Surely this was due in part to forces that had also been present in previous surges of miracles: decades of devastating war and the consequent longing to purify the world with things divine; a sense of human helplessness and desire for divine aid in the face of continuing epidemics of the plague; and exciting discoveries of new relics in the catacombs of Rome and their rapid spread around Europe. But what made this latest surge stand out was yet another force: the tearing asunder of Christianity, into Catholics and Protestants, after 1520, in the cataclysm called the Reformation—a cataclysm that brought about not only new sorts of wars, but bigger arguments about miracles than ever before, and thus more documents to boot.

Nowhere was this more true than in such fiercely contested areas as the Spanish Netherlands, which sat precariously just on the Catholic side of the shaky border dividing Europe's Catholic south from Protestant north. Between 1568 and 1648 all the Netherlands were embroiled, like much of Europe, in war—in this case civil war against their sovereign, the king of Spain, with whom they had assorted political and religious differences. By the violent end, the Netherlands were, just like Christian Europe, cut in half: the northern provinces won their independence from Spain, and were called the United Provinces, or Dutch Republic, with Calvinism the new public religion; the southern provinces were reconquered by Spanish troops and made Catholic again, and thus called the Spanish Netherlands. But while the fighting raged, this tidy outcome was hardly apparent. The political (and therefore the religious) boundaries kept shifting, and in the midst of such uncertainty discussions of religion, including miracles, grew terrifically hot.

The mountain of documents produced by these discussions, in the Spanish Netherlands and elsewhere, had made clear from the start one of the most basic meanings of miracles in the age of Reformation: Catholics all over Europe generally believed in them, and Protestants did not (at least not those of the Catholic sort). Hence, miracles were even more important to Catholic identity after the Reformation than before. And in some ways they were more important still along the northern front of Catholicism, where Protestants watched intently over shoulders, than they were in the southern and more famous Catholic bulwarks of Spain or Italy. Here was a big reason the border-rubbing Spanish Netherlands (or a region such as Bavaria) seemed an ideal place to study miracles—and many other matters of religion—in this time: its miracles, and its religious environment, would have been familiar enough to other Catholics to serve as a kind of microcosm, yet those miracles and that environment were peculiarly intense.

Besides the Catholic-Protestant divide, these bounteous documents have also begun to reveal another, more subtle meaning of miracles: that they were understood in quite different ways even among Catholics—even in sensitive border areas where unity was crucial. In other words, though virtually all Catholics assumed the reality of miracles, their particular notions on the subject were hardly one. Catholic authorities wrote as much as they did about miracles not only to confound Protestants but to assert control over their own other-believing flocks. These same authorities also disagreed among themselves—sometimes precisely because of disagreements with Protestants! And lay Catholics appeared in documents about miracles to subdue not only Protestants but fellow believers.

This very variety within Catholicism—this sometimes subtle,

sometimes bombastic arguing about defining and controlling and proclaiming and seeking miracles—was what I wanted most to explore, and finding the documents on the Jesus Oak today in the abbey gives me an idea how to go about it.

These documents, I soon realize, resulted from a big argument between Catholics. Two neighboring parishes battled to control a new wonder-working shrine that lay on unclaimed ground between them. Both parishes agreed that the miracles came from God, but could not agree at all on the question of whom God wanted to be in charge (Chapter 1).

Here was the sort of context I was looking for, featuring not only miracles but elements of geography, this-worldly interests, and flesh-and-blood personalities. And here was confirmation that to understand the miracles of another world I needed to look not only at the miracles themselves but all around them—just as when trying to see in the dark one's vision improves by looking to the side of an object, or around it, rather than straight on.

While immersed in the papers of the Jesus Oak, I decide to dig around for similar sources on still other aspects of miracle-making, and present them as a series of related, highly focused studies (or "micro-histories") under a single cover. Within weeks these sources begin to fall into my lap—through luck, or miracle, or because now I know what to look for.

In a much more crowded state archive in Gent, where I am actually required to fill out official forms and hand them over to efficient clerks in bluish coats, I find two possibilities. One stresses the roles of public opinion and theology in miracles: a woman who had no milk for her fourteenth child was cured at a local shrine, but Church leaders refused to call it miraculous—for reasons apparently unrelated to the cure itself (Chapter 2). Another addresses the problem, floating around in all miracle-believing societies, of the possibility of fraud, through the story of frustrated custodians at one shrine who began diverting pilgrims headed to a more popular shrine (Chapter 3).

Sources for the final two stories appear the next year, in the diocesan archive of Mechelen. One gives an extraordinarily nuanced face to the well-studied underworld of miracles, through the woeful adventures of a woman who desecrated the Eucharist, or Holy Sacrament, and then in breathtaking detail explained why, revealing along the way her unorthodox views of the miraculous (Chapter 4). And the last addresses that world's understanding of nature, which was basic to its understanding of miracles, through the arrest for heresy of Jan Baptista van Helmont—well known among historians of science for his legacy to medicine, but better known in his own lifetime for his less enduring, highly threatening views on natural healing (Chapter 5).

In sum, these five fresh stories, though wonderfully idiosyncratic in particulars, highlight what seem to me universal contexts of miracle-making in early modern Catholicism (and even beyond): the constants of place, images, relics, and the Eucharist, and the variables of rival theologies, rival views of nature, and rival this-worldly interests. Each story focuses on a specific context or two, but all play out against the same backdrop of miracle-hungry Catholicism during the Reformation (some even share the same characters).*

Of course there are still other ways to look at miracles: a more

**Chapter 5 has been told before in part, but is told here with new perspective, new sources, and an eye to general readers rather than specialists in the history of science. Parts of Chapter 1 were told in different form in a small Belgian journal of local history. The other three have never been told.*

systematic study might be useful, but in the end I prefer depth to breadth. There are other contexts that might be explored, or explored more fully: Protestant views, for instance, are more complex than at first glance, but I decide to focus on the even more complex world of Catholicism. There are a thousand other illuminating stories that might be told: I have files full of these myself, but eventually I choose five that seem to work best together. And finally there are countless other archives that might be searched: in many of these I still labor happily, but to sharpen most keenly my sense of other worlds I always return in mind or body to the abbey of Park, with its weathered buildings and calm lakes, where I first pondered miracles, and where I first learned of a shrine called the Dear Jesus Oak.

ONE

MIRACLES AT THE JESUS OAK

A HOLY PLACE

In the Soniën Woods, near Brussels, around 1630. The grocer Peter van Kerckhoven traveled often on the rutted dirt highway that ran southeast from his home in Brussels. Most of the time his destination was the middling village of Overijse, some eight miles away, where he was born more than fifty years before and where in his spare time he oversaw the family properties. Though the journey was by now long familiar, it was also unfailingly stressful, for it required him to pass through the Soniën Woods, deep and dark.

Despite their lofty overlord, the king of Spain himself, these royal woods were, like most woods, notoriously dangerous. Peter feared their lushness, with oaks, beeches, and elms so dense that not even a midsummer sun shone through, for this was what hid unknown enemies. He no doubt trembled at their peace, which magnified and made threatening even the smallest sound. And who would have blamed him for ignoring the freshness of their air, so less pungent than the unrelieved streets of Brussels?

For working most of all on his mind were the stories. He knew well the gruesome tales of ill-fated travelers who, on this very road, had been shot, stabbed, or strung up by professional thieves or disbanded groups of soldiers in between campaigns. To make matters worse, he knew also, like all the world around him, that such out-of-the-way places were favorite haunts of the devil and his demons. Even when companions were along, foreboding and apprehension, not calm, dominated Peter's passage through the woods.

That was why, during yet another nerve-racking trip through the Soniën, he resolved to do what many Catholics of his time did to combat dread: he would sacralize this place, or make it holy, by affixing to it a sacred object. This centuries-old practice reassured the anxious of God's presence even in the most forsaken places, thus confirming that He was mightier than the devil even on the devil's own turf. In fact, long before Peter some other believer had had the same idea, and had attached a crucifix to the most famous landmark along the forest road: a gigantic, gnarly, lightning-riddled old tree called the Devil's Oak, used for centuries as a meeting place by hunters and thieves. As long as it bore its crucifix, the oak in the forest seemed less sinister. For decades comforted travelers uttered hopeful prayers as they passed by, and even began calling the tree the Dear Jesus Oak. But by Peter's day this crucifix was gone, and he decided it was time to replace it.

After that decisive trip, Peter went to a market in Brussels and bought a small wooden statue of the Virgin, about a foot tall, with the Christ child in her left arm, and vowed to God that he would hang it on the Jesus Oak. But he grew busy and forgot his vow; children visiting his home even played with the statue as if it were a doll. Only when dying from the plague in late 1635 did Peter finally remember. Fully aware that unfulfilled vows were a danger to one's soul, but lacking both time and inclination to have his vow waived by a priest, a fading Peter whispered his secret to his grown daughter, who in turn told her brother Philip, who understood what he must do. Finally, in early 1637, Philip and two craftsmen placed the statue in a small casing, carried it to the forest, then climbed a ladder they had brought along and set the statue on the Jesus Oak.

Just as Peter van Kerckhoven had hoped, travelers began noticing the new image, and therefore crossed themselves or uttered a short prayer when passing by. Criminals must have noticed as well, but did they think twice before committing their evil deeds in the Soniën Woods? Whatever the case, by early 1642 the image was known enough that some people began attaching even greater importance to it: now they traveled to the newly sacred place for the express purpose of seeking divine aid.

The first person said to receive such aid was a three-year-old boy named Michel, from the village of Overijse, and afflicted since birth with a fist-sized hernia. His mother, Barbel Reyaerts, had tried other shrines and undoubtedly other remedies before visiting the Oak. But only at the Jesus Oak, on March 24, after engaging in the usual rituals of prayer and candle-lighting, did she find a cure for Michel. Gratefully she left behind the customary token of remembrance—in this case the wrappings she had long placed around his little body—as a witness to others that a cure had happened here.

Word soon spread, to family members and friends, from one village to the next, and a flow of pilgrims to the Jesus Oak began. Thus deep in the woods was born a shrine.

Since the late Roman Empire, a common feature of Christian miracles was their association with a specific place. To some believers this was simply an extension of the doctrine of Incarnation: thus, God had become incarnate in a particular person, at a particular time and place, in Jesus Christ, and it only made sense that He would continue to manifest His presence in still other times and places and ways. Other believers were influenced more by leftover pagan notions about otherworldly powers being concentrated in special locations and objects—including oaks. But however it was learned, just about everyone believed that though God was everywhere, His powers were more evident at some places than at others.

These special places, or shrines, were in turn almost always associated with specific saints, present in their powerful relics or—since the eleventh and twelfth centuries—represented in images of potentially equal power.* The connection of the divine to thousands of specific earthly places and holy objects helped to make God more than an abstraction in Christian minds—and after the Reformation more specifically in Catholic minds. Whatever He may have been in official theology—invisible, three-in-one, and incomprehensible—in everyday practice His powers could be seen,

*Images (in painting or statuary) of Christ and Mary were especially popular, because so few relics of them remained—though at least in the Middle Ages still too many for the tastes of some. For various theologians argued that neither Christ nor the Virgin could have left any relics, because the resurrection of each was perfect. Nevertheless, others allowed that such transitory items as Christ's foreskin, baby teeth, umbilical cord, and shed blood, or Mary's milk and clothing, may indeed have missed the resurrection. Images also increased when relics were hard to come by, as during the Netherlandish war of 1568–1648. Relics and images will be discussed further in Chapters 2 and 3.

heard, touched, smelled, and even tasted at a specially chosen place just down the road. Here people came not only in search of miracles, but to pray, to seek protection from disaster or misfortune, to find forgiveness from sin, and to make or fulfill vows. But the most popular shrines inevitably became so because of some spectacular show of divine power—in other words, a miracle, especially the dramatic cure of an endless array of illnesses.

Many such holy places—in parish or monastic churches, in cathedrals, in minuscule chapels along urban streets or country byways—were made sacred during the Middle Ages. By the time of Peter van Kerckhoven they were therefore hardly new. But what did seem new was the stunning increase of holy places, especially in such war-torn, desecrated areas as the Spanish Netherlands. Though the powers of older shrines were not denied, the new age and all its blasphemous violence called for new miracles, new intermediaries, and new places.

The stories of how these new shrines came to be closely resembled the pious accounts told for medieval shrines—namely, a shrine emerged because God's power showed itself there. Such power might be evident at the very founding, and star a host of otherworldly characters and events. The famous shrine of Loreto, in Italy, for instance, was said to have begun when angels transported across the heavens the house of the Holy Family from the Holy Land. Popular in the seventeenth century was the mysterious appearance of a statue of the Virgin in a tree, usually an oak, where miracles suddenly began to occur. Or miracles might occur, as at the Jesus Oak, through statues set in place by human hands. Whenever it occurred, the essential thing was some convincing manifestation of God's power—no miracle, no shrine.

Also essential in the emergence of a shrine, however, were influences of a decidedly earthly character, such as location, investment, patronage, or personality. These influences were rarely elaborated upon in the official chronicles of shrines because they were considered secondary, or traceable to God anyway—so why belabor them? The chronicler of the Jesus Oak preferred to focus on the place's early miracles rather than its considerable worldly struggles—not because he was unaware of those struggles, but as a matter of emphasis. If God kept his eye on such trifles as sparrows, then believers could safely assume that He was most assuredly in charge of this new holy place, directly and indirectly, and saw not only to the necessary miracles but the right earthly people, conditions, and events.

To whatever extent contemporaries saw the finger of God conducting worldly forces, they grasped perfectly well the immediate importance of those forces in the life of a shrine. They simply made plain their understanding outside of the official histories—in records rarely noised abroad or even preserved at all. But for the Jesus Oak such unnoised records survived in uncommon abundance.

THE BATTLE FOR THE HOLY

June 1–July 5, 1642. After the healing of her son in March 1642, Barbel Reyaerts told her stepmother, Anna Eregiers, about the Jesus Oak. When the fifty-four-year-old Anna developed an unbearable fever, in late May, she too made the three-mile trip from Overijse to the Jesus Oak, prayed before the image of Mary and the Christ child, and on June 1 was suddenly healed.

In gratitude, Anna did more than utter a prayer of thanks or leave a simple object of remembrance. Rather she decided to walk daily to the Oak and sell candles to passersby, in order to raise money to embellish the statue. At its most theological, lighting a candle at a holy place symbolized Christ the light of the world, or the presence of God, but at its most earthbound it was a straightforward, old-fashioned bargain: offering goods in exchange for divine help. Whatever their motives, people bought enough candles from Anna at the Oak that she could afford to hire a carpenter to build a small roof over the already encased image, thus protecting it twice from wind and rain.

After a month of this, Anna had raised enough money to do even more. At four in the morning on July 2, a time of year when the sun rose especially early, she not only walked from Overijse to her customary place at the Jesus Oak but brought along a carpenter to install a post, to which she attached a new and sturdier offer box, in anticipation of even more activity. Anna intended to affix the box to the post each morning, so that pilgrims could drop in their money for candles. At the end of the day she would then carry the box home. That she chose July 2 to expand her little shrine was no accident: it was the feast of the Visitation of Our Dear Lady, and more pilgrims than usual would make the trek to the newly popular site.

By now, however, Anna Eregiers was hardly the only person with designs on the Oak. Most interested of all in the image on the giant tree were two of the villages that lay closest to it: Overijse to the southeast (about three thousand inhabitants) and Tervuren to the north (about one thousand). Each lay some three miles from the Oak, and each had buzzed with excitement since the first healings in March. Much of this excitement was grounded, of course, in the hope a shrine offered to anyone in difficulty. But much came as well from the promise of prestige for those neighbors fortunate enough to be connected to the shrine.

Like every Catholic village, both Tervuren and Overijse already had sacred places within them, most notably a parish church and a chapel or two. But holy places even short distances away were always more alluring than the humdrum home parish. By July 1, when Anna Eregiers was laying her plans, people in each village decided it was now time to tell their particular pastor about the Jesus Oak and urge him to take charge before a rival got there first.

And so, months after the first miracles, the preoccupied pastors of Overijse and Tervuren finally learned about events taking place in the woods. It was a classic pattern that emerged over and over in the history of shrines: villagers initiated things, yet in urging pastors to take control they acknowledged that the church's stamp of approval mattered to them. And while pastors moved a bit more slowly and might have held somewhat different ideas about shrines, they too believed in the reality of divine aid and the desirability of being connected to the holy.

The pastor of Tervuren, Renier Assels, heard from his parishioners first—perhaps because the recent destruction of their church and homes by Dutch troops gave them an even stronger need for divine renewal, and, admittedly, income from a potential shrine. Upon learning the news, the pastor considered the following. The reports of miracles had aroused so much interest that perhaps they were true. A proper shrine required the direction of a priest. The area around the Oak did not belong clearly to any parish. Though the highway on which the Oak stood ran into Overijse, the Oak did stand on the Tervuren side of that highway. And, since begin-

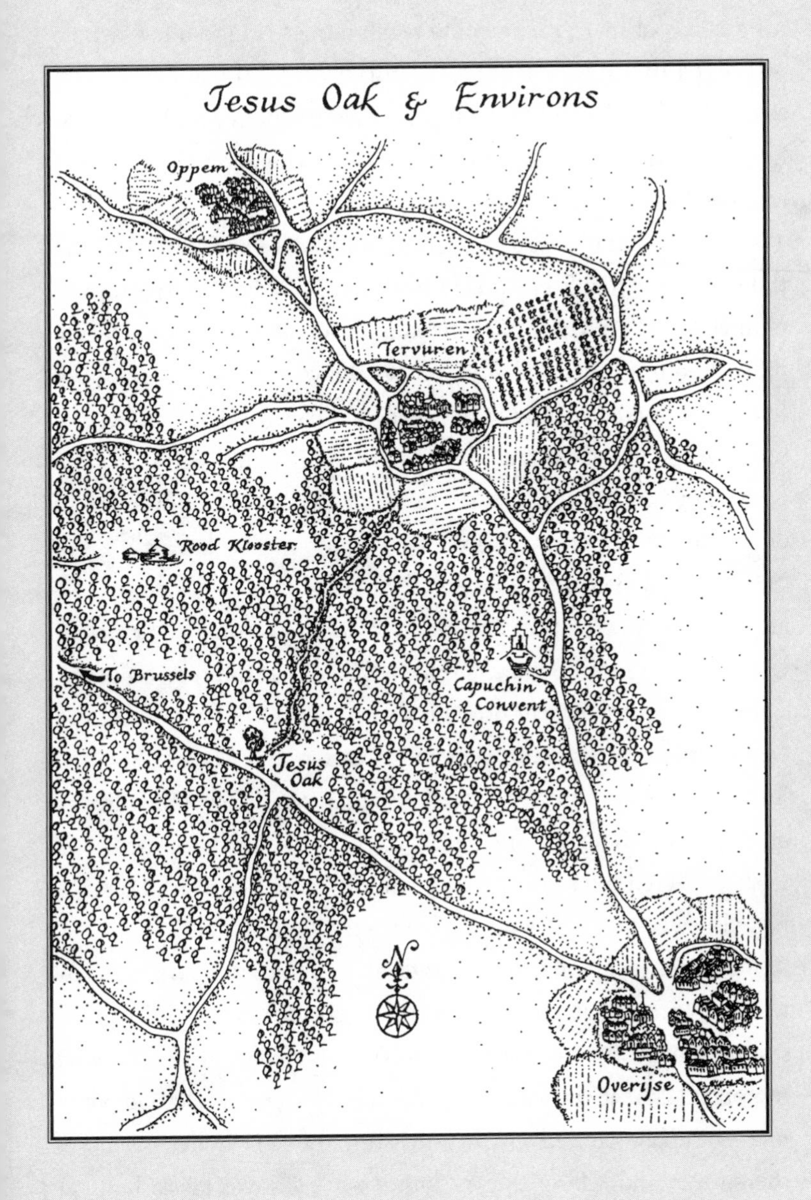
Jesus Oak & Environs
Oppem
Tervuren
Rood Klooster
To Brussels
Capuchin
Convent
Jesus
Oak
N
Overijse

ning as pastor in 1636, he could recall ministering to a few people who lived in a hut near the Oak, thus giving his parish a history there. All these things taken together led the pastor to decide that he had as strong a claim as anyone on the Oak, and would therefore heed his parishioners' wishes.

On July 2, the feast day of the Visitation of Our Dear Lady, and the very day Anna Eregiers set up her new offer box, the pastor announced at High Mass that immediately afterward he would lead a procession to the Jesus Oak. A procession was an old rite that publicly confirmed the bonds between a village and its protecting saints and holy places and God. But today it would also provide a convenient crowd of witnesses for what Pastor Assels intended to do—take control of the shrine.

Followed by many members of the parish, divided according to custom into a column of men and a column of women, the pastor led songs and sent up prayers that helped dispel the tension of the woods and set the proper tone for the occasion (for processions too easily turned, he knew, into mere recreation and worse). Arriving just before noon, the group from Tervuren saw two people already at the Oak: the enterprising Anna Eregiers, who sat near her freshly erected offer box tending things, and a peasant fellow nobody knew, who knelt weeping before the image.

The pastor ignored the peasant and directed the crucial question to Anna. "Are you watching after this shrine, or did you install this offer box, at the instigation of any other pastor?" Anna responded that it was all her own doing. Noticing the crude paper images she had crafted to sell, lamenting the meager decoration of the shrine, and seeing that no other ecclesiastical figure had yet made a claim, Pastor Assels declared solemnly to all that he was now taking charge. He commanded Anna to continue her watch over the shrine, but in his name—and to say so to anyone who might ask.

Surely by this reference Pastor Assels had in mind his counterpart from Anna's own village of Overijse, Pastor Jan Bauwens. In fact, within an hour of the events just described, Pastor Bauwens learned of them as well, thanks to three men from Tervuren who had been along on that parish's procession. These men decided, for reasons unknown (a sense of mischief? a commission from their pastor?), that before returning home they would first run to Overijse and tell its pastor what had just taken place in the woods.

The newsbreakers found Pastor Bauwens dining in the company of his assistant pastor, a couple of Franciscans, and some local civic leaders—an even larger audience than expected. Upon hearing the men's tale, Pastor Bauwens admitted that until now he knew nothing of reported miracles at the Jesus Oak, but he knew quite well his parishioner Anna Eregiers, calling her a filthy drunk and declaring that, if she was involved, then the shrine was sure to be "all superstition." Most of the other dignitaries present grumbled their agreement. Only the assistant pastor understood the importance of the news and urged Pastor Bauwens to make a visit to the Jesus Oak and claim it for Overijse. Having finished stirring the pot, the three men from Tervuren returned to their village and excitedly told Pastor Assels what they had done.

Now Pastor Assels was restless. If the pastor of Overijse, an acquaintance of his, should also make a claim on the Oak, there would be trouble. It wasn't unheard of for neighboring parishes to argue over shrines that lay on the boundary between them, or even for fistfights to break out when members of these parishes happened to reach the shrine at the same time (a regular occurrence, since parish processions often took place on common feast days). Hence, to avoid trouble and to be absolutely certain that his claim was indeed the first, Pastor Assels decided to ride to the Oak again the next day, July 3, and wait there until noon to see whether any competing clergymen might appear.

When none did, Pastor Assels rode farther on to Brussels to ask of his superior, the dean of Brussels, or even the archbishop himself, permission to establish the already budding shrine and temporary permission to direct it. For no new shrine could be officially declared, no new miracle officially proclaimed, without the consent of the local bishop. As the pastor had hoped, both dean and archbishop agreed immediately to his requests. Now he could return home with a great deal less anxiety than when he had set out. But, in fact, the matter was far from settled.

For on the very day that the pastor of Tervuren secured the archbishop's blessing, July 3, Pastor Bauwens of Overijse decided at last to act. Though he did not yet know of his rival's efforts in Brussels, Pastor Bauwens knew one thing very well: he was terribly weary of parishioners who all day long had come complaining that he had moved too slowly in regard to the Jesus Oak. That, more than anything else, determined things for him. He speedily overcame his antipathy toward Anna Eregiers, paying a friendly visit to her home in the early morning hours of July 4, then walking to the Oak itself in order to see her handiwork and stake his claim. His justification went as follows. There was no road at all between Tervuren and the Jesus Oak, while a major highway connected Overijse and the majestic tree. Peter van Kerckhoven, founder of the shrine, had owned lands in Overijse, traveled there often, and clearly intended the shrine for its inhabitants. Finally, Anna Eregiers and the first miraculously healed child both came from Overijse.

To make tangible his claim, Pastor Bauwens brought with him on this visit of July 4 two carpenters, whom the pastor instructed to fit Anna's offer box with an iron lock. By so doing, and by handing the key to Anna to watch the offer box in his name, Pastor Bauwens was of course challenging the jurisdiction of the pastor of Tervuren. He even explicitly instructed Anna that if the pastor of Tervuren should come asking for the key, then she was to refuse him, and explain that she was acting under new direction from Overijse. And so at least for a day Anna had two masters.

With all this running to and from the Jesus Oak, with all this ordering about of Anna Eregiers, with all these solemn declarations of jurisdiction, it was amazing that the two pastors hadn't yet bumped into each other there. But the inevitable meeting finally occurred on July 5, 1642, the last of four crucial days in the early existence of the shrine.

The morning began with Pastor Assels leading yet another turf-claiming procession to the Oak. More confident than ever, armed with the archbishop's decree of temporary jurisdiction, he was surprised to find a fresh, unfamiliar lock on the offer box and a very obstinate Anna Eregiers—who had now decided which master to obey.

When Pastor Assels waved the decree at Anna, she ignored or could not read it. And when the pastor demanded the key to the lock, she refused him, insisting that lock, key, and shrine belonged as of yesterday to Overijse. Now it was Pastor Assels's turn to defy Anna: because one of his purposes today was to take control of the offer box, he called forward a locksmith to break the lock and install another in its place. With this done, Pastor Assels gave Anna enough money from what was inside to finish paying her carpenters; he also offered to pay her to continue watching the shrine—under his supervision, of course. This failed to mollify Anna. She refused him again, then stormed away to Overijse to tell her own pastor the latest.

With Anna gone, Pastor Assels continued the work of strengthening his claim on the Oak. He called forward carpenters to construct a better roof over the image, and to improve its decoration: rarely in the history of processions had there been so many tools along as today. Finally, to protect against the usual assortment of unsavory persons tempted to steal the image for its powers, the pastor hired a new caretaker to replace the disillusioned Anna Eregiers.

Not long after Anna returned to Overijse, and after learning that the archbishop had granted temporary jurisdiction to Tervuren, Pastor Bauwens decided to ride to Brussels in person and lay out his own case for custody of the shrine. On the way, he of course rode past the Oak, and the two pastors met face-to-face at last. Amid the hammering and pounding, Pastor Bauwens said nothing about his broken lock or Anna Eregiers but called out casually to the workmen, "Are the offerings good?" According to those present, Pastor Assels responded that he "didn't do this for the offerings," but by commission from dean and archbishop. Then Pastor Bauwens told Pastor Assels his real business: he was on his way to Brussels to discuss the shrine's jurisdiction. He meant nothing personal by this, but was bothering to make the trip only because his parishioners had pestered him so. Then he rode on.

Pastor Assels was hardly reassured. In fact, only days later his suspicions that his counterpart was up to something unpleasant were confirmed: Pastor Bauwens had indeed gone to Brussels to discuss jurisdiction, but not, as all had assumed, with the archbishop. Instead, he had spoken with several lawyers, secular lawyers at that, about what Overijse could do in *civil* court to win the Jesus Oak. Obviously the pastor of Overijse did not think the archbishop would change his mind, and obviously the pastor was prepared to use more aggressive tactics than he had implied to Renier Assels. Thus did the newly holy Jesus Oak became the object of some very worldly squabbling.

THE BLIND SEE

The Village of Oppem, North of Tervuren, July 1642. In the middle of this squabbling, and as if to spite it, the biggest miracle yet occurred at the Oak.

When she was very young, the peasant girl Dimpna Gillis liked to make fires from thorns. She collected the usual pieces from blackthorns or sweetbriars, dragged them to the single room of her family's hut, and then, as her mother had taught her, began breaking the larger stalks into fragments that fit on the hearth. One day, when Dimpna was four, a thorn shot up and pierced her right eye, spilling three drops of blood. Her older siblings ran for their mother, who removed the thorn and comforted the screaming girl. But Dimpna lost sight in that eye.

As the years went by, some in the village heard the story of the thorn. Most knew that Dimpna was blind in her right eye. They noticed, while gathering herbs next to her in the fields, or while watching her at the spinning wheel, that to see things on her right she turned her head completely to that side. They covered her left eye and held things in front of her right, to test whether it truly was sightless. Dimpna's mother, Anna, looked on with pain when her daughter bumped into a tree she had not seen. She wept when children teased Dimpna about the unbecoming white spot on her eye, or when they called her messy eye a "loose spout."

The insults and blindness persisted for nine years, through Dimpna's childhood. But in the summer of 1642, when she was thirteen, there came talk of a new miracle-working shrine at an oak in the woods, just beyond Tervuren. Like any responsible Catholic parent of her time, Dimpna's mother had surely tried assorted physical remedies, and when those failed she had at least considered taking Dimpna to one of the dozens of shrines that dotted the region, including the medieval shrine to Our Dear Lady of the Lovely Fragrance, just two miles beyond the Jesus Oak, in the same woods. But it was the newly established shrine at the Oak, and its fresh stories, that sparked her imagination.

The widowed, fifty-three-year-old Anna called upon her sister and a friend to accompany her and Dimpna on the five-mile journey to the Jesus Oak. Setting out on a Saturday in mid-July, Anna urged Dimpna to "put her faith in Our Dear Lady, that she would help her with her blindness." As they passed through Tervuren, then into the woods, there were surely other pilgrims on the newly worn path to the Oak; most pilgrims were mothers, or mothers and fathers together, who carried on their backs sick or lame children. The presence of fellow travelers helped ease the tensions on this lonely path, which as they drew closer to the Oak was bordered by a gentle ravine on the right, and flat terrain to the left. The path went slightly uphill, then down, and they were there.

The small statue of the Virgin, sheltered by a shingled roof that peaked above her head, was attached to the mighty Oak, just as they had heard. The small party from Oppem knelt with other pilgrims and prayed at least three rosaries, which took an hour. Then they began the trip home. While still in the woods, Dimpna suddenly placed her hand over her good left eye and told her companions, "I can see you walking!" Without turning her head she also saw some cows on her right side, roaming in the woods. The three women gathered excitedly around Dimpna, administering the usual test of covering her left eye and asking her to describe what she saw with her right, which she now did successfully. Mother Anna clapped her hands with joy, and noticed that the white spot on Dimpna's right eye had vanished. After returning home, Dimpna felt for three days a sharp pain running from her right eye down to a gland in her neck—when the pain ceased, the cure was complete.

Neighbors who had known Dimpna long came to see for themselves. They looked in vain for the once-conspicuous spot in her eye. They too covered her left eye and quizzed her further, to test whether she could see. At least seven of them, especially various women friends of Anna, were satisfied enough to testify under oath to ecclesiastical authorities about Dimpna's past and cure. Some in the village were skeptical, but most regarded it as a miracle.

Those in the region roundabout were even more persuaded about the powers of the new shrine when they heard the electrifying news. They knew and cared nothing about the battle for jurisdiction between Overijse and Tervuren. Rather, they now went in droves to the Jesus Oak.

A GAGGLE OF LAWYERS

In the Courts, July 1642 to 1647. The miracle of Dimpna Gillis, and other thrilling miracles soon afterward, did nothing to diminish the earthly struggles over the new shrine but rather intensified them, for now the Oak was more desirable than ever. In the words of its chronicler, the tree, once an infamous "pit of murderers," was becoming a renowned "house of prayer."

In fact, so desirable was the Jesus Oak that Overijse and its pastor and its new team of lawyers were willing to spite their archbishop and go ahead with the plan to challenge him in civil court. Overijse's strategy was fairly simple: civil courts, not the church, had the last word on the establishment of parish boundaries. By demonstrating its long-standing ties with the area around the Oak, Overijse hoped the civil court would extend its boundaries to include the new shrine. This would not only reverse the archbishop's granting of temporary jurisdiction to the pastor of Tervuren, but would thwart any effort to make that jurisdiction permanent.

Such a plan, undertaken without the least bit of consultation, was sure to offend the archbishop. He assumed, by virtue of his supreme ecclesiastical authority, that any designation of spiritual jurisdiction he made—temporary or permanent—would be respected by boundary-drawing civil courts (not to mention his parish clergy). Hence, since he had already declared Tervuren to be temporarily in charge of the Jesus Oak, he expected courts to postpone any adjustment of boundaries until his decision was final. And if he should decide to make Tervuren's jurisdiction over the Oak final, then he had good reason to expect courts to redraw that parish's boundaries accordingly. In other words, the civil court should follow the archbishop's decision, and not, as Overijse wanted, the other way around.

The court Overijse chose to hear its case was the Council of Brabant, highest in the duchy of Brabant. At times this court was, like most others, only too willing to encroach on the turf of Church and archbishop and hear cases that the latter considered rightly his own, for such could only strengthen the council's authority. But at other times the council thought it better to cooperate with the Church, especially when, as in this case, it could hardly lose: the council would win the archbishop's goodwill if it gave him a say in the decision over the Oak, and the council's very supervision of the case would tacitly strengthen its authority over the Church anyway! Hence, the council decided not to hear the matter of the Jesus Oak, but rather assigned it to a special commission of four, consisting of two laymen and two clergymen. Moreover, it made sure that one of those clergymen was the archbishop himself—namely, Jacob Boonen, archbishop of Mechelen from 1621 to 1655, long the most powerful prelate in the Spanish Netherlands, ultimate superior over the Jesus Oak, and of course the same man who had already granted temporary jurisdiction to Tervuren, at the expense of Overijse.

Later generations would surely find outrageous the presence of Archbishop Boonen on the commission, given his prior favor toward Tervuren. But that the archbishop had already shown favor did not necessarily preclude his involvement now: to contemporaries, it obviously seemed more important that he, as superior over the place in question, should have a voice. Nor did his presence guarantee victory for Tervuren: he knew that he was expected to deal fairly and indeed his reputation suggested that he would. Hence, although the lawyers for Overijse could not have been terribly pleased that their fate was now partly in the hands of the very man they were trying to avoid, they understood that sticky webs of patronage and personal relationships were facts of life in early modern Europe, including in matters holy and judicial. Moreover, there were three other honorable voices on the commission, including the chancellor of Brabant (highest legal officer in the duchy) and a judge from the Grand Council. And so Overijse marched forward, optimistically flooding the commission over the next months and years with its particular version of the history of the Oak. The lawyers for Tervuren, taking nothing for granted, responded in like volume and intensity.

Only the highlights of the arguments need be mentioned here. Overijse insisted that the image was placed in the Jesus Oak especially for Overijse, where the shrine's founder, Peter van Kerckhoven, was born and had his lands. But Tervuren brought forward Peter's son Philip, who reluctantly testified that his father had intended the image to bless all travelers, not merely Overijse's.

Overijse held that because Anna Eregiers and her carpenter were natives, then the administration of the Jesus Oak belonged there. But Tervuren responded that since Peter van Kerckhoven lived in Brussels at the time of his donation, should jurisdiction belong to Brussels? And if the carpenter had come from Flanders, should some town there have jurisdiction?

Overijse asserted that Anna Eregiers and the carpenter had acted at the instruction of their pastor as early as May 29, 1642, while the pastor of Tervuren became involved only on July 2. Tervuren countered that this was impossible: Anna was healed only on June 1 and had no devotion to the Jesus Oak before that. Besides, Pastor Bauwens of Overijse was speaking ill of Anna up until July 4, when he suddenly needed her. But Overijse simply alleged that the pastor's disparaging remarks about Anna, though undeniable, were merely "feigned." Further, Tervuren pointed out that although there had been talk of miracles since March 1642, Anna Eregiers was the sole person from Overijse to have visited the shrine on the major feast day of July 2, a day when people with true devotion to a holy place could be expected to visit it. And was Anna really that devout, or did she have financial gain in mind, questioned Tervuren's lawyers? For she sat at the shrine "like she was sitting at her store." In short, nearly every event and character in the early days of the shrine was disputed or reinterpreted by both sides.

Of all the piles of evidence heaped before the commission, the most interesting and dramatic proved to be the testimonies meant to demonstrate each village's long-term claim to jurisdiction over the area in the woods around the Jesus Oak. During the next six months, the most important people in Tervuren and Overijse were suddenly the very elderly, some in their nineties, who came forward one after the other to tell stories that proved their parish's prior claim to the Oak.

Among the witnesses was the husband of Anna Eregiers, seventy-year-old Merten Reyaerts of Overijse, who testified that "about fifty-four years ago" a convoy was butchered just beyond the Jesus Oak, and the dead were brought to Overijse, not Tervuren, for burial by the pastor. Others testified that thirty-three, thirty, eighteen, sixteen, and twelve years before, wounded or dead travelers were found near the tree, and the pastors of Overijse, not Tervuren, had always come to administer last rites, heal, or bury. Gray, wrinkled, toothless witnesses from Overijse searched their memories to recall details of the fallen travelers nursed or buried in their parish, including details about mysterious spurs, horses with white spots, or secret hangings near the Oak—but none could recall anyone from Tervuren ever having been on the scene. Witnesses also remembered less gruesome evidence of Overijse's activities around the Jesus Oak, such as the ninety-year-old man "of sound mind" who testified that just beyond the tree there once stood a tavern, the proprietors of which always attended church in Overijse. A couple who twenty-five years before had lived in a hut near the Oak recalled that while residing in the woods they had always fulfilled their Easter obligations in Overijse, and when their children died they were always buried in Overijse.

None of this impressed Tervuren. Its lawyers discounted most of the witnesses called by Overijse, claiming that their testimonies had been bought. Moreover, even if previous pastors of Overijse had cared for the dead and administered communion, they did so not out of parochial duty but rather simple Christian charity—hardly a basis for jurisdiction. Besides, the pastors of Tervuren had also cared for wayward dead in the forest, and also administered sacraments to the few inhabitants of the woods. Because both villages had obviously long been busy around the Oak, the foundation for jurisdiction had to rest on other claims—such as which village's pastor took command of the new shrine first, a fact Tervuren thought obvious to all.

And so the arguments went for five long years.

STAKING CLAIMS

At the Shrine, July 1642 through 1647. When it became clear that the hearings would drag on longer than expected, both Overijse and Tervuren went about strengthening their claims to the Oak in more tangible ways. Ever since Anna Eregiers put up her offer box and sat watching the place, ever since Pastor Bauwens installed his lock, and ever since Pastor Assels started his processions, installed his own lock, and began the remodeling, all parties grasped the importance of having a physical presence at the shrine.

Tervuren had a big advantage here, of course, given its role as temporary guardian. When crowds became too large for the existing chapel by July 1642, it led the drive to enlarge the shrine and its administration, in ways that not only promoted the shrine but reinforced its association with Tervuren. For instance, because Pastor Assels's ordinary parochial duties prevented him from going daily to the Oak, Archbishop Boonen approved the appointment of an assistant priest, or rector, to work at the Oak under Pastor Assels's direction. This first rector, named Benedictus Piccaert, appointed a small staff, all from Tervuren, to help him at the shrine: three women to sell the usual array of candles, medallions, images, and other pious souvenirs available at shrines since the ancient world, plus a "Supervisor of the Offer Box" to clean and watch the shrine and carry the offer box daily to Tervuren.

Tervuren's claim on the Oak was also strengthened by its assignment from the archbishop, in September 1642, to conduct the usual preliminary investigations into the alleged miracles there. These had increased since the cure of Dimpna Gillis, and the investigations into all would be forwarded to the archbishop for his own investigation and final judgment. Hence Rector Piccaert located and interviewed witnesses who had known the once-blind Dimpna Gillis, or the once-herniated boy Michel, or a once-crippled three-year-old boy named Albert Raep, and still others. The rector also followed the usual protocol of gathering medical opinions as to whether their cures were natural or supernatural. When Archbishop Boonen confirmed at least Dimpna's cure as miraculous, and allowed the others to be published as "edifying," it enhanced not only the legitimacy of the shrine but its current guardians as well.

Even more tangible in Tervuren's efforts to win permanent jurisdiction over the Oak was the day-to-day, blood-and-tears, physical work by Rector Piccaert on the shrine itself. He traveled frequently to Brussels, often because of the ongoing dispute with Overijse. He also hosted visiting commissioners and their agents in Tervuren, complete with the usual pots of wine and once a special Marzipan tart carried from Brussels. He recorded meticulously the donations in the offer box, especially the monthly high of 627 florins in September 1642, or such striking gifts as that from a widow of Wavre, who "out of devotion" gave almost all she had, forty florins, "but when asked why, she did not wish to say." He recorded as well the gifts-in-kind: a silver chalice from "some Lotharingen," a silver torch from "some damsel in Brussels." He cared for the growing collection of bejeweled white, green, violet, and red dresses with matching coats that alternately adorned the image, following a custom brought from Spain to the Spanish Netherlands.

In October 1642, when rainier weather came, Rector Piccaert drew up a request to the king of Spain (through the king's governor-general in Brussels) to build a small but fully enclosed wooden chapel, which would protect the image and pilgrims far better than had the shrine of Anna Eregiers, or the makeshift additions constructed since. And when in November this new chapel proved almost immediately too small (for people now traveled to the Oak from nearly a day's journey away and were none too pleased to discover that the chapel was full or that they had missed mass or were standing so miserably in the rain), it was the rector who helped gain permission to build yet another chapel, a work that would occupy most of his time over the next five years.

Daily he tramped or rode from Tervuren through rain, snow, "and so forth." He sometimes hauled by himself, "in very awful weather," wood and other supplies. He bought traps to reduce the "multitude of mice and rats" that ran from the woods into the chapel, oil for lamps, two "black velvet cushions for the use of nobles who visited the chapel," a pair of slippers for the use of Capuchin friars who often came to say mass, locks and bolts for the chapel's new door, bars for the new windows, candelabra, a leaden roof, a red silken cloth to cover the tabernacle, a silver globe for the baby Jesus, the occasional trumpeters to accompany mass, a missal, a silver chalice, a vessel for holy water, a large cross, a bell, two angels next to the sacred image, and six carved lambs for a nativity scene. More than once he paid to have the offer box repaired after someone tried to break into it. He paid ordinary wages to nine men who smoothed the path that led to the chapel from Tervuren, to a woman who carried the church's linens to Tervuren and washed them, to a sculptor who remade the hand of the holy image (already worn thin by the touches of pilgrims), then severance wages to two workers let go because of "impoliteness," and of course fees to other priests who helped say mass (including the pastor of Overijse). He gave a beggar named Thomas half a stiver for fifty nails found in a refuse pile near the chapel, and he provided pots and pots of beer to quench the thirst of workers.

During the summer months, when the war season was in full swing, Rector Piccaert's already substantial headaches multiplied. His chief aim then was to protect the image from marauding soldiers, and more than once he carried it away to Tervuren or Leuven—never to Overijse—for safekeeping. If soldiers weren't trouble enough, then there were the semi-legal vendors who sold food and drink around the shrine. Once when Rector Piccaert tried to move the image because of the threat of war, the vendors grew furious that their major attraction was being taken away, and promised to "shoot up" the priest, who was saved only by the fortuitous intervention of an armed band from Tervuren.

Surely the rector improved Tervuren's chances as well by impressing the archbishop with his efforts to ensure the orthodoxy of the shrine. He saw to it that the Oak was noticeably reduced and situated *behind* the altar of the new chapel, thus making the image and the altar, rather than the tree (in pagan fashion), the focal points of devotion. In fact, the reduction of the tree had already been hastened, as at most shrines featuring oaks, by pilgrims who broke off pieces of bark in the belief that these alone were powerful. To diminish this desire, Rector Piccaert settled upon another favorite official solution: he had images of the Virgin carved from the scarred tree, giving devotion its proper form, and pilgrims their piece of oak.

Despite the various and often mundane burdens resting upon him, Rector Piccaert persisted—for the sake of the shrine, and to help make Tervuren's association with it almost traditional. Indeed, the longer he labored and the more he accomplished, the more difficult it became for Overijse to stake any kind of physical claim at all.

Given Tervuren's many advantages at the shrine, Overijse was forced to place all of its hopes in the commission. And here it faced yet another disadvantage: Tervuren had better connections there, especially with Archbishop Boonen.

It happened that the archbishop, long before the birth of the Jesus Oak, was good friends with the official patron of Tervuren: the abbot of Park, a prominent abbey just outside Leuven (or Louvain). The patron of a parish possessed, among other benefits and obligations, the right to nominate its pastor. If Tervuren won the battle over the Jesus Oak, the abbot of Park would therefore automatically become patron of the new shrine as well. It was quite likely that the archbishop's friendship with the abbot influenced the decision to grant temporary supervision over the Jesus Oak to Tervuren. And it was certain that the abbot, and his successors, wished to make this supervision permanent.

Especially two successive abbots of Park, Jan Masius and Libertus de Pape, became heavily involved in promoting the Jesus Oak and cementing their association with it. Masius said the first mass there, and many more afterward. Both regularly intervened with the governors-general, if necessary in person, to support the rector's repeated requests to expand the chapel or build another. Both sent endless letters and legal briefs to tell the "true" history of the Oak, including the "dubious" tactics employed by Overijse and the various miracles that had occurred under Tervuren's watchful care. Both called in theologians and canon lawyers from the University of Leuven to side with Tervuren. And most especially both made sure to intervene with their friend, Archbishop Boonen.

Again, the archbishop was only one voice on the commission, but it was a powerful voice—especially since the other sitting clergyman was the archbishop's subordinate and good friend, the dean of Brussels! And again, the friendship of abbot and archbishop did not alone assure victory: arguments and evidence and fairness still mattered. But it was precisely the archbishop's sense of fairness on which the abbots hoped to capitalize. Specifically, the abbots took care, behind the scenes, to point out how little income Tervuren had enjoyed since the fires and destruction of that village in 1635—the addition of a popular shrine would certainly help remedy that situation. And most of all they took care tactfully to remind the archbishop of an old debt he owed the abbey. Some decades before, a previous abbot of Park had freely relinquished his patronage over a popular shrine called Laken to a previous archbishop of Mechelen, and asked for nothing in return. Legally, of course, the current archbishop was not bound to repay this act of voluntary generosity by a past abbot, but the current abbot obviously hoped repayment would come in the form of the Jesus Oak. Hence, even though the archbishop would consider seriously the arguments of both Overijse and Tervuren, if those arguments were even roughly equal, then the leverage exerted by the abbots of Park could play a decisive role. Overijse, whoever its champions and however sound its arguments, had no such immediate leverage.

Growing ever more doubtful of victory with the commission, Overijse tried one last appeal to another purely secular court, this one supreme in the entire Spanish Netherlands: the Grand Council of Mechelen. But the appeal never amounted to anything. By 1647, few but the diehards from Overijse believed their village could prevail. Then in that year came a final blow: Pastor Jan

Bauwens, Overijse's strongest voice, died, and his successors proved less zealous about pushing onward.

And so, after hundreds of florins in legal costs (nine hundred for Tervuren alone, about three years' wages for a rural pastor), the commission finally made Tervuren's provisional supervision of the Oak—and therefore the patronage of the abbots of Park—permanent.

Like most victors of the time, Tervuren attributed its good fortune to the will of God. But Overijse showed, through its continuing complaints and long cries of "unfair," that in its view the matter of jurisdiction had not been decided by God at all but by the arm of flesh: it was worldly know-how and unbeatable earthly connections that gave Tervuren its hard-earned victory.

A MODEST SHRINE

1647 to 1700. With custody established at last, the only questions remaining about the Jesus Oak were how long would it survive and how great would it become?

Any shrine was by definition an exceptional place in the cruel world, but some were more exceptional than others. Some shrines did not outlive the enthusiasm of their early years, and disappeared. Others settled into a local and modest role, after a start that seemed to promise more. A few enjoyed a regional reputation. But only the very elite were able to sustain their early momentum to become truly great, with their names on the lips of believers many duchies and counties away.

The Jesus Oak did survive its early years, with miracles occurring in slightly declining numbers but still enough to attract pilgrims for a few strong decades. The chapel was maintained, visiting priests were compensated for saying mass, a permanent rector was in place. True, it was far from lavish: the first rector, Benedictus Piccaert, died around 1658, hardly a rich man, and, in fact, with many unpaid bills to physicians, surgeons, hospitals, and apothecaries accumulated in his last months. But at least his beloved shrine was still alive.

In fact, the early shrine was alive enough for its custodians to start laying plans for a full-fledged church, meant to replace a series of rapidly unsuitable loam and wooden chapels. This was no routine decision: a church required serious investment and donors, for it was rarely built from pilgrims' donations alone. And if achieved, a church built expressly as a pilgrimage center could help make the Jesus Oak at least a respectable regional shrine. The first stone was laid in 1650, and after a series of delays the entire structure was complete by 1680—on a scale large enough that no expansion was ever required again. Here was the shrine's crowning glory.

But it was also a last flicker. For by the time the church was finally finished, the great streams of pilgrims had ceased and income had dwindled. The abbots of Park, who ended up paying the great bulk of construction costs, told the governor-general as early as 1665 that they hoped to complete the church very soon, but needed help in doing so, for they had no profit from the shrine—indeed to the contrary, they had only "heavy expense and burden." Offerings alone were insufficient even to maintain the place and the rector, much less finish construction, so that without their subsidies the shrine could not continue. Clearly popular enthusiasm for the place was waning. By the time the church was completed at last, in 1680, the Jesus Oak was already merely local, just like most shrines, with its pilgrims drawn largely from surrounding villages. And it was destined to remain so.

Successive rectors still held out hopes for greatness, but less stubborn contemporaries had to look no further than the standard of all shrines in the Low Countries, the *Scherpenheuvel*, or Sharp Hill, to realize how limited the Jesus Oak truly was. Here was the greatest shrine in the land, built in the early seventeenth century and vibrant as ever. The differences between the two places were not hard to see, from beginning to end.

Like the Jesus Oak, the Sharp Hill grew up in the midst of violence and fear. But instead of the tension and isolated murders that occurred around the Oak, the towns around the Sharp Hill, close by the eastern front of the war against the Dutch, witnessed entire bloody sieges, in 1578, 1580, and beyond. The resacralizing of the Sharp Hill around 1600 was therefore an even more poignant event than the taming of the frightful old Oak in the woods.

Like the Jesus Oak, the Sharp Hill saw its early crowds suddenly grow thanks to convincing miracles. But instead of the hundreds who often walked at once to the Oak, various witnesses put the number of pilgrims at the Sharp Hill on major feast days at twenty thousand and more. Instead of accommodating its pilgrims with a modest, brick church costing some forty thousand florins and requiring thirty years to build, the magnificent, domed church at the Sharp Hill cost close to three hundred thousand and was finished in eighteen years. And instead of the church's completion marking the end of the glory days, the erection of the church at the Sharp Hill only brought more pilgrims.

Like the Jesus Oak, the Sharp Hill was born in the wild. But instead of remaining that way, and instead of the Jesus Oak's simple shack for devotional objects, a small home for the rector, a paltry 125 florins a year for his salary, a few run-down stalls and tents for vendors, no lodgings for visitors, and elevation to a separate (and tiny) parish only around 1700, the Sharp Hill turned almost immediately into a full-fledged town, built up from scratch, with a respectable home and income for a proper pastor, an abundance of food and drink and lodging for visitors, an entire group of some twenty priests (with their own cloister, fishpond, and farm) to serve pilgrims, and around five hundred communicants living permanently in the parish.

Like the Jesus Oak, income at the Sharp Hill eventually leveled off, but at a vastly different plateau. Instead of the Jesus Oak's two thousand florins per year, usually enough to cover expenses, the Sharp Hill's nine thousand florins in 1604 kept rising for years afterward, and always outpaced expenses—including an incredible twenty thousand florins of income in 1605—sixty-four hundred of it profit and most of it put back into the shrine. The Sharp Hill was still a far cry from such an international pilgrimage site as Rome, where various ecclesiastical interests engaged in furious lawsuits and even bodily assaults over the huge sums that entered the treasuries, but the Sharp Hill was nevertheless among the exceptions in the world of shrines: it regularly made enough money to cover expenses and even to expand or redecorate. In contrast, the Jesus Oak, like most shrines, sometimes made enough money to maintain itself at a modest level but usually needed help from its patron.

Finally, like the Jesus Oak, the Sharp Hill published an official history. But instead of a brief in-house work by the local priest, as at the Jesus Oak, the Sharp Hill boasted at least three lengthy histories, one of them sponsored by archduke and archbishop alike, and a second authored by Justus Lipsius, one of the greatest scholars in Europe (coincidentally a native of Overijse, and the great-uncle of Overijse's lead lawyer in the legal struggle with Tervuren).

Everything at the Sharp Hill simply seemed to happen on a larger scale than at the Jesus Oak, and to be so much grander.

Recognizing the difference in stature between the two shrines was not hard. More difficult was explaining those differences.

Just as many contemporaries invoked otherworldly explanations for a shrine's birth, so with a shrine's stature: the Sharp Hill was greater because the Virgin wanted it to be greater. The miracles at the Sharp Hill were simply more numerous and powerful. Most shrines (not the Sharp Hill) had to give way to new shrines so that new saints might bloom as well—"The Lord scatters them and divides them, as he deems that time and place require." Or, the Virgin punished one shrine in favor of another and stopped working her miracles because of greed among a shrine's keepers. But believers did not think exclusively in these otherworldly terms: just as immediate worldly forces helped to explain how the Jesus Oak came to be, so did they help to explain its inferior stature to the Sharp Hill.

The Oak's first official historian, for instance, could not go along with the explanation that other shrines were greater because their miracles were greater. Baffled that enthusiasm for his beloved Oak was waning, he wrote in 1661 to assure pilgrims that recent miracles there were just as exceptional and potent as those in earlier days, and indeed even more so than miracles that occurred elsewhere. "I will not deny that such miracles happen at other holy places, too. But I still think that they happen nowhere as frequently as here, since we have Jesus and Maria together on the throne of an oak."

This author was surely engaging in filial piety by suggesting that the powers at the Jesus Oak were superior to shrines elsewhere: the Sharp Hill could probably boast more miracles, and shrines in Germany boasted hundreds and even thousands over a longer period of time. But he was absolutely right that the miracles at the Oak were just as impressive in quality. So were the miracles by the Holy Virgin of Leuven, where Justus Lipsius marveled at the paucity of visitors, given her "numerous and great miracles." So were those at Our Lady of Groeninge in Kortrijk; Our Lady of Hanswyck in Mechelen; the shrines of Duffel, Eeklo, Bornem, Vilvoorde, Kortenbos, Westrozebeke, Melsele, Laken, and hundreds of other modest holy places and saints in the Low Countries and beyond, which could boast miracles every bit as stunning as those at the Sharp Hill. To what would this historian have then attributed his shrine's inferior status? He did not say; perhaps he left it as an inscrutable mystery of God, but surely he was as aware as others of this-worldly considerations.

The biggest worldly forces in shaping both the Jesus Oak and the Sharp Hill were location and, once again, patrons. The Sharp Hill was situated right at the front lines of the war with the Dutch, thus serving as a visible reminder of the battle between old faith and new. A visit to the Jesus Oak in the Soniën Woods was no ordinary journey, but every visit to the Sharp Hill was an even greater act of courage, for it often brought pilgrims within sight of rebel troops—if this discouraged some pilgrims, it appealed to many more.

Location also mattered in that the Sharp Hill lay far from any royal property, while the Jesus Oak sat on lands owned by the king of Spain. The miracles in the Soniën Woods put the king and his governor-general in a difficult position: the Most Catholic king surely acknowledged the Virgin's right to manifest her powers wherever she pleased, including on prime royal hunting grounds. And at least two governor-generals seemed emotionally attached to the Jesus Oak, traveling there to worship and promoting it more, for instance, than they did any existing shrine in the woods—such as the nearby Our Dear Lady of Lovely Fragrance, locally popular for the curing of fevers and for young women in search of good husbands. Yet neither king nor governors were eager to see choice lands become the site of a crowded shrine, however reverently they regarded it, and however clearly they saw the benefits that might result from a shrine. Obviously these benefits did not outweigh the disadvantages of crowding and ruin. Besides, they had already given permission for two monasteries to be built in these woods, not far from the Jesus Oak!

Hence, they would keep the Jesus Oak small. From the beginning king and governor gave no thought to killing the devotion at the Jesus Oak, but they gave much thought to limiting its size. It was they who made it difficult for vendors to set up shop at the shrine, and, when stalls finally were allowed, restricted the number to five. It was they who permitted no lodgings near the shrine, unlike around highly popular shrines. And it was they who allowed the Jesus Oak to be declared a separate parish from Tervuren only when crowds had thinned anyway and the parish was acceptably and forever harmlessly small. Moreover, they strictly limited how many trees they would donate for construction at the Oak. As much as anyone did king and governor recognize that their particular earthly influence would be a prime shaper of this holy place.

The abbots of Park likewise recognized the importance of

earthly influences on the shrine's existence and stature. They wrote to more than one governor-general to complain that if more vendors and stalls were not allowed, then people would have nowhere to repose and refresh themselves, and the shrine would die. And this without any reference to the will of the Virgin. The rectors of the shrine understood the same: they lobbied governor-generals as late as 1700 to grant the privileges promised in 1650 by an earlier governor-general, for without those privileges they feared the demise of the Jesus Oak.

At the Sharp Hill, on the other hand, royal officials early on persuaded or cajoled various persons to sell or donate lands needed for the expansion of the new town, which occurred at what seemed truly miraculous speed.

Which raised the second explanation of the Sharp Hill's superiority: its patrons. Tervuren's were greater than Overijse's, but the Sharp Hill's were greater than everyone else's—namely the pious archdukes, Albert and Isabella, who ruled the Spanish Netherlands between 1598 and 1621.* Certainly the chief patrons of the Jesus Oak, the abbots of the Park, were no minor figures. Certainly noteworthy persons visited the Oak, including the very governor-generals who restricted its growth. But instead of the occasional great one, the Sharp Hill overflowed with them, including numerous nuncios, archbishops, bishops, abbots (even those of Park), noblemen and noblewomen from the seventeenth century's golden register, many of whom argued among themselves over who should have the privilege of paying some ridiculous fee for this stained glass window or that in the new church. And instead of a mere ab-

Before and after the reign of the archdukes, the chief political figure in the land was the governor-general, who ruled in the name of the king of Spain.

bot as chief patron, the Sharp Hill had the archdukes, whose reign marked the golden age of the Spanish Netherlands.

Albert and Isabella possessed not only the intangible quality of universal celebrity, which helped to attract pilgrims, but far more political power than even such an important abbey as Park possessed, or for that matter a governor-general in Brussels: during the brief reign of the archdukes in the Spanish Netherlands, they were virtual sovereigns. And they put that power to good use at the Sharp Hill, especially when they began to see the shrine as a symbol of divine approval for their regime. When the church was planned, for instance, the archdukes, fully aware that not even the Sharp Hill could afford to build an entire church from alms alone, devised a scheme that required every province to make "donations" toward its construction. Since this was to be a shrine for all the land, all the land should help pay, however reluctantly.

The abbots of Park had no such recourse in building the church at the Jesus Oak: it was left virtually to them alone. Though they used their influence to persuade the governor-general to allow at least the building of a church, and though the governors donated lumber at critical times, the abbots won no special privileges from the governor and received from him no grants of cash to help fund the place. And this despite all the bowing and scraping before the governors by the rectors of the Jesus Oak—showering gifts upon the governors' families when they visited, saying masses for their souls, and humbly waiting in antechambers in Brussels for up to two days when calling for favors.

Of course the greatness of the patrons at either shrine did not alone explain popularity, for ordinary believers were perfectly capable of finding their own holy places. But the efforts of illustrious patrons added luster to a shrine, legitimized it, and increased its chances of longevity. By the end of the seventeenth century, the Sharp Hill remained the national shrine, while the goal of the rectors of the Jesus Oak was becoming terribly modest: simply to make of their shrine "a little Sharp Hill."

Perhaps the Jesus Oak, even with royal support rather than royal interference, would have remained inferior anyway. Perhaps it was the will of the Virgin. Perhaps the governors believed that the land could sustain only one great shrine and it already existed. But had the governors chosen to support the Jesus Oak as the archdukes had supported the Sharp Hill, there might well have been a very different shrine in the woods.

FINAL GLIMPSES

1702, Decline. In a letter to the latest governor-general, the latest abbot of Park explained the perilous finances of the fading shrine at the Oak. Though the recent elevation to a parish was a great blessing, there were so few pilgrims that donations were insufficient to maintain either church or pastor. In fact, the pastor had no income at all, not even any wood from the king's forest. As for the vendors, they were all poor and earned their living "only with the greatest trouble," selling beer to pilgrims and passersby. Although the pastor received very little from pilgrims or vendors, he had to be ready at all times to hear their confessions and say mass. The wars of King Louis XIV of France had not helped, and the Jesus Oak was surviving only because the abbots of Park still supported it almost single-handedly.

1766, Hope. The royal tax collectors reported that the seven houses around the church of the Jesus Oak in 1742 had now grown to twenty-four. This was made possible by a small renaissance in the popularity of the shrine, reflected in the new series of portrait murals on the church's walls. Grateful pilgrims, especially the parents of healed children, commissioned these paintings to commemorate the cures of their loved ones, all of which added to the intimacy and attractiveness of the place. But pilgrims did not come from much farther away than Brussels, and the shrine remained nearly as modest as ever.

1797, Terror. This was not the first time that a pastor of the Jesus Oak was forced to flee with the precious holy objects of the place, so he knew well what to do. He hurriedly prepared a document describing in detail the sacred image, so that no one would dispute its authenticity when he brought it back. He also noted that he was going to lock the image inside an oblong case of boxwood, seal the case at four distinct places, and accompany it into exile at the home of his brother, in Brussels.

Hurriedly, he folded the document, and took a final look around the church: there were the lovingly wrought murals, the peaked windows, and the usual pile of waxen body limbs left in thanks or promise. Then, like the guardians of the Sharp Hill and hundreds of other shrines under siege by the revolutionary soldiers from France, he galloped away to safety.

August 5, 1951, Celebration. The Jesus Oak survived its economic and spiritual valleys. It survived the French Revolution. It survived the industrial nineteenth century. But it never became even the little Sharp Hill that its pastors labored valiantly to make it—not even when it was declared a national monument after World War I, or when Cardinal Mercier placed a crown on the image in 1924, thereby exalting its stature. The community around the shrine was little more than the twenty-four houses of 150 years before, and was now known better for cigar-making. At the Sharp Hill, on the other hand, directors expected sixty thousand pilgrims on feast days, arranged for the pope himself to perform a special mass, and recorded 403 miracles between 1920 and 1940.

Still, here in 1951 there was cause for rejoicing at the Jesus Oak: it had survived yet another world war, and 1950 marked the three hundredth anniversary of the beginning of its church. Though this church now functioned more as an everyday parish than as the respectable shrine it once was, on this evening, at eight-thirty, villagers and friends came to see a play that recalled their miraculous heritage. The current pastor, around the thirtieth in a long line, composed the piece himself and planned to run it at least four different nights.

The audience watched as the stars appeared one by one—Peter van Kerckhoven, Pastor Renier Assels, parishioners of Tervuren, a governor-general, an abbot of Park, Dimpna Gillis, a group of sick children, and dozens of soldiers. But nowhere to be seen were Rector Benedictus Piccaert, or the pastor of Overijse, or lawyers, contractors, bricks and leaky roofs, or Thomas the beggar digging for nails, much less the first champion of the shrine, Anna Eregiers. And in addition to the mortal cast there appeared in the drama of the Jesus Oak characters from the other world, including the Virgin herself, a row of heavenly girls, dancing angels, an ascended saint, numerous elves and satyrs, some demons, and more.

These last were not exactly the same characters whose names

dominated the historical documents gathered and stored in the abbey of Park, patrons of the Jesus Oak, nor was the story presented that night the same as the one told here. But like the Oak's first historian, the pastor who wrote this drama understood well the principle of overlooking the mundane in order to emphasize the holy at a shrine—however humble it may have been, however human its earthly founders.

TWO

MARIA ABUNDANT

THE MILK FLOWS

October 31, 1657, All Saints Eve, a Poor Neighborhood in Gent. Maria Caroens, mother of fourteen, was now desperate. For her newest infant child she had produced not a single drop of milk, and so the child cried every night, all night, and was slowly starving to death. At last Maria could bear no more.

This was saying much, for suffering was an old acquaintance of Maria, ever since her girlhood in the seaside town of Nieuwpoort, where she was born forty-two years before. Maria's first husband, a fishnet maker named Jan, died during their eighth year of marriage, while the five children born to them all died young, a heartbreaking rate even in a world where often half the children died before age ten. By her second husband, the blacksmith Antony de Witte, she had given birth to nine more children, including this youngest last April.

If labor pains and grief were the bitterest themes of her life, then poverty and all its attendant burdens were close behind. Antony's wages as a journeyman smith were never abundant, so he had to travel regularly to find work, sometimes crossing the border into Zeeland in the nearby Dutch Republic and staying away an entire winter. His other job, the less common one of traveling as a proxy pilgrim for those unable to visit shrines in person, obviously required him to be gone as well, leaving Maria alone with the children most of the exhausting time.

This probably explained why Maria, who like most urban women also worked for income, tried to earn her share of daily bread by baking and selling waffles from home. But also like most women, whether they sold on the marketplace or from small retail shops, Maria's income was as meager as her husband's, so that she too was forced to travel in search of better profit—even when Antony was away. Did she take the children with her? Leave the eldest to watch the youngest? Leave some with friends? She never said, surely because the combination of children and long hours were relentless facts of life for women and thus hardly worthy of mention.

Whether alone or surrounded like a mother hen, Maria once set up a waffle shop in Poperinge, many miles southwest of Gent. And once when Antony was in Zeeland she journeyed still farther north than he to Holland, at the "constant requests" of her brother, and sold waffles there from his home. But apparently her brother wanted her there so that he might convert her, for he had become "bitterly Protestant"—and soon they wearied of each other. When Maria and Antony and their houseful of children finally settled in Gent, it was in a small house in the Savaan street, near a foul-smelling canal.

Maria knew at least one other burden as well: her chronic inability to produce sufficient milk for her many infants. With her first thirteen children, favorite home remedies had at least resulted in some milk, but for this last there had been nothing. This time when a friend named Margaret Doosens applied to Maria's breasts the usual poultice of wheat flour and boiled wheat, and told Maria once again to drink milk supplemented with wheat, as with past children, she had no luck. Even the hopeful and experienced Margaret, successfully nursing a child of her own at the moment, finally declared Maria's case "a waste of time."

Maria therefore tried the next solution of her day: hiring Margaret, who was nursing her own baby, as a wet nurse. But if noblewomen and even some working women afforded wet nurses easily, Maria could barely manage it. Neither were any charitable institutions prepared to help: some paid wet nurses to feed a few orphans and foundlings, but babies still with their mothers were on their own. Hence Maria scraped together what income she could to allow her child to stay with Margaret during the day, a large block away in the Bagatten street, then took the child home at night to lie at her breast, in the hope of stimulating some milk. Still there was nothing. After several months she had no more money to pay Margaret, and so tried to wean the child early, but the child would hardly eat the "pap" or pudding she prepared. The child wanted only milk, and without any was gradually starving.

Even Maria, familiar as she was with grief, had her limits: that she had already experienced so much suffering did not mean she was willing to stand by and do nothing while this child suffered too. Having tried every physical remedy known to her, she therefore decided, "more out of desperation than devotion," that she would now seek spiritual aid as well.

Maria's notions of this realm probably did not match exactly that of local priests, especially not if she mixed folk charms with her prayers, or chewed on a piece of bark from such a tree as the Jesus Oak, or wore around her neck a locket containing written charms, or drank an herbal potion given her by a wise woman, or sought from that same wise woman rather than her pastor relief from a possible spell that had dried up her breasts or bewitched her child's mouth. But Maria and local clergymen were, just as at the Jesus Oak, agreed on one thing: the reality of supernatural power. They might even use the same forms to invoke that power, including various charms, the drinking of holy water as a remedy against sickness, scattering holy water on fields to promote fertility, or even the form that Maria's devotions finally took: visiting a shrine. And though many churchmen might have preferred that she visit a shrine to increase her faith and piety and long-suffering, while Maria was more interested in receiving tangible aid, they would not have denied that such aid was possible.

People like Maria chose a particular shrine for a variety of reasons: it was nearby, or far away, or its patrons had the right name or reputation, or it was recommended by friends, or it was old, or more likely it was new—but most of all it was reputed to work miracles. Surely Maria heard talk, and was unable to travel far, both of which influenced her decision to venture out that day, on All Saints' Eve, toward the church of the Franciscan Recollects, just a block or two away from her home. This church was serving as temporary shelter for a special statue of the Virgin brought to Gent because of the latest war between France and Spain, and already the statue was reputed to have worked miracles from its new location within the church.

Of course Maria wished to bring the usual offering to the

shrine, but this presented a problem, for she had no money. Feeling unable to ask any more of friend Catherine, Maria stopped at the home of another friend, named Christine, in the Sacrament street, and borrowed five stivers. This Maria used to buy two waxen breasts, which she would place at the altar. Just as grateful visitors to shrines often brought waxen images of cured body parts, so did they often leave such images in advance, as part of a prayer or vow. For churchmen such an offering was justified by the Old Testament practice of sacrifice, but for more literal-minded people it represented the sort of bartering with God seen already at the Jesus Oak: goods in exchange for favors.

Whatever Maria's attitude may have been, she left her offering and prayed for one of three things: that she might be given milk, that someone might come forward to pay a wet nurse for her child, or, most desperately, that the child might die and end its suffering. Three days long Maria walked to the church of the Recollects to offer this prayer. But still there was no change.

Maria might have understood this failure as yet another test of faith; not everyone who visited shrines received a miracle, she knew. But Maria did not give up hope yet: she simply concluded from her failure among the Recollects that this was not the shrine for her, and kept looking.

This attitude came out in her next visit to the home of friend Margaret Doosen, who now had some sorrow of her own: on the very day that Maria had finished her devotions in the Recollect church, one of Margaret's children fell into the ever-dangerous household fire and suffered serious facial burns. During Maria's visit later that day, the two women consoled each other, and considered shrines where Margaret might take her burned child. Yet another friend, Mayken Bernaerts, had urged taking the child to a miraculous statue of the Virgin in the local Jesuit church, several blocks away. According to Mayken, this statue was renowned for having been thrown into a fire by an irreverent heretic, yet after "a long time" it had emerged from the fire unblemished.

Surely Mayken recommended this particular shrine to Margaret because it possessed a quality so powerful in contemporary minds: correspondence. Saint Rochus was said to have died of the plague, and thus became the patron saint of victims of the plague; Saint Sebastian was shot to death by arrows, and thus became the patron saint of archers and soldiers; Margaret's child had been injured in fire, and the image was reputed to have survived fire. What better way to cure the child than before this fireproof image of the Virgin?

Margaret probably visited this shrine eventually, but at the moment it was Maria who proved more enthusiastic about it—even if her thinking showed little correspondence at all. Upon hearing the news, she thought to herself: "If that image could heal a burned child, then it could bring milk to my bosoms *(boesems)*." Perhaps Maria was working on the common assumption that, of all saints, the Virgin was best for problems surrounding pregnancy and mothering, due to her own immaculate conception and Jesus' miraculous conception, and illustrated by endless paintings that showed her giving her breast to the Christ child. Or, Maria's thinking might have been simpler still: not necessarily the special womanly powers of the Virgin, but the power of the statue itself—quite against what churchmen wanted her to believe, which was that God worked through images but images had no power per se. However Maria understood things, she visited the Jesuit church a few days later.

This time she had no offering at all but her broken heart, and intended simply to hear mass, then pray before the image. It was kept, as at the Recollect church, in an honored place—a special chapel devoted to Our Dear Lady, just to the right of the choir. As she walked toward the image, there was much else for Maria to admire in the 170-foot-long church, even if its Gothic style was considered old-fashioned by some Gentenaars: there was an obligatory gigantic Rubens altarpiece, various depositions from the cross, paintings of Mary and Jesus, the Annunciation, the Ascension, the Holy Trinity, and Wise Men, silver and gold gilding everywhere, plus some relics of Saint Ignatius Loyola, founder of the Jesuit order, in a priceless silver reliquary—and all finely displayed, for this was a well-lighted church. But her main interest was the statue of the Virgin.

Now standing before it, Maria made the same whispered plea that she had made days before at another shrine: "Holy Mother Mary, I have no money or other offering, but I offer to you my soul and body and my poor household, if it's possible that some miracle can happen to this poor, sinful person: take my child from the world, grant me milk, or arouse someone to take in and feed my child." She followed this with saying the rosary and hearing mass, then returned home without noticing any change.

The next day she went to the Jesuit church again, to the same chapel of Our Dear Lady, and said the same words and prayer and heard another mass in the chapel. Still nothing. Then again on the third and last day. Kneeling in utter helplessness, and after the consecration of the host by the "very tall" priest celebrating, she pondered: "Lord, the mass is almost finished, and I'm still not heard." Turning to the image of the Virgin, she made a vow: "Holy Mary, if I'm heard, then I promise, as long as I'm in this city, to come and visit you here daily, with a short or long prayer, at least as long as a mass."

It was as if this was what the Virgin had been waiting for. Suddenly Maria fell into what seemed a dream or sleep. Still kneeling, and unaware of how much time had elapsed, she awoke to find herself in a heavy sweat, with milk flowing from her left breast and soaking her clothes. Her right breast was full as well, but it did not surprise her that nothing flowed from it, for it had no opening and her other children had never been able to feed from it. Yet it astonished her that so much milk flowed from her left—more than ever before, more than any of her physical remedies had ever produced.

Maria's astonishment turned to delight as she returned home and for the first glorious time satisfied her hungry child—ignoring or ignorant of medical warnings to avoid breast-feeding within twelve hours of experiencing strong feelings, lest she pass along through her milk an overcharged emotional state to her child! When husband Antony came home that evening, Maria excitedly told him the news. To her disappointment, it only made him nervous. He ordered Maria to keep quiet about what had occurred: "There are plenty of flimsy Catholics in Gent; the one will be moved to devotion, another will laugh at you." He didn't want to be the center of attention, or speculation.

But Maria persisted in her joy. She returned to the Jesuit church several days in a row, and felt something pulling inside her, like a stone falling to the floor, after which her breasts filled with more milk than ever (though the child continued to feed only from the left). She also made sure to tell another friend, a certain "devoutly inclined" patron named Miss Beeclaere, who had provided Maria with alms in the past and knew her condition. Miss Beeclaere proved to be far more excited than Antony had been. At first she didn't believe what Maria was telling her, but since she had seen Maria's breasts "when they were dry" and Maria now allowed her to inspect them again, Miss Beeclaere could see the obvious change and was convinced. She urged Maria to tell her story to her confessor, for it seemed nothing less than a miracle.

JESUITS

Christmas 1657 to June 1658. It was more than a month before Maria finally followed her friend's suggestion, probably because she did not have her own private confessor, as the Miss Beeclaeres of the world usually did. But finally, on the second or third day of Christmas, she decided to seek one out in the church of the Jesuits, where she had been cured.

Following her daily prayer in the chapel of Our Dear Lady, she walked to the third confessional from the chapel, knelt down, and recounted her story to the Jesuit on duty, named Pater van Liere. She concluded her account by expressing a desire to sponsor a mass in gratitude, but admitted she had not enough money for such elaborate thanks. Not to worry, assured Pater van Liere: he would personally say a mass on her behalf.

Maria then returned home, assuming that everything was now complete. But there was more. For once Pater van Liere informed his fellow Jesuits that a miracle might have occurred inside their church, they became annoyed that he had let Maria get away.

As a rule, the religious orders who ministered to the laity (such as Franciscans, Dominicans, or Jesuits) and the laity themselves were more enthusiastic about miracles than were the "secular" or "parish" clergy (parish priests and bishops). This may have been because the sensibilities of laypeople and these orders more closely matched. It may have been, especially for Jesuits, the result of decades of experience in China, the Americas, and Europe, which taught them that to convert or minister to people one must speak their language—and the language of most Catholics was emphatically that of miracles. But the greater enthusiasm of many religious orders for miracles was also the result of at least one quite practical cause: their intense competition for souls.

The churches attached to the monasteries of religious orders were, after all, not parish churches with a fixed, reliable audience, whose members were obligated to make regular devotions, but instead places to which people came voluntarily and irregularly, beyond their parish duties. To attract believers from parish churches, and from the churches of rival orders, one had to outdo them. This might come in the form of providing more appealing confessors, music, preaching, decor, or shrines. It might come in the form of slightly subtle competition, as when the city of Naples in 1656 declared a great feast day for the patron saint of the Theatine order and the local Jesuits deflected attention from it by announcing a pious fast of their own; or when miracle recorders at shrines were careful to note the names of other shrines that the cured had visited without result. And it might come in the form of open contests, as when Franciscans and Dominicans argued so vigorously over a set of miracle-working relics that even in the dead of winter they broke into torrential sweats; or when a parish priest in Brussels called the Jesuits "bloodsuckers," "scalp pluckers," and "black crows"* for aggressively enticing so many local parishioners with lovely preaching and empathetic confessing and innovative schools, thereby diluting and confusing loyalties to one's parish.

*"*Black crow*" *referred not only to the thieving nature of that bird but also to the vestments of the clergy.*

Because of these efforts to attract laypeople, it was hardly surprising that Maria Caroens sought her cure not at any parish church but at a Franciscan and then a Jesuit church, both of which drew thousands on great feast days. And it was no more surprising that Pater van Liere's superiors wished to find Maria: word of a miracle at their church could only enhance their already substantial prestige—especially when it involved a woman who had failed to receive a miracle at the church of their rivals, the Franciscan Recollects.

This was not to say that all such rivalry was solely political. For even obviously self-interested holy places might renounce potential advantages in the name of honesty, as at the medieval shrine to Thomas Becket at Canterbury, where some of the monks who directed the place shouted "yes, yes," to an alleged miracle while others responded "no, no!" And it was a Franciscan who denounced a supposed miracle involving the deceased Franciscan nun, Clare of Montefalco. Indeed, it was precisely in order to show that the cure of Maria Caroens was genuine, and not the result of empty self-interest, that the Jesuits of Gent wished to find her and submit her evidence to the bishop: if this ultimate and impartial judge of local miracles confirmed her cure as miraculous, then all the world would know it was hardly a Jesuit invention.

These Jesuits were likely aware that recent cases similar to Maria's had not been declared miraculous, including the cure of a woman at the Jesuit church of Kortrijk in 1641, who was without milk for fourteen days, then was filled after touching the remains of the former Jesuit Leonard Lessius. But Maria's case was far more dramatic than this and surely had a better chance—if only they could find her.

The Jesuits did not know that Maria visited their church daily.

They possibly did not know exactly what she looked like, since her discussion with Pater van Liere had occurred in an identity-obscuring confessional. Hence they began a word-of-mouth search around town.

One of the people they put on alert, in early January 1658, was a woman named Little Adrian, who sold butter and cheese at the Wal-gate, and who therefore had frequent contact with all sorts of people. Adrian admitted that she did not know any women who had given birth to fourteen children and were without milk for the last then were suddenly restored, but, "being devout," promised she would ask everyone who entered the shop about such a person.

It was Maria herself who finally entered the shop one February day in 1658. That it took these two long months was somewhat surprising, for Adrian's butter shop stood conveniently at the end of the Savaan street, where Maria the waffle maker lived—perhaps Maria preferred another purveyor. In any case, Adrian greeted Maria with, "How are you?" Maria gave no typically perfunctory answer, but responded in full: "I'm having a hard time making ends meet, but I thank and praise God and the Holy Virgin Mary for the benevolence that I've received of being able to suckle my child." Adrian exulted, "Our Lord must have sent you here, for I promised to find you." She urged Maria to return to Pater van Liere at the Jesuit church and tell him where she lived, because the Jesuits wanted to know more.

The next day Maria did so. She did not remember exactly in which confessional she had originally called. Like most Jesuit churches, this one overflowed with confessionals, fourteen to be exact, but finally she found Pater van Liere at his usual place in the third, and told the delighted man where she lived: at the waffle shop in the Savaan street, with the small sign jutting into the street, plus a second sign advertising Antony's availability as a proxy pilgrim. Pater van Liere noted all this and promised that someone would visit soon.

Another Jesuit, a Pater van Delft, arrived within days to interview Maria. He also heard husband Antony, and Margaret Doosen, and Margaret's husband, confirm the story, though he would not bother to record their testimonies in detail. In addition, he hired Antony to make a three-day pilgrimage for someone to a shrine near Brussels, for a *daelder* a day.

On February 15, 1658, Pater van Delft returned to Maria's home with a notary and a neatly written copy of her testimony. Maria could not read the document herself, but she and Antony listened as it was read aloud. It took the form of most miracle accounts: the detailed medical history, the crisis, the physical and spiritual remedies attempted, the network of family and especially women friends involved, and finally the miraculous cure, sprinkled with orthodox rituals of praying and hearing mass. It would hardly have been unusual for the Jesuit editor to make small corrections, to eliminate contradictions or omit mention of any unchurched remedies Maria might have tried—not necessarily out of deceit, but lest such small matters preoccupy judges and detract from the reality of the miracle. Finally, in the presence of the notary, Maria signed her mark, a simple cross, attesting that it was true.

Like most people seeking official confirmation of miracles, the Jesuits also went to the trouble of gathering the opinions of medical doctors. Their testimony was always important, but it would be unusually so in Maria's case.

Physicians doubtless enjoyed their privileged status as expert witnesses in miracle investigations: *their* opinion of what constituted a natural or supernatural cure, rather than the opinions of such rivals as wise men and wise women, was the only expert testimony bishops relied upon, and was often decisive. In fact, without the confirmation of physicians that a cure was more than natural, it would have almost no chance of going forward to the bishop for consideration as a miracle.

But it was also doubtless that when cases did go forward, physicians hardly enjoyed testifying of "their own helplessness"—or in other words admitting that they did not know how a supernatural cure actually worked. They tried to deal with this by granting glory to God for such cures, or insisting that physicians complemented divine power rather than competed with it. But that miracles highlighted their incompetence, or that witness after witness named the various unsuccessful medical practitioners they had visited before receiving divine aid, could have been no more pleasant for physicians than the frequent enemas they so routinely prescribed for their patients.

Still, because there were very few cures for which physicians could imagine no possible natural explanation, when they spoke, bishops listened. The Jesuits therefore sent copies of Maria's testimony to eight different physicians, some in Gent and some in Brussels, including the physician to the governor-general, and asked for their opinions on the case. This, rather than a personal examination of the patient, was typical, largely because it saved time and money, and because most physicians would have been able to see the patient in question only after a cure, not before. Hence, they worked from the position, "assuming the evidence is true and complete, was this cure natural or not?"

The medical opinions about Maria came trickling in during May and June 1658, and it pleased and gratified her Jesuit advocates. It went "beyond nature," concluded every single physician, for a forty-two year-old woman who had borne fourteen children and produced little milk or other bodily fluids to suddenly and instantaneously have her "depressed and languid" breasts filled with milk, "without any pressure," and that one of them should flow so freely for so many months. Therefore, the cure "depended upon a higher source."

This was just what the Jesuits hoped to hear. Now they could send the case forward with confidence that the bishop and his men would consider it seriously. And if Maria's cure were confirmed as a miracle, it would mean full publicity—for the event itself, and incidentally for the shrine in their church.

It was not clear how much Maria was aware of all the efforts on her behalf, or whether she cared. But certainly she continued to be amazed, for though none of her usual physical remedies had worked this time, she was after many months still producing more milk for this once-starving child than she had for any of her other thirteen.

THE BISHOP'S MEN

August to October, 1658. Because Gent was currently between bishops (the last having died in May 1657), the Jesuits delivered their documents to the still-functioning bishop's vicariate, or council, in charge of the diocese until a new bishop could be appointed.

Though swamped by countless other matters, the five members of the vicariate were impressed enough by the testimonies taken thus far to proceed further, which meant first of all interviewing Maria herself.

On August 19, 1658, she walked several blocks north to the bishop's palace and told the vicariate her story, much as she had to the notary six months before. When she was finished, the members posed questions. They did not physically examine her, as was done in some cases (including the infamous "trial by congress" of various impotence cases, carried out in the presence of judge and lawyers), but the vicariate did ask Maria the sort of highly personal medical information that dominated miracle investigations.

Vicariate: "Was the one as well as the other bosom dry before this occurrence, so that there wasn't the least bit of milk inside them?"

Maria: "I don't know for sure, but I do know that I did all I could and I felt no milk and saw no milk, and I couldn't feed my child, and the child wasn't content with whatever it got, but kept crying, and had to be fed *pap*."

Vicariate: "During this alleged filling of your breasts with milk, did you feel no movement, or force, or pain in your body, or around your breasts?"—a question reflecting the common assumption that a sharp pain always accompanied a sudden cure.

Maria: "As I said before, I fell into something like a dream or sleep, and coming out of that I found that my breasts were swollen with milk, in each one, and the day after it first happened, I fed my child, and then visited the shrine again. And while I was in the church doing my devotions, I felt something like a pulling, then a falling into my bosom like a stone, so that my breasts were more full than the first day, and the third day they were even more full. And since that time I've kept up my devotions, and I've continued to nurse my child." This response contained another assumption:

that miracles happened most often while a person was asleep or in an unconscious state.

And so on. When the questions ceased, Maria volunteered that she had never produced as much milk for any of her children as this one, hinting that she too was eager for her cure to be declared miraculous.

However wary the councilors may have been about what caused the change, or however suspicious later observers might be that her story was quite formulaic in its structure and contents, no one, at any level, ever disputed that Maria had been suddenly and surprisingly cured. All that remained was for the vicariate to consult and announce its decision.

The vicariate did not leave behind many clues of its deliberations, which would end up taking a modest couple of months. But combined with evidence of the broader mental world to which the vicariate belonged, these clues were enough to suggest how they proceeded.

One thing was certain: Bishops and the men around them were, as already mentioned, usually less enthusiastic than Jesuits or laypeople about alleged miracles. In fact, their feelings could be described as resolutely mixed.

In part of their hearts and minds, these men believed as deeply as the simplest member of the flock that miracles occurred. Miracles were the "most energetic language of God," even more than creation itself, because miracles were dazzling and unpredictable. Miracles were also a sign of Christ's true Church, her "adornment, glory, magnificence, and confirmation:" Augustine said that the authority of the Holy Church began and ended with miracles.

Hence bishops and their helpers regularly denounced those Catholics who were skeptical of all miracles. Moreover, after the

Reformation these churchmen recognized the appeal of miracles in the struggle for souls, for Protestantism's transcendent, distant God had little to match Catholicism's God-with-us-and-all-around-us. These churchmen therefore did not shy from proclaiming genuine miracles to the world, including the learned Bishop Torrentius of Antwerp, who criticized a nun in his diocese for refusing to let her wondrous cure be announced.

Yet in another part of hearts and minds these same believing churchmen were wary of shouts of "miracle!" by their flock. Too many dubious claims predisposed churchmen to be skeptical, and to consider the laity as gullible, impressionable, and superstitious, and some of the religious orders as little better. They would have agreed readily with Thomas More, who gloomily concluded that if some priest wanted to "bring up a pilgrimage to his parish," all he had to do was convince someone to claim a cure, then ring the church's bells, and everyone would come running. These churchmen were even more skeptical about claims from women, who took the initiative in so many cures but not to their glory, for women showed too much "enthusiasm" for the otherworld. These churchmen tended from the thirteenth century onward to stress internal religion, and to discourage believers from running here and there for bodily cures and temporal fortune. They also feared that believers, through their zeal for good fortune, were likely not only to fall into innocent superstitions but to try more sinister forms of supernatural aid, such as magic and witchcraft. And last, these churchmen fretted that exaggerated claims of miracles would give ammunition to Protestants, who in the minds of many churchmen sat waiting pen in hand at their local print shop, just across the border, for the next Catholic foul-up.

To leading Protestants, the age of miracles was past: they had been needed to establish Christianity in ancient times, but their usefulness had ceased, just as the Israelites ceased needing manna once they entered the Promised Land. The miracles of Christ, said John Calvin, were real but "temporary testimonies," not meant to be a "permanent condition" of Christianity. Martin Luther and many others agreed, insisting that Catholic "miracles" were in truth lying wonders of the antichrist, "rascalities" of the devil himself.

Criticism of genuine miracles Catholic churchmen were willing to bear, like a cross, or to refute with published defenses. But what these churchmen could neither bear, nor defend against, were vague and dubious "miracles" held up by believing Catholics as genuine, and which Protestant rivals inevitably howled about in print, pulpit, and tavern. Here was a big reason why bishops and their councils proceeded cautiously, and were less enthusiastic than religious orders about miracles. Indeed, they generally favored an attitude, expressed by one of their kind, that "all novelty is dangerous and all unusual events are suspect." Only if the evidence was "irrefutable" would they defend a particular miracle. This was quite in contrast to the image portrayed by Protestant critics, who suggested that Catholic leaders proclaimed miracles on the slightest pretext in order to dupe and shackle believers. Rather, it was bishops who were deluged by the laity and religious orders to promote miracles, and bishops who tried to rein them in.

The way bishops did this was to insist on their exclusive authority, affirmed by the Church's monumental Council of Trent (1545–1563), to investigate and pronounce upon cases of alleged miracles, and to establish rigorous procedures for the process.

Hence the bishop of Roermond appointed at the shrine of Kevelaer, in the eastern Netherlands, a committee of twenty-four to decide on the many miracles claimed there. Most bishops at least consulted their vicariate, or a few others, for every alleged miracle sent to them. Any of these committees might call several, or dozens, or scores, or even hundreds of witnesses in order to ensure thoroughness: 133 witnesses testified about miracles surrounding Anna of Saint Bartholomew, while 659 told of wonders allegedly performed through the late Pope Urban V! The questioning was thorough as well, recorded often by numerous clerks, and with translators provided as necessary. All this helped to give the impression of great care, in cases large and small.

In control of the official process, bishops naturally emphasized their particular assumptions and ideas about miracles, and measured what they heard accordingly. It wasn't as if their views diverged drastically from those of ordinary believers: both accepted, for instance, a basic distinction between natural and supernatural forces. And it certainly wasn't as if churchmen agreed among themselves on a single view of miracles: Augustine, for instance, declared that all things we see in nature were miracles from God, while others, especially from the twelfth century on, sought to define the spheres of nature and miracle more clearly so that "God's special, miraculous interventions" might be placed in "sharp relief." The view that generally prevailed among miracle watchers by Maria's time was articulated by the most famous thinker of the Middle Ages, Thomas Aquinas (d. 1274), who insisted on distinguishing among events that were (1) *natural*, or part of the ordinary course of nature; (2) *preternatural*, or rare and marvelous but still part of the ordinary course of nature; and (3) *supernatural*, or above and beyond the ordinary course of nature.

This approach did not necessarily deny Augustine's point that God was behind all things. It simply wished to distinguish between things God did *directly* (outside of nature) and *indirectly* (the ordinary course of nature)—or, more formally, between primary and secondary causality. As one fellow put it, a miracle was the "extraordinary action of God" while nature was God's "sustained and uniform operation."

The trick, of course, was to identify each, and here was where disagreement and problems typically occurred. Both churchmen and lay believers asked: Was this cure, though wondrous, directly from the hand of God, or the result of a force in nature? And if it was supernatural, was it from God or the devil? Further, was a malady truly incurable by natural means? Was the cure sudden? Was it lasting?—for "cures" by the devil disappeared (which helped explain why investigators deliberately dragged out proceedings). Generally, churchmen were more inclined than other believers to see nature at work in these matters. Then, the churchmen posed even more questions to test the miraculous quality of a cure. They asked about orthodoxy: Was the cure surrounded by religious rituals, such as prayer, or mass, or a vow, or an invocation of God, or some other pious act, or had a "superstitious" incantation been used (thus one not approved by them)? Churchmen also asked questions of morality: Was the person truly penitent and humble? They further asked legal questions: Were the witnesses reliable and numerous? Did witnesses agree closely enough on the date of the cure, the length of the sickness, the remedies tried, and other details? And finally, churchmen asked theological questions: Did the cure promote true faith and demonstrate "God's majesty," for "cures" of the devil and his kind could be detected by their uselessness—the merely strange or unusual was not enough.

There were still other possible criteria for miracles, but from these alone it was clear that very few events could pass every barrier put up especially by churchmen and physicians. In fact, miracle-investigators spent far more energy looking for natural explanations than supernatural, just to be sure of the latter. Moreover, they put the burden of proof on those advocating a miraculous rather than a natural explanation: even a slight possibility that something might have a natural explanation was sometimes enough to render it unmiraculous.

All this, and more, the investigators into the cure of Maria Caroens knew and assumed.

Sensing that the vicariate was dragging its feet, the Jesuits tried to speed things along.

One of them persuaded a member of the vicariate to push his fellow councilors for a decision on Maria's cure. During a meeting in early September 1658, all five men, in fact, agreed to move Maria's case forward again—but not to announce a final decision just yet. Instead, the vicariate decided to seek still more information. Specifically, it wanted to gather its own set of medical opinions. Perhaps this was routine, or perhaps something about Maria's cure was bothering them. Whatever its reasons, the vicariate sought the fresh views of four experts—all from Gent, and two of them among those already consulted by the Jesuits last May.

On October 18, 1658, these new medical opinions arrived, delivered in person by the leading physician, William Thijs. And the outcome this time was much different from the last. Now three of the four doctors, including the two who had previously called Maria's cure supernatural, declared without further explanation that although the restoration of Maria's milk was "exceptional" in nature (*preternatural*), it was not necessarily "above or against" nature (*supernatural*).

This declaration by the physicians decided things for the vicariate. A medical declaration of "supernatural" did not ensure that a cure would be judged as miraculous, but a medical declaration that a cure was possibly natural (which included preternatural) doomed its chances. Upon receiving the medical opinions, the vicariate immediately called an extraordinary meeting, with Dr. Thijs still present, and announced its decision. "Having examined the expert judgment" of the physicians, the vicariate yielded to it and held that the restitution of the milk of Maria Caroens was "not miraculous, neither should be had for such, nor proclaimed as such." All papers relevant to the case were to be preserved in the episcopal archives. Case closed.

The Jesuits were baffled: in their minds this was no vague miracle or half miracle, like the once-lame man healed enough to walk slowly with a cane, or the once-speechless girl who could now say a few words. This was a dramatic, complete, and inexplicable change, enough to impress even the most skeptical investigator. The Jesuits therefore sent representatives to the vicariate over the next month to retrieve various documents they had submitted, and to find out what had gone wrong, but to no avail: the case, repeated the vicariate, was finished and the documents belonged to the vicariate. The Jesuits even tried to bring the case before the ecclesiastical court of the diocese, but this too amounted to nothing.

Frustrated, the Jesuits wrote in their house history for 1658 that a woman had been miraculously cured in their church, that her case was confirmed by numerous respected doctors from Gent and Brussels, and that the vicariate seemed close to confirming it, but then for "dubious" reasons did not.

NEIGHBORS

The Jesuits did not specify what they meant by "dubious," but clearly they suspected there was more to this decision than merely definitions of nature.

Perhaps the two physicians who had already reviewed Maria's case and now reversed themselves genuinely meant it: new cases similar to hers might in the intervening months have come to their attention and placed Maria's cure in a new and natural light. Or perhaps they had in the meantime read a recent work by Paolo Zacchia, a physician from Naples, who explained that one technique for distinguishing the truly miraculous cure was that it in no way even resembled a natural cure—thus a suddenly mended broken bone or a straightened bent leg resembled no natural remedy and could therefore be miraculous, while a cure that involved a crisis followed by an "evacuation," such as vomiting, hemorrhaging, diarrhea, purging, sweating, or urination, resembled the sorts of effects physicians saw or caused all the time and therefore could not with certainty be regarded as supernatural. Was not Maria's profuse sweating during her cure an "evacuation," not to mention the flow of milk from her breast? If interpreted this way, it was at least possible that Maria's cure came from God's handiwork (nature) rather than God himself.

But that these two physicians had just months before been convinced of the supernatural quality of her cure, that fewer physicians were consulted this time (again, all from Gent), and that no explanation was offered in the final decision, all caused the Jesuits to scratch their heads. Also suspicious were the vicariate's unusual decision to interview no other witnesses besides Maria herself, and the urgency it felt to summon an immediate meeting after hearing the new medical opinions.

The best clue that other forces were at work in this verdict—both with the vicariate and perhaps the physicians—lay in a stack of documents filed with the official papers of the inquiry into Maria, but whose contents were never mentioned during the proceedings. These documents were the product of yet another inquiry, undertaken in 1655 almost exactly two years before Maria's cure, into the origins of the Jesuits' special statue. And what the earlier inquiry revealed was that the supposedly miraculous origins of this statue, before which Maria would utter her life-changing prayer, were at best doubtful, and likely ridiculous.

The statue, discovered those investigators, came to the Jesuit church around 1625, the gift of a noble and pious Catholic couple, who had in turn received it decades before from a priest forced to flee Protestant Holland. This priest told the couple that during the 1580s a heretical brewer had mockingly thrown the statue into a fire, but it would not burn. The ability to resist fire was an old sign of a holy object, and so the priest asked to have it. The brewer responded, "Take your Mary, take her, she's useless for heating my oven."

The Jesuits of Gent loved such faith-promoting stories. They took great satisfaction, for instance, from their church's having been built triumphantly on the very spot where the fallen Calvinist leader, Hembyze, had lived in the 1580s. And they were proud as well of their special statue of the Virgin, given by the Protestant-defying Dutch priest and displayed in their church from at least 1631. In 1644 Bishop Antoon Triest even came to the church and bestowed the title Our Dear Lady of Mercy on the statue, and consecrated an altar for the chapel in which it now stood. Finally, in

September 1655 the Jesuits decided to "elevate" the statue, an old ceremony that involved moving an object to a more sacred and honored place, "from one cosmic world to another." In the case of the statue, elevation meant that it was no longer merely a decorative piece, a symbol, or a "prototype," but an object through which God actually performed miracles.

The Jesuits carried out this elevation during the first weekend of October 1655. Preceded by much publicity from the pulpit and large posters, the event was replete with a solemn procession, much prayer and song, enthusiastic preaching, memorable masses, recounting of the statue's miraculous origins, and the setting at the statue's base of a commemorative plaque repeating those origins. Now believers could be sure that the image was worthy of veneration as a holy object and potential miracle worker. There was just one major problem in all this: the Jesuits neglected to ask Bishop Triest in advance for permission to perform the elevation. Just as no new miracles were to be proclaimed within a diocese without the permission of the bishop, so no new images were to be called miraculous until approved by him first.

Bishop Triest knew about the elevation even before it occurred, thanks to one of the posters put up by the Jesuits, but decided not to stop a ceremony already announced, lest he provoke public curiosity. Instead he decided to investigate both the Jesuits' failure to ask permission and the veracity of the claims about the statue, then act quietly. But from what he knew already, he saw no reason to call it miraculous.

It was certainly possible that Bishop Triest decided to investigate the Jesuits and their statue out of personal spite and rivalry. The bishop and his vicariate belonged, after all, to the secular clergy, and thus their sympathies and interests lay more with parish priests than Jesuits, who not only upset the routine of parish life but were in many things "exempt" from the authority of bishops—sometimes acting more freely than bishops thought they should. In the case of miracles and images, for instance, exempt orders were not free to declare their own as they pleased—this right still belonged to the local bishop.

There was an even more specific point of tension between Bishop Triest and the Jesuits, especially in the years preceeding the elevation of the statue. Many members of the parish clergy, cathedral clergy, and vicariate, plus Bishop Triest himself, were associated with the loosely organized spiritual movement within Catholicism called Jansenism, whose chief rivals were none other than the Jesuits. So called because of their namesake, Cornelis Jansen (d. 1638), former bishop of Ieper and author of a famous treatise supporting Augustine's view of grace, Jansenists emphasized internal religion and condemned Jesuits for their supposed willingness to placate most believers with such undemanding "externals" as pilgrimages and miracles. Jansenists insisted that one should go to confession only with true contrition, or love of God, while Jesuits held that most believers could attain only attrition, or fear of God, and that this was good enough for now. Jansenists claimed that Jesuits were leading believers into a false sense of security, and "colluding in the ignorance of the peasantry rather than reforming them," while Jesuits feared that strict Jansenism would not only exclude most people from heaven but tempt them to convert to Protestantism. And Jansenists, along with many others, resented the Jesuits for their tendency to act first and ask permission later—Jesuits were not unique in this, but simply the most notorious.

This rivalry was no mere academic tussle, but had tangible

consequences—in the form of numerous Jesuit victories. Rome condemned Jansenism various times after 1640, and Bishop Triest personally in 1653. At almost eighty years of age he was forced to endure the humiliation of seeing posted on his own cathedral doors the placard announcing his ban from the sacraments. Months later he was reconciled, but the event left a scar on his otherwise spotless life and a bitter taste in his mouth, especially as he was forced to endure still other humiliations, each worse than the last. Many Jansenists in Gent, where the battle was arguably fiercest, blamed the Jesuits for his treatment.

Precisely because he had lost that battle, however, Bishop Triest could not appear to take action against the Jesuits for purely personal reasons. In fact, ever since his condemnation, and even before, he had gone out of his way to smooth things. He had already authenticated various holy objects within the Jesuits' church, and he had been the one to bestow a special title on the very statue that was now under investigation. Moreover, he had asked the Jesuits to minister to soldiers quartered in Gent, consulted various Jesuits on thorny cases of conscience brought before him, given the Jesuits a thousand florins to help decorate their new church, and soon after his condemnation by Rome willingly consecrated the new anti-Jansenist bishop of Antwerp. Hence, at least in appearance, and even genuinely, given his keen spirituality, Bishop Triest would not act arbitrarily against the Jesuits. When he opposed their efforts or claims, he made sure to do so on principle. And when he decided in October 1655 to question their statue, he therefore moved carefully, with every sign of fairness.

One way he demonstrated that fairness was by not moving alone, but rather bringing in many others—including Jesuits. First he consulted his vicariate. Then he wrote eleven theologians (three of them Jesuits from outside Gent) to ask their opinions of the image and its recent elevation.

Answers came back over the next month, during October and November of 1655, and they were all negative. That the four Augustinians consulted denounced the elevation was perhaps predictable: their Jansenism caused them to clash often with the Jesuits, especially those of Gent—and most especially Pater van Liere, the confessor of Maria Caroens. Here was an emotional preacher, notorious for such inflammatory statements as that the Jesuits, not the Augustinians, had been chosen by God to teach the true principles of Saint Augustine, and that Jansenists were heretics, tempters, and wolves for whom he would not say one Hail Mary or Our Father when they died! Also predictable was the condemnation of the elevation by the Jansenist D'Aubermont, who in 1654 had given a sermon in Gent at which Bishop Triest and friends sat on the front row "ready to applaud," according to a scornful report of the event by the local Jesuit superior. Finally, the condemnation by Peter Marchant, a Franciscan Recollect, major rivals of the Jesuits in Gent, was likewise predictable. But that the three Jesuits consulted by Bishop Triest also condemned the unauthorized elevation of the statue by the Jesuits of Gent suggested that there were indeed serious flaws—not only in the failure to ask permission, but with the statue itself.

In fact, concluded all eleven theologians, there was no evidence that the statue had actually been thrown into the fire and survived it, or that the Dutch priest had actually seen this himself. It was more likely, they continued, that the heretical brewer had simply made the story up and passed it on as a blasphemous joke to the gullible priest, then laughed about it with his friends. Stories of the statue's miraculous origins should therefore be halted immediately and the image itself destroyed or removed to more modest surroundings, to avoid further damage, following Aquinas, who said that "when holding up false images . . . the Church can receive much injury." The injury they had in mind was obvious: scandal to the faithful, and propaganda meal for nearby Dutch Protestants.

What, worried the theologians, would believers think when they learned that the story of the image was based on such flimsy evidence? Although the faith of some might indeed be shaken, perhaps the theologians overestimated the importance of solid legal evidence to the laity or even the Jesuits—if the statue gave evidence of real power, that was the best proof of all of its veracity.

Regarding Dutch Protestants, however, the theologians were on firmer ground. They were indeed watching. If Spanish and Italian Church leaders could worry about the effects of criticism from faraway Protestants, how much more concerned were leaders in the Spanish Netherlands, who lived only miles away from the nominally Protestant (but highly mixed) Dutch Republic, and who knew that some of these Protestants lived secretly within the very walls of Gent. A Catholic investigator at a Catholic shrine in Vught, once part of the Spanish Netherlands, wrote that some practices there needed reforming but he would not mention them in writing lest his report fall into the hands of Protestants. In fact, many internal investigations into Netherlandish Catholic shrines were motivated by what nearby Protestants would think.

Dutch Protestant leaders were vigorous in large part because there were so many Catholics in the Republic: they wanted to provide those Catholics with reasons to convert, and Protestants with reasons to stay where they were. Hence, these leaders sponsored missionary work and encouraged religious debate and exposés.

They retold scandalous and often unfounded stories of the Catholic clergy, such as of the Jesuit in 1570 who supposedly carried a picture of a woman secretly under his clothes and through his lust became pregnant and produced a child, which caused other Jesuits to call it a miracle and establish a shrine in commemoration. They promoted satires about Catholic holy places, modeled after Catholic devotional books, such as *The Holy Virgin of Halle, Her benevolence and miracles translated from the Latin . . . to the ridiculing of Popish Roman Idolatry*. They winked at marionettes of Our Dear Lady of the Sharp Hill, sold as comic toys. And they railed against images of all kinds.

To Protestants all images were "stupid." "We've never been taught to pray to the tail of the ass on which Jesus rode, or Martin's boots, Gregory's skull, Crispin's cutting-knife, Rochus' dog, or Anthony's pig," for by honoring the objects of the world "we commit idolatry," explained one author. Moreover, the true Christian would do better to devote time and resources wasted on images and rituals to feeding the poor. Hence Protestants would hardly hesitate to pounce on such a spuriously miraculous image as that promoted by the Jesuits of Gent, about which they were sure to learn through Catholic family or acquaintances, who in all sincerity would explain why they visited this image and then the laughter would begin, bringing unnecessary dishonor to the Church and the Virgin.

Plenty of Catholics, including bishops, were as prepared to defend images as they were miracles generally. Apologists argued that the Old Testament passages against idolatry that Protestants so loved to quote did not condemn images as such but rather those regarded as idols, and that for every passage of scripture condemning images another could be found supporting them. What, for instance, of the serpent held up in the wilderness through which God healed the children of Israel? (Numbers 21:8)

More practically, images helped believers to recall the virtues of various Saints (better than words alone), instructed those who could not read, and excited many to devotion. Even the literate and famously devout Teresa of Avila relied on tangible images, because she had "so little aptitude" for imagining things in her mind. "This is why I was so fond of pictures," she explained. And those who were not did not "love the Lord, because if they did they would enjoy looking at His picture in the same way as worldly men enjoy gazing on portraits of those whom they love." And this was why even Bernard of Clairvaux, who did not like any images in the bare churches of his Cistercian order, allowed them for ordinary believers.

As for the possible abuse of images, the sun and moon might become objects of abuse and idolatry as well—should humans be rid of them too? Thomas More admitted that abuses were real, but still trusted that the "simplest fool" knew that Our Lady was in heaven and that her image here with us was merely an image. Others likewise insisted that believers knew the difference between a statue of a horse and a real horse, between a thing and its shadow, between a portrait and the actual person, between a map of Brabant and Brabant itself. And if Catholics spoke among themselves that a statue of the Virgin "healed this one or that," they understood well that the statue was not doing this itself but rather God through it.

But though Church leaders continued to acknowledge the usefulness and even miraculousness of images, and to say that only abuses needed fixing, they also showed hesitation and even disagreement. In fact, there had been arguments from the beginning of Christianity about images, with some insisting early on that veneration "of all inanimate objects" was wrong. During the fifth and sixth centuries a movement arose to decorate tombs with simple Christian symbols, such as crosses or lambs, rather than elaborate sculptures and paintings. Differences over images played a leading role in the growing rift between eastern and western Christianity during the eighth and ninth centuries. And in later medieval centuries the Church even destroyed some of its own images as false, and worried whether the distinction between an image as a prototype or as a worker of miracles really mattered to ordinary believers.

In the age of the Reformation, debate within the Church continued still, if less dramatically than debate against Protestants. Renowned bishops such as Carlo Borromeo and Gabriele Paleotti in Italy or Antoon Triest in Gent insisted that images be historically reliable, in origin and appearance, out of fear that believers would grow disillusioned from revealed frauds and that Protestants would ridicule. But contemporary Jesuits such as Giovanni Ottonelli, an artist himself, emphasized that above all else paintings were meant to inspire devotion and faith in believers—the classic Jesuit subordination of means to ends—and was content to weed out only those images that reflected a questionable sexual ethic. The Jesuit Antonio Possevino said much the same, admitting that it was desirable to render an image correctly, but the real purpose was devotion, not historical accuracy. This wasn't far from a more extreme attitude voiced centuries earlier by Paulinus of Nola, that "misguided piety was better than no piety at all." The Jesuits of Gent showed that they were willing to take a similar approach, and regarded the demands of history or canon law as secondary to the task of instilling faith.

But Bishop Triest would not go that far. Bolstered by the opinions of his eleven theologians, he concluded in November 1655 that the claims about the miraculous statue in the Jesuit church would have to stop. The only question was how to proceed.

Because the origins of the statue had already been announced at its elevation, if it were suddenly removed merely a month later, then the chance for questions and scandal among the faithful, and Protestant observers, was real. One of the bishop's consulting theologians, Peter Marchant, did not care. He favored halting the cult immediately and destroying the image. It was, after all, he argued, begun not by popular clamor, as so many cults were, but by the Jesuits themselves, who should have known better. Moreover, "you say that scandal will occur if the cult is not allowed to continue, but more scandal will occur, indeed sin and peril, if it *is* allowed."

But the bishop's other consultants, including the Jesuits, advised moving discreetly, a style the bishop himself preferred. As he and many other bishops knew from long experience, it could do more harm than good to suppress with full fanfare an already well known devotion. More than once had the bishop compromised with various parishes and churches in his diocese on the issue of popular rituals by telling them in essence that they could keep a dubious custom if they toned it down. Like more and more bishops since the Middle Ages, he did not "seek violent confrontation" with popular beliefs, but rather tried to deal flexibly and quietly, simply ignoring things if they were small enough. He and his men wanted the last word about the miraculous and otherworldly, but they would not or could not enforce it absolutely.

Some rituals and holy places were indeed quashed from above. But others were adopted under public pressure, such as the procession of the miraculous Holy Blood at Bruges, begun around 1250 by popular demand and continued ever afterward. Others were reluctantly tolerated by bishops, such as the common and wondrous resuscitation of babies who died without baptism, were then quickly baptized, and finally buried in consecrated ground. And others were ignored if they didn't go too far. This is why one historian would later suggest that ideas about the otherworldly were usually the "outcome of some sort of interaction between clergy and laity, center and periphery, learned culture and popular culture," or why another would portray miracles as taking shape within a "dynamic system of negotiation," involving pilgrims, leaders of sacred places, parish clergy, and the various religious orders.

This dynamic system was evident in every step of what happened next in the saga of the Jesuits' statue. First, Bishop Triest summoned the local superior of the Jesuits on November 17, 1655, and informed him that the new cult around the statue must cease.* Second, because the statue already enjoyed some renown among believers, it was not to be removed nor destroyed, simply deemphasized: thus, all claims in sermons were to cease, the plaque proclaiming the miraculous origins was to be removed, and the statue was to stand merely as another image, or prototype, of the Virgin. Third, and most important here, despite the bishop's best efforts to suppress the statue, Maria Caroens heard about it anyway in 1657 and was healed.

Were the Jesuits still quietly promoting the statue by then? Or did people simply remember the stories and elevation of 1655? Whatever the case, Maria's faith and her wondrous healing put the

*If Bishop Triest took any personal delight or revenge in this apparent subjection, it was perfectly hidden. Or perhaps not, for when he died in April 1657 he remembered in his will every religious order in Gent save one: the Jesuits.

bishop's vicariate in a very difficult position. Who could deny that she had been healed? Yet how could the vicariate go along with the promotion of such a dubious image, in light of the inquiry completed in 1655?

The announcement by the new set of physicians in October 1658 that Maria's cure had been natural must have been especially welcome to the vicariate, for it solved in one stroke their complicated problem.

But it made at least the Jesuits just as quickly suspicious. The new medical opinion appeared to them as nothing but a cover for the vicariate's true objections, which were never made public and which not even the Jesuits knew for sure, even if they might guess.

On the one extreme, perhaps the vicariate simply believed the physicians' verdict about Maria. On the other extreme, perhaps the vicariate simply acted politically—refusing to take Maria's cure seriously merely to spite their rivals, the Jesuits, and compelling the physicians to do their dirty work for them. Each member of the vicariate knew the notorious biblical example of acting politically, in Acts 4:14–18, where various leaders of the Jews "could not deny" the miracles of the apostles but they *could* order the apostles to cease lest too many be converted. Was the vicariate, made up of secular clergymen one and all, acting likewise against their frequent rivals the Jesuits?

The unrecorded motives and thoughts of the vicariate were probably more complex than either of these scenarios. They might have believed privately that Maria's cure was genuinely miraculous, but because the image was false the miracle could not be publicized. For they were likely familiar as well with a sentiment articulated by the medieval thinker Caesarius of Heisterbach, which admitted that one might be cured by a false relic if one believed in it enough—for God might choose to smile upon heartfelt devotion. Yet it was more likely that yet another sentiment prevailed in the minds of the vicariate and the physicians: namely, that Maria's cure *could not* have been miraculous, precisely because of the scandalous origins of the statue, and was necessarily attributable to some natural cause. This went beyond merely not *wanting* the cure to be miraculous, or merely spiting the Jesuits. As one of Bishop Triest's expert theologians concluded about false statues, miracles associated with them were "absolutely dubious."

When the fifteenth-century German shepherd boy Hans Behem was at the center of miracles that displeased the local bishop, that bishop was sure the miracles could not have been real, for this would mean that the Virgin was behind the shepherd and against the bishop—an impossibility. When Joan of Arc claimed to have experienced angelic visions, her judges (some reluctantly) declared her a witch instead, for to confirm those visions as genuine would have been to say that God was with her, and that was impossible. When later Jansenists in France, condemned by Rome and the king, began to claim miracles of their own, everyone understood that if these were confirmed by the Church, then it meant that the Church had been wrong, and this was impossible, for it would "strike at the root of the whole papal authority." In all these cases, the authorities were not necessarily dishonest but simply predisposed toward a certain order of the universe and church, which convinced them that there were other explanations for seemingly wondrous events.

Similarly, the uncertain origins of the statue likely made it at least difficult for the vicariate to see Maria's cure as truly miraculous. In approaching the second set of medical doctors, in September 1658, the vicariate likely shared the news of the statue's origins with them, along with the facts of Maria's cure. Not that doctors and theologians always agreed—far from it. And not that doctors routinely did the Church's bidding—although it was possible in this case, for all four doctors were local and thus subject to some pressure from Church authorities. But rather that these doctors shared a worldview that had more in common with the vicariate than it did with such simple believers as Maria Caroens. Because the statue was not miraculous, there *must* have been another explanation for Maria's cure. Had the eight physicians consulted by the Jesuits in May 1658 also been privy to the information about the statue's problematic origins, they too might have been motivated to look harder for natural causes and thus have effectively stopped the inquiry right there.

Certainly the Jesuits were disappointed by the announcement of the vicariate's decision regarding Maria, especially when they learned a couple of years later about a woman at the Jesuit church in Mechelen who was without milk for a mere eight days, then was cured after placing the relics of Saint Francis Xavier on her chest for one hour. But they were characteristically not discouraged for long, for in this very year of 1658 the Jesuits of Gent began enlarging the classroom building for their school, and in 1660 they completely remodeled the inside of their church in the latest Baroque style, just like other Jesuit churches across Europe, and presumably to the satisfaction of their many local visitors.

Perhaps Maria was disappointed as well. Or perhaps she and Antony were indifferent to the official decision, and simply marveled as they pleased at what had occurred. Perhaps her well-fed fourteenth child lived, unlike most of her others, to adulthood. Perhaps Maria bore still more children. But we know nothing else of her, nor her friends, except that by late 1658 Margaret Doosens was a widow, left alone with several children, including the burned one who was not cured—not even when Margaret took it to the statue in the Jesuit church, still on display, which some still said had survived fire, and which Margaret was still certain had cured her friend Maria Caroens.

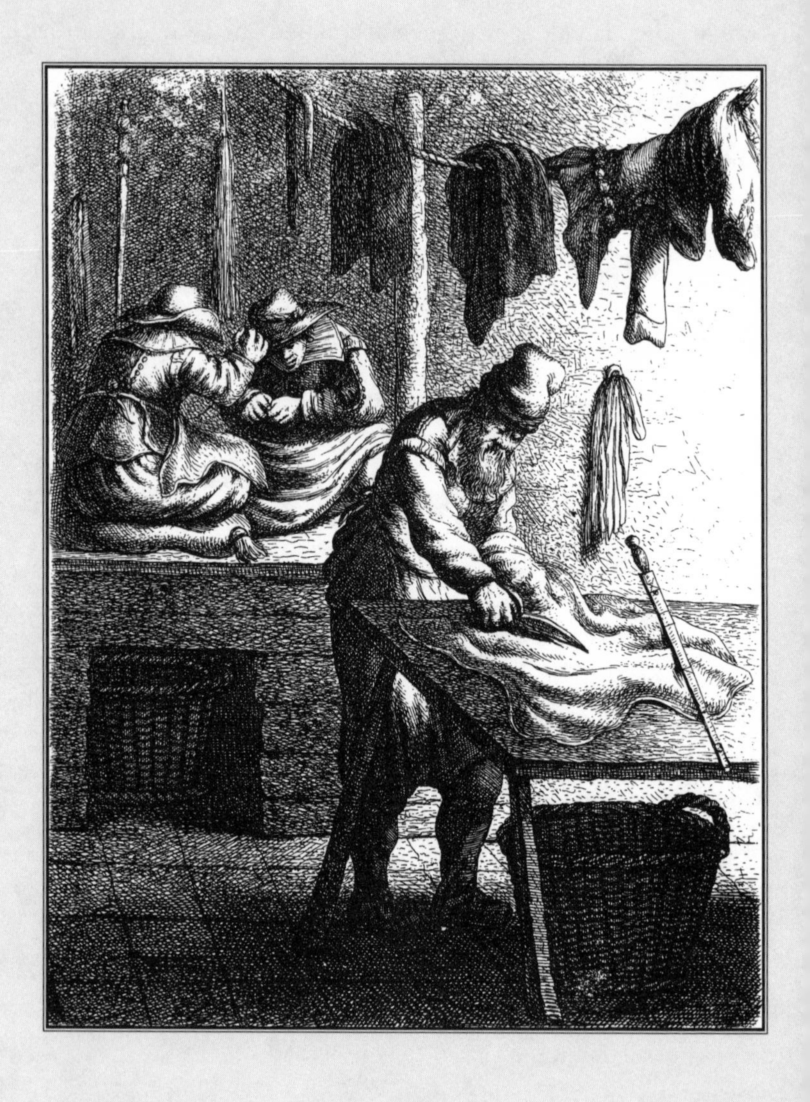

THREE

THE CHAPEL OF POOR TAILORS

UNHOLY DIVERSIONS

March 5, 1660, a Friday, on the Streets of Gent. Two years after the healing of Maria Caroens, and some ten blocks north, another anxious mother carrying another sick child walked hopefully toward yet another shrine.

Her destination was the church of the convent called Groenebriel, near the city's northern walls, where she had heard were preserved a few small relics of Saint Fiacre, a holy hermit who had died a thousand years before in France but who at the moment was suddenly enjoying newfound fame as a healer. Most of Fiacre's precious remains still lay in France, around Meaux, but even the fragments on display in Groenebriel were said to draw people from surrounding villages and beyond, especially on Friday, market day, when peasants brought their goods to town and thus their sick children as well.

This mother and child managed to find their way through Gent's narrow, cluttered streets and past many of its seventy-five other religious institutions. Only when they were a mere block or two away from their destination did serious confusion set in.

It happened just after passing the convent of the Augustinians, on their left, and directly in front of a modest chapel nearby. There before the chapel sat a woman, carding wool, who glanced up at the two, guessed their business, and asked: "Have you come to visit Saint Fiacre?" Hesitant to address this stranger, the mother grudgingly admitted that this was indeed their purpose. The wool carder then motioned behind her and said, "The blessings are now done here," in the tailors' chapel, named in honor of Saint Fiacre, where the relics had recently been moved. Unfamiliar with the city, unsure whether to believe this woman or friends who had told her where to find the saint, and determined to get her child to the right place, the pilgrim hesitated again. But persuaded at last, she went inside to have the child blessed.

This scene was repeated numerous times over the next two weeks, such as on March 19, when the same wool carder stopped three passing pilgrims, used the same arguments as before, and again succeeded in persuading them to change directions and head toward the tailors' chapel for their blessings. This time, however, a neighbor girl overheard the exchange and interrupted. She informed the out-of-towners that the wool carder was mistaken: the relics of Fiacre were indeed in Groenebriel, just around the corner, just as they had heard. Hence the pilgrims changed directions once more and continued to the convent, where they told attending nuns of their strange encounter.

Even more enduring in Christianity than miracle-working statues were the relics of such saints as Fiacre.

The cult of the saints dated from the second-century Roman Empire, when believers gathered around the tombs of Christian martyrs to honor them and bask in their holiness. As the empire gradually accepted Christianity and martyrdom declined, believers in search of holiness turned then to honor those dead who had led exceptionally virtuous lives. Celebration of heroes and the "very special dead" were not unique to ancient Christians, but Christians added their particular twists. They buried their dead right among them rather than far away: to believers, the remains of the saints were still alive and powerful, just as the risen Christ was alive and powerful—another example of God's presence in specially chosen places and objects of this fallen world. Christians also regarded the saints as active intercessors with God: because the saints were once "one of us," they were easier to approach than God Himself, yet because the saints' extraordinary virtues made them no ordinary human beings, God was especially inclined to listen to them, His closest followers, for a whole variety of purposes.

Long before the seventeenth century, relics were paraded about in times of war, natural disaster, celebration, and other community occasions. They were used to prevent and fight fires, and marched through fields to promote fertility. People swore oaths on relics, and sometimes took such oaths more seriously than those sworn on the Bible. And of course relics were extraordinarily popular in healing, according to a saint's reputed gifts: Saint Denis for headaches and rage; Saint Blaise for throat pain; Saint Barbara for burns, explosions, and sudden death; Saint Giles for epilepsy, sterility, and pos-

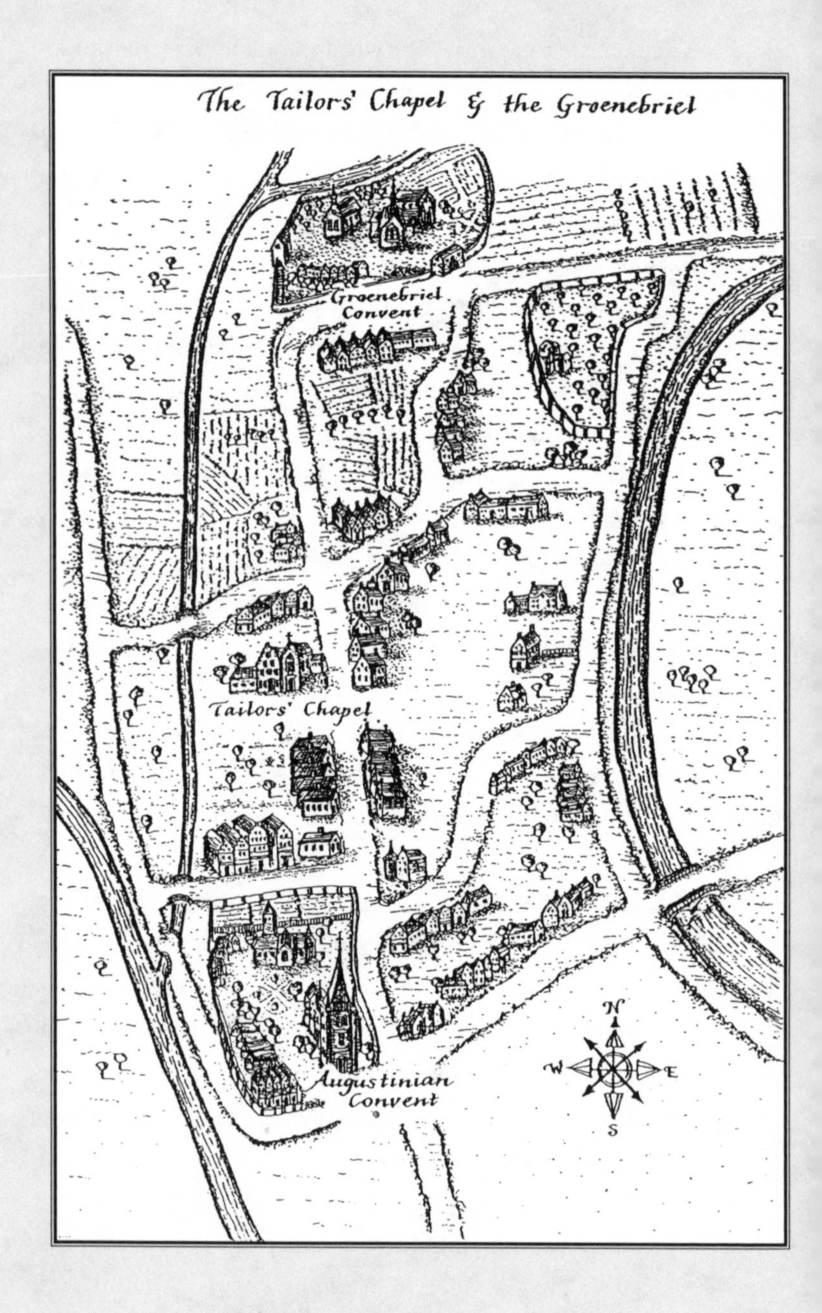
The Tailors' Chapel & the Groenebriel
Groenebriel
Convent
Tailors' Chapel
Augustinian
Convent
N
E
S
W

session; Saint Christopher for sudden death and travel; Saint Margaret for difficulties in childbirth; Saint Catherine for protection of young girls and students; or Saint Fiacre for gardening (his own favorite pastime), skin problems, and such inglorious afflictions as hemorrhoids, venereal disease, and difficulty urinating (though he was also known as a general healer).

Believers sought favors among the saints for themselves but mostly for their infants and young children, usually (in miracle accounts) those under four, who were most susceptible to the illnesses of the day. These young ones were also more susceptible to accidents, particularly (according to the same accounts) in wetter northern Europe, where they fell into more lakes, ditches, wells, canals, streams, pits, cesspools, and springs, along with suffering widespread accidents involving farm equipment or collapsed ladders and walls. But it was especially illness that set Catholic parents on the road to find the right saint.

The popularity of individual saints waned and peaked according to their effectiveness. Fiacre himself seemed most potent right at this time in the seventeenth century, and was sought out in France even by an ailing Cardinal Richelieu. But though many saints declined in popularity, and though Rome attempted to prune the vast tree of saints of its more historically dubious members, there was no thought among Catholic believers of giving up saints altogether: if one failed, there was an entire multitude of others waiting to be tried, from such widely famous relics as pieces of the true cross, or Mary's milk, or the shroud of Turin, to obscure local saints. In French lands alone during this time, there were 123 different saints good against fever, 48 against lightning, 43 against headache, and so forth, and, in fact, so many all around in statues and relics that along one six-mile stretch of road connecting several French villages a believer had opportunity to invoke 149 different saints.

The way people sought out divine help for their illnesses and accidents, or gave thanks for cures, was to draw near to the saints, and to pray, and especially to touch—usually their bones, but also other objects connected to them. Perhaps by kissing a relic, or drinking water that had been washed over it, or seeing the relic, or sleeping near it, but certainly by touching it, one might be healed or blessed. The moment of touching was awe-inspiring, prepared for with cleansing rituals, and often accompanied by trembling. Pilgrims might also weep, and kneel nine times, and remove their shoes, and light candles, all in the midst of incense. Like Maria Caroens in Gent or Anna Eregiers at the Jesus Oak, they almost always left alms, in gratitude or anticipation. And they always made a vow, to go on pilgrimage, or to fast, or to feed paupers, or to offer candles, wax, jewels, livestock, and even children to God, in exchange for help from their saint.

When ancient Catholic critics complained that these rituals, meant to promote healing and good fortune, were also observed by pagans and wouldn't Christians do better to find others, defenders could point to such biblical examples as the Ark of the Covenant helping Israel cross the River Jordan on dry ground. When other Catholic critics argued against relics just as they had against images—namely that inanimate objects should not be venerated by Christians, lest they commit idolatry—defenders insisted that relics were not inanimate at all. When still other Catholics remarked that most believers were ignorant of the distinction similarly made for images—that relics did not themselves possess power to do miracles but rather God signified by miracles through them the virtues of that particular saint—defenders did not think this or even more flagrant abuses sufficient grounds to throw out the whole. When Protestant critics insisted that true believers should go directly to God and that scripture did not specifically teach relics, defenders of the saints could point to Paul's bidding the Romans pray for him, and the woman who touched Christ's robe and was healed, and those who touched Paul's sweat cloth and were cured. Besides, scripture did not specifically teach the Trinity either. In short, despite centuries of criticism within, and new attacks without after the Reformation, the saints remained the most familiar and reliable way for believers to seek divine help—so familiar and reliable that not even all new Protestants could completely quit their saints, to the chagrin of Protestant leaders.

That believers still valued the saints, and that the saints worked for them, could be seen not only in how frequently they visited existing shrines but in how eagerly they attacked the physical remains of the newly deceased holy, cutting off the wrappings around their corpses, or their nails, extremities, and organs, even boiling and decapitating them to have their bones more quickly. It could be seen in how relics were eagerly collected, divided, and subdivided, for each piece was believed to have the same power as the whole (though to possess the whole was highly desirable); especially princes became great gatherers, with Philip II of Spain alone possessing some seventy-four hundred different relics, managed by a full-time caretaker. It could be seen in rules that required relics to be displayed only in protective reliquaries, lest they be stolen by the unscrupulous or simply crushed in the crowd of pilgrims moving forward to handle them, and by placing the more precious reliquaries up high, out of reach. It could be seen in the great lengths to which people went to possess relics, including the payment of astonishing sums of money, or even theft. And finally it could be seen in a literal way, for relics could bring benefactors, alms, and prestige to the shrine that sheltered them—not only at such large and medium complexes as the Sharp Hill or Jesus Oak, but on a smaller scale at such convents as Groenebriel.

UNSMILING NUNS

The abbess of Groenebriel was, to say the least, peeved upon hearing stories of diversions by the tailors.

Head of the convent since 1648, Mother Anna Maria van Hamme was long acquainted with trouble, but she had never seen anything quite like this. She immediately sent two lay sisters (whose task it was to run the convent's errands in the world) to have a look around the chapel, and if possible to arrange for someone to snoop around inside. The news brought back from these reconnaissance missions was as upsetting as Anna Maria had feared. Satisfied that her convent was the victim of foul play, she now turned for help to the vicariate of the still bishopless diocese of Gent, the same body in which Maria Caroens had placed her hopes only months before.

During March 1660, Mother Anna Maria wrote twice to the vicariate to tell what she had discovered: that certain dependents of the tailors' guild, most notably one Elisabeth de Mey, wife of the guild's servant, were misleading pilgrims about the location of Saint Fiacre. That this had occurred with "scandal and deception of good pilgrims," who had often traveled "many miles" to seek remedies "for their ills and infirmities" at Groenebriel. That, in fact, there were no relics at all in the chapel of the tailors, much less any relics of Fiacre—nothing but some tiny, vague objects the tailors claimed were relics. That she suspected the tailors themselves had put their servants up to these deceptions, and were not innocent bystanders. And that there could be no doubt that the relics of Fiacre in Groenebriel were genuine, for various bishops of Gent had said so. Certainly, concluded the abbess, the Church ought not tolerate such deceits.

There was no need for Anna Maria to state the reasons why, because they were obvious, and indeed were the same reasons that had applied in the case of Maria Caroens: scandal among believers and Protestants alike. Neither was there need for Anna Maria to state that the tailors' deceptions also damaged her particular convent: the vicariate's own interests in suppressing scandal would be enough to move them. But certainly the foremost priority in her mind in reporting these deceits was the damage they did to the convent, especially in potential loss of friends, prestige, and even income.

On this last point, Anna Maria explained further: her complaint was not about simple greed. The tailors played that game, she said, for they pressed diverted pilgrims to leave eight or nine stivers apiece at their chapel, and even boasted that they hoped to earn thousands of florins a year from their "relics." The convent, on the other hand, asked of visiting pilgrims to cover only the cost of consecrated water and bread distributed to them. Its chief interest was not gain, but to protect its reputation and the honest devotions of pilgrims.

There is no specific reason to disbelieve Anna Maria's claim, but the true motives of any shrine keeper were rarely perfectly clear. Moreover, even those with the purest motives were keenly aware that it cost money to run a shrine, not to mention a convent, and those in charge of either valued every donation made—especially if they were even close to the thousand or so florins a year the tailors supposedly hoped to garner from devotions at their chapel. Unfortunately the account books for the convent church did not survive (nor did those for the tailors' chapel). But other records from the convent show that the nuns of Groenebriel could have used every last bit of income brought in by their special saint.

All convents, male or female, contemplative or active,* survived on an original endowment, annuities and dowries brought by new entrants, income from the common work, and gifts from new friends. Of course these amounts varied from place to place, so that some convents were better off than others, but, generally speaking, male convents were better off than female, and the female were chronically short of funds.

This was true even in Groenebriel, founded in 1372 as a contemplative Victorine convent (a branch of the Augustinians) and more prosperous than most. After all, Mother Anna Maria's recent predecessors had managed to undertake various building projects,

The contemplative vocation focused on prayer, labor, and physical separation from the world, while the active centered usually on sick care and education. About half the houses of women in the Low Countries at this time were contemplative and the other half active. Because cloister was stricter for contemplative women than for active women, or for all men, one might regard this as yet another disadvantage in procuring funds. But, in fact, cloistered houses, such as Groenebriel, tended to be better off than active houses, whose members were able to go out. That active women were usually poorer suggests that the ability to go into the world and seek alms was less important in attracting benefactors than the contemplative life, which most contemporaries regarded as superior.

the nuns generally boasted loftier social origins than those in the thirty other female houses of Gent, and some neighbors even considered the convent "rich." Yet the nuns did not think themselves rich at all—only fragile: Mother Anna Maria marveled aloud in her accounts for the bishop that she was expected to support a community of forty-five and continue a rebuilding program (necessitated by war and age) on such a piddling income as theirs, as if Our Dear Lord with his few loaves and fishes had more to start with in feeding the multitude than did she.

Indeed, with the annual accounting almost always in the red, it wasn't enough for Anna Maria merely to watch carefully the endowment, cast a discreet eye at the size of annuities possessed by potential entrants, and ensure that the common work of the nuns brought in profit as well as discipline. In addition, she, like other superiors, had to court outside friends almost constantly. One way to do this was through entertaining these friends at the convent's grille, with food, drink, conversation, and occasionally even plays or other recreations. But she could not go too far in such pleasantries, lest she thwart the second great means of attracting friends: namely, inspiring them. Outsiders did not know exactly what went on inside convents, but they cared much and they knew the rumors, good and bad—including that the last abbess of Groenebriel was during her short reign possessed by demons. In other words, Anna Maria van Hamme understood well the need for piety as well as hospitality. And if the best place to entertain was the grille, then the best place to inspire was the convent's church.

Fortunately for Anna Maria, Groenebriel's original, crumbling church had been rebuilt into something respectable only years before, thanks to a few choice benefactors sent, the nuns were sure, by God. For these benefactors included none other than the archdukes, Albert and Isabella, who laid the first cornerstone in 1613 during memorable ceremonies, and who so inspired the many great ones in attendance to give generously that the church went up quickly. This church not only provided a pleasant place for nuns to worship, but its decoration, its comfort, its heavenly music, and its celebrated patrons made it a major attraction for still other new benefactors. Not even the devil's striking the church tower with lightning, causing part of the roof to collapse, or breaking the windows with his hailstones right during Vespers so that the nuns had to run for cover, could dampen the convent's enthusiasm for their special place. Especially not since the church contained yet another attraction, its crowning glory, even more powerful than fine architecture, music, or statuary: namely, a relic of Saint Fiacre reputed to work cures.

Virtually all churches possessed one relic or another, plus statues and crucifixes, but as seen at the Jesus Oak or the Jesuit church of Gent, the possession of a holy object that attracted genuine crowds was a rare thing. The first bit of Fiacre in Groenebriel arrived in 1592, and was long regarded as just another relic, one of eleven in the convent's possession. Twenty years later, several sisters even seemed unaware that part of Fiacre rested among them. But obscurity had vanished by 1648 when Fiacre was clearly the main attraction of the convent—surely in part because his reputation had in recent decades spread from France, where most of his relics still lay, and surely in part because of some well-reported cure in Groenebriel itself.

Anna Maria van Hamme recognized from the start of her reign

the importance of Fiacre to the convent. In 1648, her very first year as abbess, she sought from Bishop Antoon Triest of Gent a highly desirable indulgence for Fiacre's shrine, which offered to those who visited a release of so many days from purgatory. Impressed by the crowds of pilgrims who brought their children "from miles around," the bishop readily granted it. As Anna Maria had hoped, this indulgence caused even more pilgrims to come serve Fiacre. Her acquisition of yet another piece of the saint, in March 1659, stimulated interest still further. Hence by March 1660, when the trouble with the tailors began, Fiacre's presence was stronger than ever in Groenebriel, with fresh relics, irrefutable documents of authenticity, an indulgence, rumors of cures, and enough pilgrims that some nearby tailors grew weary of seeing them all pass by.

Anna Maria was hardly one to sit still and watch all her efforts fall victim to a few scheming tailors, especially now, when her convent happened to be in the middle of yet another major building project: the floodproofing of its cellars near the river, and the completion of an encircling wall—over one thousand feet long, five feet wide, and ten feet high. During projects such as this, every stiver mattered more than usual, and every affront to the public or the convent might have tangible consequences for potential benefactors. That was why Anna Maria could not afford to have it said by tailors or anyone else that the nuns of Groenebriel were cheating or stealing, or that the relics of Fiacre no longer rested in the convent church but in some run-down chapel.

Admittedly, her worries and attentions made her less than pleasant at times: it was no small thing, even in "ordinary" years, even with the aid of subordinate officers, to decide how many and what kinds of shoes, stockings, linens, pigs, cattle, peas, salmon, beer, almonds, plums, or anise should be bought, much less worry about walls and tailors. With the new problems added to the mix, no wonder some sisters now began assigning to Anna Maria less flattering labels than those they had assigned upon her election as abbess: then she had been pious, discreet, loving, understanding, peaceful, disciplined, and humble; now she was unfriendly, strict, stingy, and small-hearted.

These might have been genuine flaws. They might have been expressions of petty resentments. Either way, the resolve and hard experience that Anna Maria had gained from penny-pinching and from beautifying the convent were precisely what helped her stand up so forcefully to those scoundrels the tailors. And on this matter at least surely all the nuns of Groenebriel stood with her.

DEFIANCE

In addition to its forceful abbess, Groenebriel wielded another weapon in its struggle with the tailors: one of its two confessors, Jan Baptist le Monier, happened to be one of the five members of the vicariate of Gent. He would ensure that the convent's appeal was at least not ignored, or swept under the table with piles of other urgent pleas from around the diocese.

On March 23, 1660, shortly after the first complaints from Groenebriel arrived, the head of the vicariate assigned one of its members, plus a secretary, to visit the chapel of the tailors and investigate the complaints of Mother Anna Maria van Hamme. Three days later the delegates were ready with their report, as follows. Inside the chapel they saw no genuine relics at all. The chaplain, who said mass weekly, was not present during their visit. Instead there was only a woman, who told the delegates that she and others sprinkled pilgrims with water blessed in honor of Saint Fiacre. Unimpressed, the delegates ordered the woman to cease all such "blessing," to abstain from anything having to do with relics or blessed water, and to stop molesting pilgrims or calling them to visit their chapel, all on pain of the chapel's being closed. Nearly satisfied with this report, the vicar-general asked the delegates, as a final precaution, to go speak with the pastor of St. Michael's, in whose parish the chapel of the tailors stood, to "preclude all scandals." That, assumed the vicariate, should solve the matter.

But it did not. Only a week later, on Friday, April 2, there were new attempts at diversions, this time including tailors themselves rather than merely their servants. Hence, Anna Maria again sent two lay sisters to observe things, and to find witnesses who had seen anything suspicious. She recorded their testimonies the next day and forwarded them to the vicariate immediately.

Sister Cathelyne D'Auwe testified that she saw one of the tailors' servants obstruct the way of a peasant woman and commit "all kinds of scandal" in order to prevent the woman from walking on to Groenebriel, "whooping and hollering to the amazement of neighbors, and yelling that the nuns ought to be ashamed of themselves, taking people's money like that, deceiving them," and "using all means" to get the woman to enter the tailors' chapel.

A local cabinetmaker passing by the chapel saw an elderly tailor standing near the Augustinian convent, who not only spoke to a woman with a sick child but touched her, and tried to take her inside the tailors' chapel. Amazed that he would touch her, the woman stopped and insisted that she was continuing on to Groenebriel to visit Saint Fiacre, because she had taken her child there before and knew it was the right place. But the tailor persisted, saying, "Come with me, I've already led another woman into our chapel, which is the right chapel," and he pulled the pilgrim inside anyway, despite her protests.

The longest testimony came from Alexander de Caboeter and his wife, Louise de Rave, who lived near the chapel and showed an even keener interest in it than other witnesses. They had seen suspicious activity not only the previous day, April 2, but also the Friday before, March 26, the very day the vicariate had ordered all wrongdoing at the chapel to cease.

On both days the couple saw two different "poor tailors" working a four-way intersection near the Augustinian convent, where they intercepted pilgrims as they walked by and diverted some of them with the same old story.

On April 2, Mr. Caboeter stood outside a store chatting with the new chaplain of the tailors, who lamented (and thus admitted) that the chapel had no relics of Fiacre, but only water blessed in his honor. With a relic, he claimed, they could easily obtain an indulgence and attract more pilgrims.

Nearly every day the couple saw Elisabeth de Mey trying to divert anyone headed to Groenebriel, using any and every means to do so, "calling and shouting" that Saint Fiacre was to be served and honored here, not elsewhere.

And more than once were both husband and wife approached by puzzled people emerging from the chapel, who repeated what they had heard inside: namely, that if the nuns of Groenebriel possessed any relics of Fiacre it was only because they had stolen them from the tailors, and that Elisabeth de Mey had told her son to "go tell the nuns that the tailors will come themselves" to the convent and proclaim the truth for all to hear. One of the tailors, a Paulo Saleere, had even said to Louise de Rave, "I'll go to the convent myself and if one nun sticks her head out the window I'll kick her in the ass"—which would have been a remarkable feat indeed, but yellers of such threats do not bother themselves with details.

When the vicariate saw the latest reports from Mother Anna Maria, they were as incensed as the nuns, if for different reasons. They did not like being disobeyed, and they liked even less the growing possibility of scandal that inevitably followed the slightest whiff of deceit around the holy. It was bad enough when Protestants perpetrated such deceit, as they possibly had against the Jesuits of Gent, but worse still when that deceit came from Catholics themselves.

The vicariate recognized that the very popularity of saints and their relics was what allowed the unscrupulous and ignorant among Catholics to blossom—the unscrupulous ready to take advantage with outright deceits and subtle imitations, the ignorant prepared to believe just about any claim they heard. As the famous French thinker Blaise Pascal would soon observe, and as the martyr Thomas More had said more than a century before, it was experience with genuine miracles and relics that led believers to be duped by so many false ones.

As with miracles and statues, it rested upon the local bishop to investigate relics, but this was perhaps the hardest task of all. From the beginning there were Catholics who passed off fake relics as genuine, even to fellow believers. From the beginning there were enterprising dealers and well-meaning believers who to spread the wealth broke genuine relics into smaller and smaller pieces, greatly multiplying the already staggering number in existence. And from the time of the Reformation and its often violent confusion, there was so much more splintering and scattering and hiding of relics that keeping perfect track of all proved impossible. In short, determining the authenticity of relics was an eternal problem, but perhaps never more difficult than now.

Protestants were going to mock genuine relics anyway, but they would trumpet from the rooftops any cases of outright fraud—such as the priest in Brussels around 1600 who forged imitation relics from originals in Rome and passed them off as genuine, including the lance that had pierced Christ's side, or a few of Judas's thirty pieces of silver. Protestants also mocked the sheer number of relics, especially those from the same source: how many pieces of the true cross could there be, and how many skulls could a given saint truly have? Even Catholics puzzled over this: one popular preacher lamented that "one hundred cows couldn't produce as much milk" as that supposedly produced by the Virgin Mary in reliquaries around Europe. The staunchest believers might put forward supernatural explanations: God multiplied relics as He pleased, they contended, or God would reveal which relic was true in his own good time. But not all Catholics, especially not all churchmen, would toe this line, and therefore took a variety of specific steps to combat deceit, in all its forms.

In early centuries they tried to prevent the dividing up of relics, to preserve both wholeness and order, but this was violated so often that objections were dropped.

They also insisted that relics be displayed regularly, to guard against fraud, but frequent displays led to thievery—even when protected in reliquaries—and to shutting the relics up again, so that few knew what the originals looked like.

They always preferred that every relic be accompanied by a glittering document of authenticity, but because so many relics were lacking these (especially before the sixteenth century), other tests of authenticity had to suffice: smell, for the holy simply had a pleasant odor about it; or the character of the relic holder; or the logic of one's story; or further investigation—though this might only complicate the problem, for traveling investigators sometimes returned with still other relics that they claimed were real, rather than the originals in question.

Finally churchmen tried, especially toward the Reformation, to emphasize the virtues of saints rather than merely their healing powers, hoping that this would curb the fever for the objects themselves. But for most people, such as those who came to visit Fiacre at Groenebriel, healing and wonders still mattered most—how many of them could recite the details of Fiacre's virtuous life?

Clearly there were few rational tests on which all could agree or which all could see for themselves. Belief, intuition, and hope often mattered most in authenticating relics, especially for ordinary believers, whose main test was simply whether the relic worked. And as long as origins and questions of authenticity remained even fairly vague, the environment for fraud flourished.

In the case of the tailors and their chapel, however, there was for the vicariate of Gent no vagueness at all. The small unidentifiable bits in their reliquary were not about a difference of opinion or disputed provenance. Rather, the tailors were simply trying to dupe people, and therefore should be stopped.

After reading the latest reports from Anna Maria, the vicariate summoned on April 7, 1660, the dean of the tailors' guild, plus a few tailors to represent the several hundred who worked in Gent at the time. With little or no questioning about who was actually involved, the angry vicariate simply held all present responsible for events around the chapel, and gave five specific instructions: (1) remove Elisabeth de Mey from the chapel, and anyone else involved in misleading pilgrims; (2) bring the current reliquary, with its highly suspicious contents, to the secretary of the vicariate, who would place inside it at least a suitable Agnus Dei and perhaps even a small relic or two, so that visitors could be sure something genuine was inside; (3) cease telling people that the relics of Fiacre lay there; (4) quit trying to divert pilgrims; and (5) decorate the chapel's altar in more seemly fashion, as befitted the Holy Sacrament. No protestations by the tailors were recorded, and hence the vicariate assumed their agreement.

Yet once more did chastisement fail to solve the problem. A mere two days after this meeting, tailors and their dependents were at it again, reported the nuns of Groenebriel. On Friday, April 9, neighbors and pilgrims reported that there was "continuous and great confusion" around the chapel, as old tailors and their servants stood on every corner of the busy street, some of them far up the road in order to catch pilgrims early, so that anyone braving the journey to Groenebriel was confronted on the way by two, three, or four persons from the tailors' guild. As usual, a number of persuaded pilgrims went inside the chapel for their blessings, while some, who had visited Groenebriel previously with other children, continued on.

The vicariate heard the now familiar news at its meeting of April 12, and once again ordered representatives from the guild to appear the next morning, including the dean, the "house masters" Paulo Saleere and Francis Sateau, the chapel accountant Gillis

Daniels, and four regular members of the guild. How could they explain this disobedience?

This time the representatives were less submissive than before, claiming that they themselves had not bothered anyone on the day in question and refusing to take responsibility for what others might have done without their knowledge. But this gave no "satisfaction" to the vicariate, which once again ordered the guild and its members to behave in a seemly manner. If they violated this order again, the chapel would be put under the interdict (the sacraments withheld), and each of them would be punished as necessary.

The best that could be said about this decree of April 13 was that the reports of diversions merely slowed. Over the next four months, dozens of people reported their continuing adventures among the tailors, with only a few startling variations worth repeating here. One pilgrim was told by a woman at the chapel that there had been a lawsuit over the relics and the chapel had won. Another pilgrim explained that she decided to visit both chapel and convent, just in case, but after exiting the chapel an old tailor and a woman prevented her from continuing to the convent, and even led her by the arm in the other direction for two blocks. Other pilgrims heard various custodians of the chapel, including the chaplain, claim that Fiacre had been served at the chapel for one hundred or even three hundred years (technically true, since the chapel was named in his honor). And when one suspicious pilgrim observed that there were no nuns present at the chapel, for she had heard that Fiacre was in a convent, a woman at the chapel explained that children were taken to the convent, but they weren't healed; instead they were brought immediately afterward to the chapel and healed indeed.

Not even the installation at last of Gent's new bishop, Karel vanden Bosch, in July 1660, put enough fear into the tailors to cause them to stop. Nor did a formal summons issued on July 12 by the ecclesiastical court to the tailors' house masters, Paulo Saleere and Francis Sateau, now seen as the ringleaders.* Nor did a summons in September for the chapel's new chaplain, Joannes van Loo. In fact, if the tailors themselves slowed down, the chaplain picked up the pace, as more and more pilgrims complained that it was he who tried to deceive them to come inside, or had them look "at all the people" already there—obviously the diversions continued to work. And at least one pilgrim heard a woman say, while standing next to the nodding chaplain, that "as true as God was in heaven," this was the right place to visit Fiacre.

The nuns were flabbergasted at the escalating claims being made by the tailors. And these were only the complaints they heard—how many more pilgrims and stories never reached Groenebriel at all?

Accordingly, Mother Anna Maria, though continuing to send reports to the bishop and vicariate and diligently asking every arriving pilgrim about encounters with tailors, decided to take matters into her own hands. First, she again wrote to her contact in France, who promised on August 12, 1660, to obtain yet another small relic of Saint Fiacre for the convent. The precious piece arrived two months later, in October, with all the necessary documents, and was declared genuine by the new bishop. Next, Anna Maria arranged for a new translated edition of the life of Fiacre, the

The convent also talked of taking the case to the Council of Flanders, the highest civil court in the county of Flanders; apparently this threat had little effect as well, and the case was eventually concluded by the bishop's court.

title page of which proclaimed that he had "been visited for long and over many years in the renowned abbey and convent of Groenebriel in Gent, where various approved relics of the same lie resting." This received the required approbation from the vicariate, on November 3, and was published soon after, reassuring all the world that Fiacre was in the convent, not with any tailors. Yet even after these efforts, the diversions continued, and nuns and vicariate continued to gnash their teeth.

WHOSE FRAUD ANYWAY?

What could possibly have moved the tailors to be so stubborn toward nuns, and even to defy their bishop and his vicariate?

Critics within and without Catholicism believed that the most common motive for holy fraud was greed. The desire for notoriety or the spirit of pure evil might play their roles as well, but greed was paramount. Was this what drove the tailors of Gent?

When the tailors built their chapel, in 1300, they were in the heyday of the Flemish cloth guilds. Guilds of all kinds were born in the Middle Ages to control the manufacture, quality, and prices of goods, and to offer social support to members and their families; guilds also often played a direct political role in medieval towns. But there were guilds and there were guilds: greatest of all in wealthy medieval Flanders were the cloth guilds—weavers, fullers, tailors, and so on—whose number constituted about half of all guild members in medieval Gent.

Yet by 1350 the glory days of the cloth guilds had already faded, as rivals arose to outshine them. Their influence was reduced officially in 1540, when *all* guilds in Gent were stripped of political power, in retaliation for that city's brief rebellion against its native son, the legendary Charles V. As for the tailors' guild, although always one of the largest guilds in Gent and other big towns, its individual members were always among the poorest. In fact, most of the several hundred tailors (including masters, journeymen, and apprentices) who lived in Gent at any given time during the seventeenth century existed on the edge of poverty.

Unlike their cousin stocking makers, for instance, the tailors' market was local rather than international, their trade made-to-order and slow rather than ready-to-wear and mass-produced, and hence their prices expensive rather than cheap. Moreover, their large numbers made for intense competition. No wonder they worked longer hours than most guilds, received lower wages, and often worked at a loss just to attract clients.

If competition with one another wasn't enough, there was also growing competition from other sources. More private individuals were choosing to make their own clothes, or have their servants make them. More and more women were sewing from home for income, especially making underclothing and lingerie. These practices were marginally tolerable to tailors. But absolutely intolerable were the numerous "patchers sitting on the corners of streets who for money patch up old clothes and stockings," for they did not belong to the guild and undercut its prices. Just as guilty were "unfree" tailors, more skilled than patchers but also outside the guild, allowed to exist only because they proved useful in labor shortages, or when profit-hunting masters violated their own rules and hired them because they were cheaper than bona fide journeymen.

Unfair competition only added to the stress of an already stressful job. Tailors had to attract new clients, take measurements, decide how much credit to extend, work around the numerous religious holidays of the Spanish Netherlands, and most of all had to cut things right. If most people still preferred tailors to cheaper servants or the unguilded, this was why: cloth, usually provided by the customer rather than the tailor, was the greatest single expense in making new clothing, and there was only one chance to cut it correctly.

All around their quarter of the city, skilled tailors sat cross-legged on big, immaculately kept worktables, usually next to big windows streaming with light, supporting the cloth on their knees to keep it clean while they carefully cut it, or mended and fashioned suits, vests, pants, robes, coats, cloaks, military uniforms, and religious habits, for people of all ranks. But however well they cut it, and however much hope they had for wealth, tailors never earned much.

Of course there were exceptions: some tailors fared well working exclusively for wealthy clients. But the overwhelming majority, even in richer Antwerp, were still too poor even to be taxed, much less to accumulate capital with which they might actually buy cloth and resell it in raw or finished form (a method by which they might have greatly increased profits). Instead they remained stuck in a vicious circle of slow work, expensive prices, small margins, and unpaying credit customers in a trade dominated by credit. Tailors said among themselves to beware of "crown, sword, and plume," or in other words royalty, nobility, and clergy, yet precisely these groups ordered the finest and most expensive clothes. When they did not pay, tailors suffered even more.

No wonder tailors had a reputation for being poor and skinny: a saying in Brabant went, "two tailors, one man." Some tried to supplement their income by other means, perhaps as a tavern keeper, or a fellow who put up posters announcing local plays, or one who sold tobacco. Was it so unlikely then that some enterprising tailor might look out his spacious windows, see all the pilgrims passing by his own undervisited chapel, and try to lure them inside for the donations that usually accompanied a religious visit? Especially those "poor tailors" who lived right around the chapel, and who received special mention in the accounts of eyewitnesses?

Part of a guild's function, again, was support of its own, such as sponsoring communal dinners or aiding widows and other poor. In Gent, where support for tailors was less generous than elsewhere, it came in the form of housing six poor members of the guild in six modest homes—located right around the chapel. It wasn't clear why the lucky six were chosen, for many members of the tailors' guild could qualify for poor relief—but those who were chosen were invariably old, elated, and tremendously obligated to the guild and their "house masters." If the house masters Paulo Saleere and Francis Sateau should therefore have suggested a plan to increase the income and status of the guild's chapel by drawing off some of the pilgrims headed to Groenebriel, the lucky six had plenty of incentive to go along. In fact, they had incentive to develop such a plan themselves! The same could be said of the guild's few hired servants, also indebted to the guild for their livelihood and also, according to witnesses, residing around the chapel. Increased alms in the chapel would not only boost corporate income and prestige (and thus ultimately benefit poor tailors and servants individually), but it was a way of repaying the guild to which they owed so much.

Hence, for certain tailors, economic and social motives might well have explained their action. But these could not explain the actions of the vast majority of tailors, some of whom also apparently participated in the deceptions. This majority would have received very little individual benefit from any increase in alms to the chapel. Instead, what they needed most was more customers, and the biggest factor in attracting new customers was a tailor's reputation. They could therefore not afford to suffer rumors that members of their guild were misleading pilgrims.

Tailors were keenly aware of the stereotypes people already assigned them—not only that they were skinny and poor, but especially that they were deceitful. Tailors, went the stories, bought old clothes then remade them and passed them off as new. Tailors supposedly kept back small and large scraps of the material provided by clients, then used the scraps to fashion, at no cost, hats and other small objects, sold for big profits. Caricatures of the period showed tailors with snips of material hanging out of every pocket and on every piece of clothing, while a common saying went, "The tailor has eyes bigger than his scissors." Their petty thieveries were even celebrated in verse, alleging that when tailors made a new suit of clothes, they first cut a few pieces of cloth for themselves.

Most tailors worked hard to undo this image. They emphasized instead their skill at cutting, at saving customers money, and promoted such reassuring sayings as "measure thrice, cut once." Their own official manual was entitled "The Honest Tailor." To demonstrate their sincerity and reliability, they joined the local civic militia, which helped explain why tailors kept so many guns and swords around their shops. And they held bigger funerals than they could afford, all to boost their status and to say to potential customers, "You can trust us." Hence, they would hardly engage without cause in such a socially risky behavior as misleading pilgrims, or defying the vicariate and bishop of Gent.

Only other and compelling reasons, then, might have motivated some tailors to participate in this game against innocent pilgrims. Perhaps they simply saw it as a way to support their new chaplain; for there had been no chaplaincy there even fifteen years before, and funds were still undoubtedly short. Besides, more and more pilgrims were accusing him of direct involvement in the diversions; and the diversions started up soon after he was named. Or was there a less practical motive among tailors—namely that their chapel had indeed been cheated by the nuns, and thus they felt justified in cheating back?

A full three centuries before the convent of Groenebriel linked itself to Fiacre by procuring his relics, the tailors' chapel had already placed itself under the protection of that saint (along with Saint Maurus). The tailors apparently never possessed the relics of either—the cost or connections of obtaining any were surely beyond their declining means—but a relic itself was not absolutely necessary to make a place holy: one might still benefit from association with the saint honored. As the crowds to Groenebriel grew larger after 1600, and especially after 1648, the tailors must have felt that one of their two saints was being taken from them: here was perhaps the origin of the tailors' claim that the nuns had stolen Fiacre, rather than any literal theft.

Still, whether literal or figurative, if the nuns' actions were seen as theft, then the participating tailors would have felt perfectly justified in using whatever means necessary to win their share of pilgrims. For when it came to the holy, and especially to relics, the usual rules were thrown out the window, as if the actors were suddenly in another realm.

Most basically, the ordinary rules of property and theft could not apply to relics, for they were alive and possessed a will of their own. For instance, if one could steal a relic successfully, it was only because the saint allowed it; if Fiacre did not wish to move, nothing in the world could move him. Could this not have applied, with slight variation, to a saint's name as well? That is, if Fiacre no longer wished to protect the chapel of the tailors, then he would hardly have granted them so much success in bringing pilgrims inside.

Moreover, the typically vague origins of holy objects, and even the vagueness of holiness per se, made it sometimes difficult to say what was absolutely fraudulent or not. Some people regarded as holy were declared saints by the Church, while others seemingly as pious were accused of "simulated sanctity." But was such a state always objective, or did one's predisposition make all the difference, as in the cure of Maria Caroens? Guibert of Nogent in the Middle Ages exposed a number of relics as dubious, then turned around and celebrated as genuine others that had no more rationally convincing proofs but that he held dear anyway.

There were still other ways that deceit around the holy was muddied. If a fraudulent relic was not known by pilgrims to be fraudulent or deficient, then what harm did it do, especially if it truly helped to cure them—as Caesarius of Heisterbach had already suggested was quite possible? Recall as well Paulinus of Nola's sentiment that he would rather see misguided piety than none at all. If the tailors and their chaplain were bringing people to deeper devotion, then for some that was enough. And if the tailors truly had an old gripe against the nuns, then this was one way to justify their behavior.

In their public defenses on the matter, however, the tailors did not bother with unearthly justifications. In September 1660, they denied to the diocesan court ever having said that Saint Fiacre rested in their chapel, but claimed only that their chapel was the old chapel of Saint Fiacre, which it truly was. As for displaying false relics, all they showed people was what the secretary of the vicariate had recently given them! Finally, the tailors claimed that the nuns of Groenebriel were the party now doing the misleading, even taking people from the tailors' chapel to the convent.

In the end, the tailors found it hard to persist with their public claim that nothing improper was going on around their chapel, especially as the ever vigilant nuns continued to gather testimony from pilgrims, even in January and February 1661, nearly a year after the first condemnations. Pilgrims recounted that the tailors were still telling the same stories, still blessing diverted pilgrims with the reliquary while suggesting that it contained the relics of Fiacre, and still leading people by the arm into their chapel. Surely the diocesan court would not be content forever with merely slapping them on the wrist, but would take real action.

By February 1661, that day of action was drawing closer. Sensing defeat, the tailors tried in this month another strategy to avoid public condemnation by the court. They drew up a confession admitting that questionable things had indeed occurred around their chapel, but in exchange for this confession asked the court to let them handle the matter on their own and discipline the guilty as they saw fit. When there was still no positive answer from the vicariate, the tailors delivered personally another document in March. This one was even more explicit in admitting guilt. Having learned that two of its members, and its chaplain, had been summoned by the court for making false claims and expressly contradicting the court's orders, and wishing to avoid the continued expense of a trial, the tailors hereby admit to the world that they have no relics of Saint Fiacre, and promise to do all in their power to prevent further misleading statements and actions in the future.

But even this admission was too late, or not enough. For the diocesan court decided that it would reserve its right to punish the guilty, an action that, even if it were restricted to a few tailors, would hardly improve the reputation of all. The sentence of June 1661 was as sharp as the tailors' needles. Paulo Saleere and Francis Sateau were ordered to refrain from diverting anyone else in the future, to cease pretending that their chapel possessed the relics of Fiacre, and to pay one hundred Parisian pounds each (or about fifty florins, a sizable sum for a tailor, perhaps one-sixth of his annual income), plus expenses, to the convent of Groenebriel. Father Joannes van Loo, the chaplain, was fined thirty Parisian pounds (or about fifteen florins, perhaps one-tenth of his annual income as chaplain), plus expenses, as were the tailors' servants Paul van Driessche and Elisabeth de Mey.

The sentence must have worked, for the accusations of diversions never appeared again. The streets of Gent were once more safe for pilgrims wishing to visit Saint Fiacre in Groenebriel, even if they were watched enviously from the shadows of the tailors' chapel.

The chapel continued until the French Revolution, though without any improvement in status and though it never did get any sort of relics. Its permanent altar even fell into disrepair, so that its chaplain came to use a cheaper portable model. The tailors tweaked the nuns of Groenebriel at least once more, by planting a dividing hedge between their houses and the convent, but here too the nuns had the last laugh, for the hedge was on public land and the tailors had failed to ask permission: the city made them tear it up.

Thanks in part to alms from pilgrims, Anna Maria van Hamme finished the convent's massive wall by 1663, and continued to promote the flourishing cult of Saint Fiacre, even obtaining from Rome, shortly before her death in 1676, a supremely desirable plenary indulgence for visitors. Some nuns still complained about her occasionally harsh ways, but those who composed her obituary were careful to include as well her achievements—especially her decoration of the church and her embellishment of the reliquaries fashioned for saints Margaret and Fiacre, whose remains pilgrims still came to see. In fact, pilgrims were still coming for Fiacre in 1708, according to other observers, and even beyond, so that Anna Maria's efforts and her occasional stepping on toes were rewarded.

When the convent was ruined forever, during the French invasions of 1793, the last abbess took care to save Fiacre's relics. These were brought out of hiding again in the friendlier days of 1811, and were a final reminder of the once popular shrine. But in later years the relics were forgotten, and Fiacre became better known as the name for horse-drawn cabs in Paris (they picked up their fares near the Hotel Fiacre), which were later sentimentalized in a polka of 1860 and "The Clip Clop Song" of 1949. By then almost no one knew the origins of the word, or anything about the saintly hermit whose remains were once the cause of great comfort to a multitude of parents, yet for a time the source of so much trouble near a small chapel in Gent.

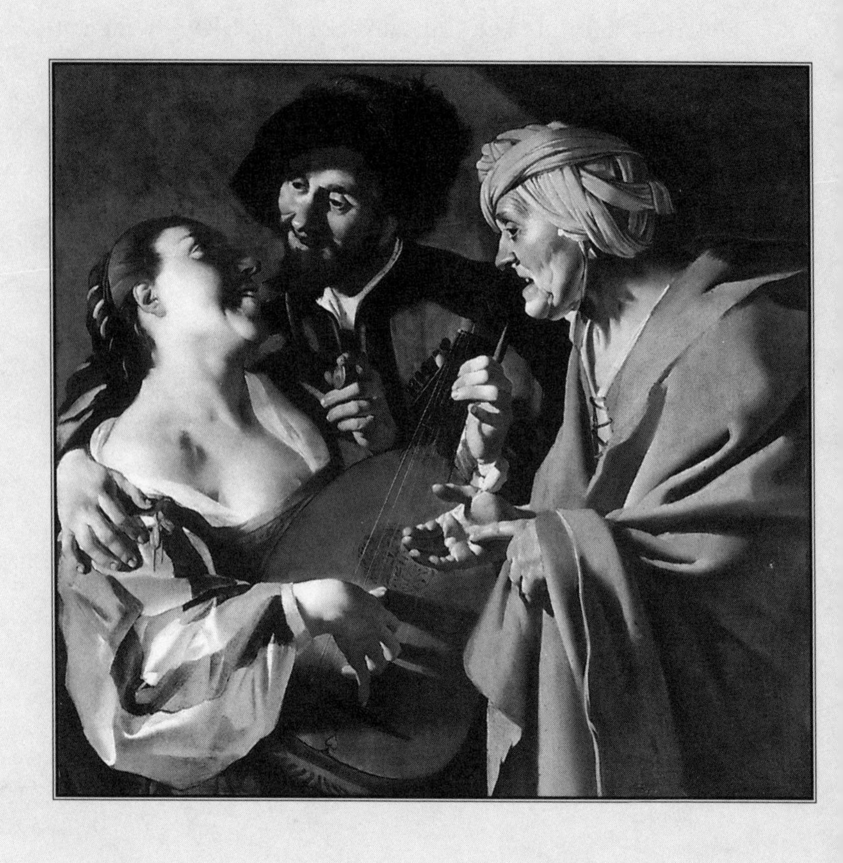

FOUR

ALDEGONDE IN THE UNDERWORLD

HIDING THE HOST

Brussels, Holy Sacrament Day, May 31, 1652. In the chapel of the House for Penitent Daughters, the line for communion moved slowly forward. Near the end of that line, twenty-two-year-old Aldegonde Walre moved more reluctantly than the others, but their momentum pulled her steadily along.

Confession the day before had been torturous enough. Aldegonde had tried to delay it by requesting a special confessor instead of the regular man attached to the house, saying she wanted someone besides a Dominican, but that was just a ruse, for, though Catholic from birth, she hardly knew the difference. The real cause was that deep inside she feared all confessors: they asked more about her shameful past than even loquacious she cared to reveal, they passed along (she suspected) her secrets to the headmistress, and worse. But her ploy had failed. There would be no special confessor, came the reply. And so Aldegonde had appeared like everyone else before their usual confessor, the Dominican Pater Ambrose, offering as ever only a perfunctory and incomplete statement of her sins.

And now communion today was even harder. She had tried sly means to avoid this as well, saying she had no veil or cap to wear. But the headmistress provided one and encouraged her, reminding that it was a great feast day—what better time then to receive Our Lord? Hence Aldegonde went grudgingly along with this ritual too, pondering all the while what to do, as she sat among the others during mass, awaiting the awful moment, and surely distracted from the sights and sounds and smells all around her.

Like many others in chapel today, Aldegonde had entered this house for wayward women (especially ex-prostitutes) halfheartedly—persuaded, threatened, or forced inside by ecclesiastical and civil authorities hoping to reform her. Such houses were first established in the Middle Ages, spread widely thanks to the zeal of both Protestant and Catholic Reformations (plus growing fears of syphilis), and by Aldegonde's time were more numerous than ever around Catholic Europe. There were houses for married prostitutes, for girls at risk of becoming prostitutes, and for younger single prostitutes such as Aldegonde. Some taught the women skills to help them return to the world and make a marriage or an honest living, others offered a traditional conventual life of penance and spirituality, and still others, such as Aldegonde's, were essentially prisons or asylums, designed to teach discipline but especially to keep these women off the streets, for months or years.

While some residents had begun to appreciate a solid roof over their heads and regular meals in their bellies, and showed signs of wanting to improve their ways, Aldegonde was not among them.

It wasn't clear how free these women were to leave, as this varied from house to house, but certainly if it were up to Aldegonde she would have been gone by now: after a year in the place, she had concluded that she much preferred the risks of prostitution or thieving to the rigors of discipline. She regretted having entered, the walls that kept her in, and the mistresses who supervised her life and worked mightily to save her soul by compelling her to do such things as confess and commune.

Finally during the mass had come the miracle-working words, "*Hoc est enim corpus meum*," this is my body, soon after which all the penitents, all in white, stood together in their screened-off part of the church and shuffled toward the Irish priest who awaited them at the communion window.

Aldegonde, of medium height and large frame, was next to last in line. Over her black hair she wore the silken veil given her to help achieve a reverential state of mind. When her turn came, she approached the window and knelt on the bench before it, to receive the consecrated wafer, or host, which the priest placed on her tongue. At least one of the watching mistresses, named Anna, prayed fervently for Aldegonde's wretched soul.

Returning to her seat, Aldegonde leaned her head against the wall. Suddenly, she bent at the waist and made a quick motion with her hands toward her mouth. Then she asked permission to leave the chapel, before mass was finished, complaining that she was ill.

But in truth Aldegonde left because she wanted to hide her misdeed, which was this: she had taken the consecrated host from her mouth in order to discard it in the privy, or to hide and later sell it. For the moment she placed it in a handkerchief, which she took back to her room, then laid the handkerchief and its holy contents inside a small chest.

Aldegonde's roommate Jennie Poisan, at nineteen always somewhat intimidated by her more experienced friend, returned from mass an hour later. Finding Aldegonde petulant, Jennie bravely offered a small admonition that reverence ought to be the order of such a marvelous day, for they had just received "a glorious God" within them. Aldegonde pursed her lips to Jennie and spat out, "Pooh."

Around lunchtime, Aldegonde decided to tell Jennie what she had done. After all, the two had shared confidences before, the biggest being their agreement to break out of this tiresome house together at the first opportunity. Taking Jennie by the arm, Aldegonde whispered in French (Jennie's first language) that she had something on her soul that was tormenting her, and would Jennie swear to tell no one else, including Pater Ambrose or the mistresses? An anxious Jennie promised.

When Aldegonde finished her story, she showed the handkerchief and its contents to her roommate. According to her own account, Jennie immediately began to weep and reprimand. How could Aldegonde do such a thing? And how could Aldegonde even consider making things worse by throwing the host in the privy? Aldegonde said nothing. But within Jennie a great struggle commenced: she had promised Aldegonde to say nothing, yet this misdeed was so great that surely it could not go unreported. She would ask the headmistress for advice.

That evening, around ten, she approached Mistress Marie and tearfully explained the dilemma of her promise. Marie responded that if Jennie had vowed to conceal something that was wrong, then she could rest assured, on the safe authority of the most learned lawyers in the Church, that her vow was automatically invalid. This news opened the floodgates for Jennie, who now felt free to tell all.

Upon hearing this tale about Aldegonde, Mistress Marie grew wary; she asked questions and appeared skeptical. But she could not dismiss the possibility that it was true. Hence, Marie required Jennie to make another promise, this one binding: she was to tell no one else what she knew, but go back to her room and see whether Aldegonde was asleep. In another direction, Marie sent Mistress Anna to tell Pater Ambrose what had happened and to ask his help. For though the mistresses were accustomed to handling most of their own affairs, the holy Eucharist was officially the business of priests.

Jennie did as instructed, and discovered that Aldegonde was indeed in bed, but not yet asleep. Feeling trapped, and apparently moved by both fear and affection, Jennie immediately blurted out her betrayal. "I am lost, I shouldn't have told anyone in the world," cried Aldegonde in response. Seeing such anger, and remembering Aldegonde's threat to get rid of the host, Jennie acted on impulse. She grabbed the little chest with the host inside it, then ran out the door and down the stairs as fast as she could. Aldegonde got out of bed and went after Jennie—some said with a knife in her hand—but was too slow.

Within seconds a frantic Jennie was safely within the chambers of Mistress Marie. Together they opened the chest and saw the linen handkerchief, sewn shut with a black thread, and the host inside. It was now wrinkled, and stuck to the linen because of moisture from Aldegonde's mouth.

In the meantime, Mistress Anna returned with a message from Pater Ambrose: he would come to the house first thing in the morning, but in the meantime they were to keep a candle burning next to the host all night, for since it had not been swallowed it was still consecrated, and was to be treated like all hosts left over after mass—preserved in a tabernacle, a light burning next to them to signify Christ's presence. Leaving the chest, host, and burning candle inside Marie's room, the three women locked the door and went to bed. Jennie presumably did not return to the room she usually shared with the angry Aldegonde.

ABUSING THE MIRACLE

The Next Day, June 1, 1652. Despite Mother Marie's efforts to keep things quiet, most everyone in the house soon knew about the crime.

One of the other residents, Elisabeth Peeters, had noticed Aldegonde's strange behavior during mass—specifically the sudden movement of her head after sitting down and her "greatly altered" countenance. Immediately it occurred to Elisabeth that Aldegonde had spit out the host. When Elisabeth confronted her about it the next morning, Aldegonde was more impressed than offended: "You must be a witch," replied Aldegonde, who confirmed Elisabeth's suspicion, then freely admitted that she had committed many misdeeds such as this.

Mistress Anna likewise sought out Aldegonde, to inquire why. "I could not swallow it," was Aldegonde's rather meek answer. When Mistress Marie moments later also asked Aldegonde why, Aldegonde became obstinate, and said angrily that her plan was actually to gather together as many hosts as possible, for she knew well what to do with them. Then she yelled that she would never trust Jennie again. Soon afterward Pater Ambrose arrived and took the soiled host away, to dispose of it properly.

After lunchtime, two other priests arrived at the house, both of them apparently canons of a local chapter, and most likely sent by the vicar of Archbishop Jacob Boonen, who had been put on alert by Pater Ambrose. Their task was to conduct a preliminary interview with Aldegonde in order to determine what everyone wanted to know: Why had she taken the host? This time she proved more willing than before to talk. She had always experienced trouble in swallowing the host, she admitted. Did she have any idea why? wondered the visitors, who most certainly had ideas of their own. She did not. The visitors tried to help her: Had she, for instance, suppressed any sins in her confession, or taken food and drink that morning, before communion? Just as they presumed, the answer to both questions was yes—and not only yesterday, but each of the few times in her life that she had confessed and communed.

Aldegonde also volunteered that she had desecrated the host before—once in Mechelen, when she hid it inside a small book, then threw both book and host into the privy. And another time with a "comrade" in Antwerp, with whom she had visited a parish church, received communion, hidden the hosts, then sold them to a procuress, or "coupler." In fact, her real intent in concealing the host yesterday, she confessed, was to add it to others she planned to take when she escaped from this prison, then sell them.

That was as far as the visitors searched for now, but already it was enough to get Aldegonde locked up in even more secure quarters than the House for Penitent Daughters: inside a tower of the Laken gate, part of the walls of Brussels.

Besides holy images and relics there was a third type of miraculous power in the Catholic world: the consecrated host of the Eucharist.

Most Protestants saw in the earliest accounts of Christian communion, especially the Last Supper, primarily a symbol of community—both among believers, and between believers and Christ. Catholics recognized as well the communal aspect of the ritual, but saw in the gospel accounts that described it even more: namely, that the consecrated bread and wine were not merely symbols but themselves objects of holiness—even the literal flesh and blood of Christ, as suggested by His words "This is my body" and "This is my blood."

Because the custom developed of giving communion to the laity in one kind only, namely the "body" or bread, it was natural that popular devotion to the Eucharist came to focus here. By the ninth century some Christians, inspired by religious women, were reverencing consecrated hosts (the special wafers that replaced ordinary bread) in much the same way that they reverenced relics. By the eleventh and twelfth centuries, some consecrated hosts were credited with performing miracles, just like those involving relics. And when the Fourth Lateran Council in 1215 confirmed the Real Presence of Christ in the Eucharist, it formalized the tendency to regard the host, itself the product of a miracle, as a potential *worker* of miracles—and indeed the most potent of all.

As some theologians explained, a relic or image was merely a symbol of divine holiness, whereas the consecrated host was Christ himself. Further, the host was not only superior to other miracle-working objects but the Eucharist the "most excellent" of all seven sacraments—the other six went to work only when the believer received them, while in the "sacrament of the altar" there resided independently, "really, truly, and substantially the author himself, the fountain and origin of all grace." Certainly relics might work miracles and other sacraments bestowed grace, but Christ's own body was more powerful and gracious still.

The elevated status of the host was reflected in the care taken by monks and others who shaped and baked the hosts—frequently washing, carefully cleaning the millstone, keeping any saliva away from the flour, reciting psalms throughout the process of preparation, and using only the purest wheat.

It was dramatized by the priest's raising the host high above his head during consecration, by the audience's kneeling, by the incense and candles that heightened senses, by the purple or black curtain placed behind the altar to highlight the white host even more, and by the bell that rang at the moment of consecration.

It was reinforced by the priest's placing the host directly on the tongue of the recipient, to avoid spilling (lest the flesh of Christ be desecrated), by withholding the wine altogether from the laity (even easier to spill than the host), and by preserving leftover hosts in vessels made of precious metal, which were accompanied by burning candles symbolizing the presence of Christ.

It was refined by the care theologians took to discuss, at heroic length, such perplexing questions as whether host and wine each contained separately and fully the body of Christ (they did), or what to do with accidentally vomited (and thus undigested) hosts, or at what point between mouth and stomach grace was actually transmitted, or how long it took for the host to be digested in the stomach so that one might safely eat and defecate again, or how to proceed against mice or other animals that somehow managed to eat a spilled crumb of the host (for even the smallest crumb was fully the body of Christ), or to refute those who said that the transformation of the host could not be miraculous because a miracle by definition was neither regular nor predictable.

And it was confirmed by the growing realization that the elevation and consecration of the host represented the high point of mass, more even than the transformation of the wine, causing priests to complain that as soon as the miracle was accomplished, many people headed for the door to go their own way, or to watch still other elevations.

After the Reformation, many Protestants, insisting on the strictly symbolic role of the Eucharist, ridiculed all reverential attitudes toward the host, calling them idolatry,* or wondering sarcastically how Christ could be both at the right hand of the Father and inside so many hosts at the same time? But in response, Catholic churchmen only confirmed and elaborated the supreme status of the host among all other objects of holiness. Thus: relics and consecrated hosts could no longer be preserved together in tabernacles, as they had been until 1525, for hosts had precedence and were now to stand apart. When a priest visited the sick, the host was now to be reverently displayed along the way. Priests were now encouraged to hold up the host (rather than relics) high to stop riots or change the weather, and believers to look to the host for their healings. Churchmen promoted more opportunities than before to see the host outside mass, especially during wildly popular processions featuring large, star-spangled monstrances (from the Latin word "to show") fashioned to hold and highlight a host. And

This must be qualified for some Protestants. Martin Luther believed in a spiritual presence of Christ in the host, and the English church declared that the Eucharist was both a miracle and a symbol. But the special devotions to the Eucharist were more characteristic of Catholicism than any Protestant version of Christianity; Luther, for instance, despised Corpus Christi as no other feast day.

churchmen revitalized the Church-wide feast day devoted exclusively to the Eucharist, "Corpus Christi," or Holy Sacrament Day—the very feast on which Aldegonde abused the host, and a feast with special meaning in her native southern Netherlands, where it had originated around 1264 at the instigation of a few religious women.

But this emphasis on the host and this zeal for it also had some unexpected consequences, not always pleasing to churchmen. A small number of Catholics—especially female religious—were so in awe of the host that they wished to receive it more frequently than ever, even weekly. Or they sought out unusually large hosts, supposing (unorthodoxly) that these conferred an extra dose of grace. Or they experienced Eucharistic visions, such as Christ appearing on a platter of food, Christ Himself celebrating mass, or Christ slipping the host onto their finger in marriage rather than a wedding ring. Or they consumed only the host and nothing else so that they wasted away (just the opposite of a large-bodied Aldegonde, who ate everything except the host). Such zeal always raised the eyebrows of bishops and theologians, who believed that excessive enthusiasm too easily led to the sorts of errors, deceits, and superstitions already seen among the Jesuits and tailors of Gent or at countless shrines—not to mention more work for overburdened churchmen.

Also worrisome was that majority of Catholics whose awe for the host had the opposite effect: namely, they were now so anxious about receiving it unworthily that they preferred seeing the host to consuming it, and thus communed less often. This same majority also often preferred *using* the host to consuming it—and for quite private purposes. It was easy enough for a believer so inclined to attend mass, receive communion, then keep it in his or her mouth until later—when it might be placed in a bed or field to promote fertility, concealed in a wall to shield against fire, worn around the neck to protect against illness and misfortune and evil spirits, crushed into powder then sprinkled over beehives and cabbage patches to increase yields, or placed under a beer barrel to stimulate sales. Believers also secretly hid objects under the altar during mass, in the belief that the prayers of consecration by the unwitting priest would bestow on these objects genuine healing power. They went forward after mass to gaze into the chalice and cure themselves of jaundice. And they buried children who died too young for communion with a host in one hand and a chalice in the other.

It did not matter to churchmen that many of these purposes were worthy. Nor that they themselves had enthusiastically taught believers the miraculous powers and grace of the host—even claiming that those who merely saw its elevation were protected the rest of the day from "fire, blindness, infectious disease, sudden death," and hunger pangs. Nor did it matter that many popular rituals resembled those learned at church, and were therefore called "sacramentals." It did not even matter that believers had seen priests performing similar rites—walking through fields with the host to bless crops, and of course giving the host to the dying and ill. What mattered instead to churchmen was who was in charge of the sacraments: those who presumed to use the sacraments privately violated the clergy's sense of exclusive guardianship over them, and thus were bound to find their private practices—however similar or worthy—labeled magical, superstitious, or heretical.

If this were true of even the best sorts of private uses, then it was even more true of the worst: when the host was deliberately desecrated, often for blatantly sinister purposes. No doubt this was what motivated the priests who detained and interviewed Aldegonde—in their minds she was likely more than an innocent, ignorant Catholic. She had already admitted pondering at least two thoroughly evil sorts of desecration—destroying the host, and selling it—and actually performing such desecrations in the past. If she were guilty, then there was virtually no greater crime she could have committed in her world.

Jews and Protestants were the favorite suspects of host desecration by now—Jews since the thirteenth century for supposedly treating the host as they had Christ, slicing it up and mutilating it,* and Protestants more recently for hundreds of genuine instances of scattering, tramping, tearing, and mocking "the pastry God." But some Catholics were also guilty of desecrating the host, as Aldegonde's interviewers knew too well. Many desecrators were likewise accused of being witches, who were believed to be especially covetous of the host's miraculous powers (which ironically only confirmed the Church's teaching that the host was indeed miraculous), for use in their spells and evil deeds or even to give to the devil himself. In fact, investigators often distinguished simple evildoers from outright witches by determining whether a host was involved, while priests were warned that women who received the host with unusually wide-open mouths and greedily protruding tongues just might be witches. Non-witches could be guilty as well, by providing hosts to witches or even trying to sell hosts to Jews.

Witch or not, those caught desecrating the host in Catholic states (and some jurists believed that selling the host was even worse than stealing it) could be sentenced to mutilation, strangu-

As historians have shown, more likely was that Jews were indifferent to the host, and Christians simply misunderstood various Passover rituals (burning and breaking and affixing various sorts of ceremonial bread to synagogue walls) as desecrations of the host.

lation, and burning, all carried out willingly by secular and religious authorities—appalled by the enormity of the crime, and fearful of God's wrath if such went unpunished. Such executions had occurred around Europe since the Middle Ages, including in Brussels only months before. There, in February 1652, Archbishop Boonen defrocked a priest for "blasphemous thefts" (what was more blasphemous than stealing the host?), then watched with a large audience as the priest had his right hand cut off and was strangled and burned. Also in Brussels in 1613, Protestants were said to have stolen hosts from the church of the Carmelites, but the culprits were, in fact, two Catholics, who had sold the hosts in Antwerp; these men were tortured, had their right hands cut off, and were hanged. In Valenciennes in 1607 Margot Pierre was burned for abuse of the host, and in Mechelen in 1642 so was Katlijne Janssens, who was said always to commune twice: one host for herself, one for the devil. And if such violent treatment stopped in later centuries for heretics and even witches, it endured for host desecration, as in Italy in 1723, when a man who stole a *ciborium* (for leftover hosts) and ate 215 particles in order to have their power was executed.

Given this context of reverence for the host and horror at its misuse, it was not surprising that Aldegonde's deed prompted immediate action—far more immediate than for most crimes against the Church, or other crimes she had also committed in her life. This explained why after her first interview she was moved without delay to the tower at the Laken gate. She had certainly committed a serious crime, but she was perhaps as well a witch in league with the devil. And was there more? Answers would emerge only through further questioning.

A SORRY TALE

June 13 to 15, 1652. After letting Aldegonde sit for nearly two weeks in her new cell, located ironically next to a brothel, two other investigators from the diocesan court arrived to begin a new, more thorough round of interviews.

Their intent was not only to establish with certainty what Aldegonde had done, but, in keeping with the long-standing influence of the sacrament of penance on Church law, to determine her degree of guilt. In other words, what circumstances or events in the person's life established, compounded, mitigated, or excused guilt? This was why the interviewers spent so much time on Aldegonde's past, long before getting to their main concern, the desecration of the host. In her past they might find condemnatory or exculpatory explanation.

For her part, Aldegonde was more willing to talk than ever, and to take the interviewers on a long walk through her wretched life in the underworld of sin and the supernatural. That underworld was both spiritual and temporal, for it consisted not only of views about the supernatural at odds with official positions, but also a social underclass that felt very little connection to the existing order, religious or otherwise. Yet despite social and intellectual gaps, the interviewers were far from ignorant of this underworld. Their task of helping the bishop to shape the contours of official miracles involved as well defining the dark side of the supernatural, which occurred through regular contact with scores of other-believing people from all parts of the social spectrum.

Moreover, the interviewers' notions did not completely differ from those of such people as Aldegonde: churchman and poor prostitute alike believed in the reality of magic and demons, even if they disagreed about definitions. Yet whatever the familiarity of interviewers with such ideas, it was rare for even the most seasoned to be confronted by such a miserable and full-bodied story as that told now by Aldegonde Walre.

Aldegonde was raised "godless and wild" in Mechelen by her father, the cobbler Martin Walre, and her stepmother Anna Hannar, who had migrated north from the war-torn French-speaking provinces and married the widowed Martin when Aldegonde was two (explaining Aldegonde's proficiency in both Flemish and French). One of at least five children, Aldegonde received little catechism, made no special devotions or pilgrimages, recited few prayers, and probably did not even engage in such ordinary youthful activities as planting May trees or attending spinning bees to tell and hear stories of love.

At age twelve, continued Aldegonde, before the onset of menstruation (or "the flowers"), she was violated by a drunken Martin, who regularly slept with Aldegonde because wife Anna was long ill. In sickness and in health, Martin treated Anna little better than he did Aldegonde herself. And Anna in turn took out her anger at Martin on Aldegonde: Anna showed her no respect, much less love, and could hardly bear her presence. To get back at her stepmother, Aldegonde told neighbors that Martin had once called Anna a witch. But one of the neighbors, angry at Aldegonde, told Anna what Aldegonde had said, and enmity deepened.

Sometimes Anna and Aldegonde caused such disturbances with their arguing that neighbors complained, members of the civic militia arrived, and the two women were hauled into court. Anna yelled at Aldegonde that she would grow up and die a whore, for "once a whore, always a whore." Aldegonde's hatred for her stepmother grew to the point that she decided to poison her. Everyone knew that Anna, long ill from the dropsy, would soon die anyway. But Aldegonde hastened the process by stealing five stivers from Anna's small money chest (which she forced open with a knife) to purchase some arsenic at one of Mechelen's hundred-plus seedy barracks,* or tents, an establishment called the Rat. When asked by the seller her intent, Aldegonde replied that she wanted to kill some rats. But on returning home, she placed some of the arsenic in Anna's beer. Anna died hours later, and Aldegonde was never caught.

The interviewers, cautious, asked Aldegonde for details: what color was the poison? White, replied Aldegonde, like flour, and she kept it in a paper sack, but she couldn't remember what she did with the rest. How had she administered it? Early in the morning she mixed some arsenic, white bread, and a bit of wine into a mug of beer; when Anna could not swallow the bread, Aldegonde filtered the concoction through a cloth, into a tin mug, from which her stepmother finally drank the deadly brew.

Did the neighbors know about the poison? No, none of the neighbors suspected anything—though it was possible that Anna's oldest daughter, Marie, might have, because she cared for Anna near the end. In addition, Aldegonde once admitted the poisoning to her father, who was not "completely happy" about it but laughed anyway, and continued to sleep "dishonorably" and openly with Aldegonde for about a year—and, by the way, here was something the neighbors knew for sure.

Again the interviewers were slow to believe. How did the

**The word was used to describe not only the quarters of soldiers, but also temporary tentlike structures in which such poor people as Aldegonde lived, or from which shopkeepers sold their goods; this latter sense applied to the structures erected by the vendors at the Jesus Oak, for instance.*

neighbors come to suspect that Aldegonde's father was sleeping with her? That was easy: everyone knew her father was a drunk and when he "called her to his bed" they could hear him, because the walls of the Walre house were made of loam. She might have added that neighbors of the time had no qualms about assuming "the sins of one were the business of all," lest they be smitten by God for the evil deeds of a few, and that they regarded "eavesdropping and peeping through windows as a duty." In any case, the neighbors in the Guldeboom street, Anna, Catherine, and Maria, all "spiritual daughters," or semi-religious women who lived in the world, even questioned Aldegonde closely about their suspicions. But Aldegonde, being "bad," denied all, as her father had ordered.

Despite Aldegonde's denials, the neighbors passed their opinions on to the parish priest. When this man came to question Aldegonde, she finally admitted her arrangement with her father. Largely because of the pastor's subsequent threats against him, Martin Walre fled to the village of Walem, just north of Mechelen, where he would eventually live with another woman, named Teunken Brauwer, who had once been tried for witchcraft by the diocesan court. Aldegonde meanwhile was placed by the pastor in the home of a nearby carpenter, named Gesper, where the pastor helped with expenses.

After this move, Aldegonde never slept with her father again. Over the years she visited him occasionally at his new home in Walem, and once Aldegonde and her father drank together in a café called the Zuerzee, where her father still owed seven florins for beer. Some years ago she heard that Martin had died at a hospital in Douai. But neither his departure from home, nor his death, freed Aldegonde from his crimes against her. If her account of her father was true, then her next step in life was quite in line with studies centuries later that would link the promiscuity of adolescent girls to early abuse at home: she became a prostitute.

Or maybe she decided on this course simply because she disliked the family that took her in and wished to be free. In any case, there were few secular occupations open to the many unmarried women of the Low Countries and western Germany (10 to 15 percent never married), but prostitution was one of them. Hence, two months into her stay with the Gespers, thirteen-year-old Aldegonde packed her meager belongings and fled to the city of St. Truiden, where she began her career as a prostitute, "giving her best" to men both married and unmarried, at a tavern called the Rose. By day she walked the streets near the church, trying to attract clients with her teasing and laughing. Some passed her by; some stopped to talk, buy her a drink, and more.

From St. Truiden, Aldegonde moved to Tienen, then Antwerp for three years, and finally back to her hometown of Mechelen. Here she usually stayed in the Rat, the tent where she had bought the arsenic, and the lowest sort of dwelling around. The pastor of St. Jan's, who lived just down the street, reprimanded her more than once for prostitution, but she persisted and ran around with "all sorts." She never said, but like most prostitutes surely she made little money. And surely she never benefited from the parish poor table, which aided the "traditional" or "respectable" poor of Mechelen's population (about 10 to 13 percent): widows, especially widows with children, received help, but not unreformed prostitutes.

The investigators interrupted and asked for names of men who visited her, especially in Mechelen, under their jurisdiction. This was in part to test Aldegonde's reliability, but also in keeping with efforts since the Reformation to increase pressure not only on prostitutes but on their clients and panderers.

The biggest name among Aldegonde's regulars was a lawyer named Leempoel. How long had she known Mr. Leempoel? Many years, but the first time she "had to do" with him was only two or three years ago, around 1650, "in the churchyard of St. Rombout's," right next to the home of the underpastor, "at about ten in the evening," right after Leempoel returned from the café called the Harecatchers. She even walked Leempoel home, coming close enough to hear his wife screaming at him soon afterward.

There was also a dye merchant called Riccart (whom the investigators perhaps knew had already been accused in the diocesan court of running a brothel), a nobleman named Marres den Fourier, "other married men" whose names she'd forgotten, and Adam "in the Beffer street, with red hair." With Adam she had "sinned in a stable" that belonged to another man "in the tent," who was married and with whom she had also "sinned—at least fifty times." The same man had further "sinned with Anna van Duffel," a girl of sixteen who lived with Aldegonde in the barrack. Aldegonde had met him through another "easy daughter," Antonette, who received his presents, his conversation, and his abuse, the last of which led Aldegonde to conclude that he was not "honorable."

Interest piqued when Aldegonde named two priests among her clients, for the diocesan court was especially concerned with the behavior of the clergy. The first was a man from "Pitzemburgh," a monastery housing a military religious order in the city, who came twice a day to her barrack, wore short clothes, spoke French to her, acted with an air of sophistication, gave her "good exhortations" to reform herself, but nevertheless invited her to come visit him some time.

More flagrant was a Spanish priest, chaplain in the local Spanish hospital, whose name she couldn't remember. The interviewers again demanded at least some details about the man: he was "old, short of stature, with large eyes and a long face," recalled Aldegonde, and "when he sleeps he smells remarkably awful." He gave her several gifts—including a piece of gold, silver medallions, sheets, and a woolen blanket. To boost her credibility, she even offered to tell the investigators where she sold the sheets for cash.

She was also prepared with numerous details of his behavior. This priest not only led her into his room at the hospital by night, but to be sure that no one guessed his business, he threw his baggy sleeve around Aldegonde's head, put a hat on her, and told her to walk "manlike" so that people would think she was another priest coming to visit. He repeated this farce on the way out of the hospital as well. Sometimes she stayed in his room all day and night, though he left occasionally to say mass. Once she stayed two days and three nights, and he always provided her with food and drink, including wine. He also instructed her that she was never to confess this liaison to any other priest, nor tell her friends. But she couldn't resist telling a few people, including her pastor.

The interviewers were again skeptical—not necessarily that a priest was incapable of such, for enough were brought before Church courts to answer such charges—but because they wanted more proof for such serious tales. Hence, they asked for details, now of the priest's room. It was in a narrow hall, she responded, with green bedding, a chest of books above the table, and on the table he always placed his pistol. She added, unprompted, that she could name another woman with whom the priest was familiar: one Cecilia, who now lived somewhere in Brussels, and who had run away from her marriage. The Spanish priest had "preached" to Cecilia to visit his rooms, saying that he would like to "speak" with her, and that he was good, quiet, and well paying. The investigators asked whether others could confirm that Cecilia had been busy with this man: Aldegonde could not say, but anyone asked would confirm that Cecilia was a "public daughter."

Besides furnishing the names of her clients, Aldegonde was no less shy about revealing the names of other women who practiced her trade, as well as their places of business. Most towns since the Middle Ages had one or more legal houses of prostitution, usually restricted to certain neighborhoods, in keeping with the long-standing notion among theologians and churchmen (at least since Augustine) that banning prostitution altogether would create more problems than it solved—for among other things its absence would subject respectable women and unmarried daughters to the aggressions of men. Better to let men expend their passions on a few lowly women, and save the rest. That theologians tacitly accepted the practice even as they condemned it was also reflected in the insistence by some that prostitutes charge a "just price" and use no deception in displaying their wares, or in the debate over whether the Church should accept tithes from prostitutes (most decided it should not).

Despite this acceptance of prostitution in practice, there were still limits: prostitutes who operated outside approved neighborhoods ran the risk of prosecution. So did those who operated after the Reformations, when both Catholic and Prostestant churches began to question the value of social "benefits" from prostitution and thus opposed it vigorously. Though opposition was made complicated in such large cities as Antwerp, where secular magistrates benefited economically from its 125 brothels, the seventeenth-century Church would show few signs of weariness against prostitution (that came only later), and so the investigators made notes.

The café run by Losse Maye was nothing but a brothel and Losse Maye herself a "coupler" (or panderer), claimed Aldegonde. So was a woman named Catherine, who ran a brothel right from her home. The Waffle-house was a brothel, so were the Woods and the Spigot. The brothel of the already-named Cecilia stood right next to the churchyard of St. Jan's. One of the girls employed there was named Lisbeth, widow of a former brickmason, plus a "girl who died from the filthiness" (syphilis). Everyone, "ripe and green," found service there, until they were run out by the pastor of St. Jan's. None of the women were ashamed to perform in front of others, and their best clients were "the aforesaid Leempoel and Riccaert," both of whom liked Lisbeth.

Also busy in Mechelen was a certain Marie Pantouffer, who was married to a Spaniard, but who "ran with every man" during Lent of 1651, and who was friends with the daughter of the executioner of Brussels—not surprisingly, since the town executioner was also often in charge of watching over brothels. Aldegonde knew that Marie was living in a barrack next to the Spigot, had seen her "great with child," and soon after saw her with "a child on her arm." There was a "married woman named Anna," who had no firm place of residence in the city," but whose husband Francis was branded and whipped in Mechelen, then hanged "either in Gent or in Brussels." Anna was twenty-five, tall, and with brown hair, and liked to think she was a lady. Mr. Leempoel "had also been busy" with this Anna, for Aldegonde saw them "on a Spanish chair" in one brothel just before Lent one winter. In fact, despite

Aldegonde's own relations with Leempoel, he seemed most devoted to Miss Anna, "because she can sing very well, usually lighthearted songs."

The investigators reflected on these revelations, noted the names given by Aldegonde, and then asked what they considered a logical question in such matters: If Aldegonde was a prostitute for so long, then where were her children? Methods of birth control and abortion circulated regularly among women, especially prostitutes, and Aldegonde responded that she had been pregnant more than once but whenever she felt that she was missing her menstruation, she swallowed a drink that "would chase the fruit away." For the first drink she had paid thirty stivers, for the second thirty-six, and for the third twelve.

The first drink, she volunteered, she took at the demand of her father, because he was the first to make her pregnant and kicked her out of the house until she ended it. Hence when two and a half months along, she bought a special drink at the Rat, left the city in the late afternoon, and walked a mile toward Antwerp. That evening she slept in a barn along the way. Because the process called for an early morning dose, or because she wanted to be seen by no one, Aldegonde arose at four in the morning to prepare the drink, which had to be taken warm. Within two hours she noticed a discharge from her womb of "various things," which she gathered with hay, then buried in the ground next to the barn as the sun came up. The whole process made her very ill, but upon regaining her senses she returned to Mechelen.

The investigators wondered how she knew for sure that she was pregnant. This was easy: her "breasts became very large, and swelled almost up to her chin," and the "neighbors saw that she was getting fat." But the investigators did not pursue it any further, perhaps because they did not believe her, or perhaps because at this time the moment when the fetus gained a soul, or was "quickened," was believed to be in the fourth or fifth month of pregnancy—after Aldegonde had ended hers.

Prostitution and the termination of her pregnancy were only two of the deeds Aldegonde was prepared to confess. Besides being briefly imprisoned for theft (falsely, she added), Aldegonde also considered carrying out another poisoning: she was once so angry at a prostitute called May With the Evil Eyes that she purchased more arsenic at a store across the street from the Jesuit church in Mechelen and planned to use it on her. But one of the Jesuits, a Pater Grinsel who had tried to help Aldegonde and even gave her money (and would ultimately arrange her stay among the Penitent Daughters of Brussels), saw her leaving the store and grew unhappy that she had bought something other than yarn—he wanted her to sew something and sell it rather than her body. So he made her return the bag, though he didn't know what was inside. The interviewers wondered whether Aldegonde knew that the doses of arsenic in question could kill someone. Of course, she told them, because her two brothers were soldiers, from whom she had learned all kinds of "evil and impoliteness." They had even taught her to swear and curse.

Finally Aldegonde admitted to other murders. About two and a half years before, while she stood at the St. Catherine's gate, a strange woman asked Aldegonde to watch her nine-month-old baby for half an hour, while she washed the baby's linens. But the woman never returned. Aldegonde admitted that she had had an aversion to children since her own girlhood, and thus did not treat the child well. Although it was "happy and very friendly," she hit the child "until it was crippled and lame." So awful was her treatment that others called her "the executioneress," and the city, after five or six months of complaints, took the child from her care. They placed it with a certain Margaret Capiteyns, but the child died soon afterward anyway. Aldegonde added that had it been her own child, she probably would have treated it worse.

More dramatic was Aldegonde's next killing. During Lent of 1651, she "sinned one evening" with two soldiers in the barrack of a baker, located on the great bridge. Finishing around ten, she went out to seek "further fortune." Walking across the Sluys bridge, she met another soldier who "wanted her with him." But here was one person Aldegonde wished to avoid—partly because she didn't believe he had money, and partly because he and a friend had once kicked in her door and threatened to throw her into the river. Now on the bridge, he drunkenly threatened her and tried to force her to come with him, even drawing a pistol. Unruffled, Aldegonde took it from him and threw it into the river. Furious, the man started to draw his sword, but Aldegonde attacked him with a knife—stopping at this point to explain to the interviewers that at the time she usually carried two long knifes on her person while out at night, one "in her bosom," and the other "in her left sleeve." Anyway, she pulled the knife from her sleeve and stabbed him in the back, which caused him to fall over backward and scream. She did not mean to kill him, but he was obviously badly hurt, and, fearing arrest, she ran away. Later she learned that he was taken to the hospital across from the Jesuit church, where he died of his wounds. Soon afterward he was buried in the churchyard of St. Peter's, next to the wall near the home of the president of the Grand Council.

Asked where the knives were now, Aldegonde responded that the knife used to stab the soldier she left at the scene; the other, which had a cloven handle, was taken from her when she entered this house of reform, and was being kept for her, as they spoke, by the headmistress in the House for Penitent Daughters.

THE HEART OF THE MATTER

Aldegonde's tale was so wide-ranging and riveting that even the interviewers might have momentarily forgotten what it had to do with miracles and the Eucharist. But not for long. However distracting her revelations may have been, their chief purpose was of course to serve as background to her greatest crime: her desecration of the host. And to that they now turned.

Here again was Aldegonde prepared to admit a lengthy string of self-incriminating details. Her most recent episode with the host wasn't the first, she explained. That had come with her very first communion, just a few years before (and much later than most Catholics) in the Jesuit church in Mechelen. On that occasion, after receiving the host, she secretly took it out of her mouth and placed it in a tiny book given her by Pater Grinsel. Upon returning to her room in the hospice of St. Julian, across the street from the church, she tried to remove the host from the book in order to throw it into the privy, but it was stuck to the pages. Hence she threw in the entire book (just as she had told the first interviewers). For two days this caused her great distress, so much that Pater Grinsel somehow came to suspect her deed and thus asked her about it. When she admitted what she had done, he quickly assembled a search party to go look in the privy, but they found nothing "because it was very deep," and because "in the meantime other people had used it."

The second occasion was in Antwerp, eighteen months ago, as she had also told the other interviewers. This time, a half-drunk Aldegonde received the host at mass, placed it in the folds of her dress, and gave it to her comrade Antonette, who then sold it to a coupler in the Fortune.

And of course the third time was only two weeks before, at the House for Penitent Daughters in Brussels.

Why did she do this? Just two weeks before, when asked why she could not swallow the host, she had no answer, but in the meantime, confined to her cell, she had come up with several.

First, she was simply "naturally evil." Second, she was angry that the mistresses had forced her to confess and commune, and abusing the host was a way of getting back at them. And third, she had theological reasons—namely, she did not believe that God was present within the host, as the Church taught, because there was but one God and a huge multitude of people who took communion: how could they all receive God, when there was only one?

It was a question the interviewers had heard before, from outside the faith and even occasionally within. Catholic devotional writers had long urged the faithful simply to accept the mystery of the miracle of transubstantiation (the moment when host and wine changed in essence to Christ's flesh and blood), and not to ponder it too long when inevitably ridiculed by skeptics and especially Protestants. In fact, it was from Protestants, continued Aldegonde, that she had first gotten the idea that God could not be present in the host, during a three-month stay in Holland, "giving her best" to sailors there. The investigators supposed that she must have learned such ideas by attending Protestant sermons in those cities, but Aldegonde said no: she had picked up her anti-theology of the

Eucharist directly from her seagoing clients themselves, in cafés and in bed.

She held still other heretical and blasphemous ideas. Before coming to the House for Penitent Daughters, she had not even believed in God. From her father she had learned that there was no need to pray for the dead, and that there was no hell but only a heaven for all people, good and evil. The investigators stopped her: What about devils? This brought her back to her tutoring from sailors in Holland, who had told her that devils were merely "tall priests, what else?" Sailors also told her that a priest had no power to forgive sins, and that priests couldn't be trusted with secrets: the material for their public sermons came straight from the private confessions of their flocks.

This last point Aldegonde believed most of all, and it led to yet another explanation of why she did not like to commune: she hated to make the required confession beforehand. In fact, she had never uttered "a good confession." This was based in part on a fear that "confessors would assault her," a fear reinforced by the priest at the Spanish hospital in Mechelen, who told her that all confessors desired young women. It was also based on the shame she felt in telling someone her misdeeds. And finally it was based on her suspicion that confessors would reveal her secrets: what she uttered in the confessional would be repeated to the mistresses within minutes.

Aldegonde was not alone in these fears, and her interviewers knew it. They lamented lecherous confessors who made carnal advances; indifferent confessors without wisdom, mercy, and affection; unskilled confessors who upon hearing sins grew wide-eyed with astonishment, thereby increasing shame and halting confession; harsh confessors who served up more vinegar than honey; or loose-lipped confessors who dared to break the sacred seal of the confessional. All of these caused people to avoid confession, or to confess incompletely.

But the interviewers also knew that such misdeeds by confessors were hardly universal, and that fear of confessing was often the result of the penitent's own deserved sense of shame—especially when sexual sins such as Aldegonde's were involved—to the point of losing sleep, or falling to the ground, or becoming desperate. Whatever the source of her reluctance, and though she had communed far less frequently than one might have expected of a Catholic her age, Aldegonde nevertheless reminded her interviewers that she had confessed and communed at least five or six times in her life anyway—twice in Mechelen, once in Antwerp (without having confessed first), and twice in the House for Penitent Daughters.

Still, she continued, these were not out of devotion. In fact, there was only one positive attraction for Aldegonde to taking communion: she could sell the host for money. She and her friend Antonette (a Protestant, no less) had gone to mass in Antwerp for the express purpose of gathering two hosts, which Antonette took immediately to the coupler in the Fortune for sale. This woman then used them for her own purposes, unknown to Aldegonde. Neither did Aldegonde know where Antonette was now (only that she had blond hair and was short of stature). Nor did Aldegonde know that the coupler in the Fortune was, in addition to her pandering, also suspected of sorcery. But Aldegonde knew well that the selling of consecrated hosts was another source of income for poor prostitutes, and other poor or enterprising people, and this was what she had in mind last Holy Sacrament Day.

Though Aldegonde testified that she did not know to what uses the coupler in the Fortune put the host, she knew well enough the popular world of magic around her and the prominent role of couplers within it. Couplers and sorceresses (surely interchangeable terms to the interviewers, as the woman from the Fortune confirmed) were among the most active practitioners of magic, especially in the black market for hosts—not only using them to cause obvious harm (to pigs or crops or barns or persons) but to effect love matches that were the heart of their business. One portrayal of such women compared them to bats, knowing no rest, especially at night, emerging from their dark hiding place to knock on the doors of convents, brothels, and taverns, to haul away a nun here, a monk there, another man or woman there, this one to a whore, the other to a widow, and yet another to an unmarried woman, all by means of their spells and charms and potions, involving herbs, magical formulas, and hosts. Love potions were considered evil because they violated free will, and because they often involved demonic magic; such potions did not necessarily require the host, and often consisted of placing powders in food and drink, or charms on paper inside apples (in imitation of the temptation of Eve), but the possibilities of a miraculous host hardly escaped the notice of enterprising couplers.

Magic involving the Holy Sacrament was not the only sort of magic in which Aldegonde—and most other people—participated. She also admitted to interviewers that she had used special amulets—usually charms or formulas worn in a locket around the neck—to keep herself "stab-free" in the violent world of prostitution. She learned about these particular amulets from a German soldier in Kortrijk, now dead, who had recommended them to her because she was prone to fighting and needed extraordinary protection. Some time ago she had handed over the amulets to Pater Grinsel, who burned them. This might have been because he considered them superstitious—and thus ineffective, a waste of time. But if he thought the amulets indeed effective, then he would have burned them because they were magical.

Like most churchmen he called supernatural effects caused by God "miracles," while all other supernatural effects (with the host or without) were necessarily caused by the devil and thus "magic." In other words, to most churchmen magic was the opposite side of miracles. Unlike superstition, magic worked. But unlike miracles, the source of magic necessarily came from the devil—for it was clearly supernatural, and it clearly did not come from God. Such an attitude likely occupied the minds of Aldegonde's interviewers as well, and only compounded evidence of her willingness to deal darkly.

But most people, perhaps even Aldegonde, possessed a more nuanced view of magic, which distinguished between "demonic" and ordinary or even good magic. To these, magic wasn't *necessarily* demonic (though the desperate or thoroughly evil might resort to such), but simply sought to take advantage of vaguely understood supernatural forces, in order to prevent and combat misfortune. This included not only protecting themselves with amulets and hosts, but placing spells in posts and doorways, or treasure hunting with special objects, or healing with charms, or uttering Church-inspired prayers, from the simple to those with mysterious (and thus magical) words. "Worm, worm, flee, flee, It is Jesus of Nazareth who commands it of thee!" "Chamo, Chamo, Chamo, I commend God and all God's dear saints, three choirs of angels, and all that concerns heaven and earth, in Chamo, Chamo, Chamo." "Matthew, Mark, Luke, and John, Bless the bed that I lie on." "All you rats! All you ugly beasts! I command you by sun, moon, air, stars, and firmament to depart from my house, stalls, barn, garden, as sure as Mary gave birth to the Son of God." "Burning, burning, fly from the fire to the sand, Fever disappear in the name of God. Glory be to the Father, the Son, and the Holy Spirit." As much as these and many other practices might frustrate and even infuriate churchmen, for mixing magic and religion, to practitioners there was no confusion or distinction at all—and not necessarily any mixing of the devil.

But was this sort of less malevolent magic what Aldegonde had in mind? For if anything she seemed to prefer more blatantly sinister sorts of practices—akin to those preferred by witches. For while working in the town of Dunkirk, where she had also traveled to "give her best," she learned from a ropedancer (with whom she fell genuinely in love) not only his mysterious dances, but how to use a small, magical charm helpful in her trade: it served to attract "men and young men" to her, and to make "wives jealous of their husbands"—much like the love potions so often condemned by churchmen. The charm was also useful in the event that she found herself in unpleasant company: if a fight started, she could turn the amulet the other way around on her heart, and slide away undetected. Finally, the same amulet was useful in helping her to appear as if she were possessed by the devil, which she once put to good use in Mechelen (no doubt seeking to remove blame from herself for some misdeed, because possession was involuntary, out of one's control).

This last effect was only feigned possession, but such constant flirting with the devil could hardly have endeared Aldegonde to her interviewers, who in any event would hardly have bothered to make any distinction between innocent and demonic magic—all magic would have offended them. Moreover, Aldegonde wasn't yet finished: she couldn't help musing that had she stayed with the ropedancer, he would have taught her many other useful things, for he was "a fortune-teller," and while reading her palm told her things that would happen to her "and in fact they happened." Namely, he told her that she would suffer greatly if she ever left or ignored him, and eventually in desperation would give herself to the devil—all of which had occurred. Here Aldegonde made clear that she meant nothing innocent at all by her sort of magic.

She concluded her story of the ropedancer, and her entire testimony, by saying that she had slept with him but had never "known him" because "his instrument was too small." And though he was Protestant, he hadn't taught her anything about his religion.

THE SEARCH FOR CORROBORATION

June 15 to 24, 1652. The crimes that Aldegonde admitted were all obviously troubling—from prostitution to thievery to murder to magic to abusing the host. Yet the interviewers might have seen in her story at least one bright side: the goal of judicial interviews was to extract a confession from the accused, for confession was the "queen of proofs," and this confession was queen of queens. In fact, getting such a detailed confession was usually much more difficult than it had been with Aldegonde, sometimes even requiring the threat or reality of torture, especially in dealing with witches, as Aldegonde practically claimed to be. But because she had been so willingly forthcoming, no such measures had been necessary. Thus, the interviewers might have ended their work there.

Yet in Aldegonde's case confession did not end things at all. Instead it only made interviewers skeptical. Precisely because of her fantastic stories, and her unusual eagerness to talk without compulsion (not to mention the famous dictum by Gratian, the twelfth-century father of canon law, that one could not trust the word of a harlot), the interviewers decided to spend a great deal of energy confirming Aldegonde's tales. In other words, the central point of this case remained her abuse of the host, but now there was much more at work as well—especially how truthful she was, and how guilty.

The interviewers therefore called at least twelve other witnesses over the next ten days to answer questions about Aldegonde's story. Had her own father truly deflowered her? For there was no sign that he had ever been reported by the parish priest, excommunicated, subjected to public humiliation, or thrown in prison, as should have occurred. And, though stepparents were stock evil characters in the stories of the day and though Aldegonde's fit the stereotype, had she really been provoked to the point of murder? How extensively had Aldegonde engaged in prostitution and such irreverences as carnal relations in the churchyard? As for the desecration of the host, this was in the most recent instance indisputable, but what about the others? Or her related claim that she had given herself to the devil?

The interviewers started with the mistresses and other residents of the House for Penitent Daughters in Brussels, moved to Mechelen (to interview neighbors, Aldegonde's girlhood parish priest, the supervisor of the hospice where she had stayed, her stepsister, and some of her old partners in crime), then returned to Brussels to interview Aldegonde again.

The easiest thing to establish from these testimonies was that

Aldegonde had told all of her stories before. This did not make them false, but simply meant that rehearsal and embellishment had to be considered. Only Jennie Poisan, her roommate in the House for Penitent Daughters, stated that Aldegonde never spoke of her past—but this was perhaps a belated attempt to protect Aldegonde, for every other witness testified that Aldegonde could not be shut up, including in the House for Penitent Daughters, where it was a cardinal rule to keep silent about one's inevitably sinful history. Several witnesses testified that others often clustered around Aldegonde and sat spellbound as she spun her tales. In fact these tales helped one witness, the director of the St. Julian's hostel in Mechelen, to understand why Aldegonde looked so much older than her twenty-two years.

Another conclusion easily drawn by investigators was that at least some of the things recounted by Aldegonde had actually happened, and most of the people she had named truly existed. Hence, Aldegonde was not completely fabricating. But the investigators wanted especially to know how truthful she had been on four particular topics, and thus questioned witnesses even more closely about these: her upbringing in the home of Martin Walre and its connection to her promiscuity; whether anyone had evidence that Aldegonde poisoned her stepmother or others; whether she had killed babies or anyone else; and of course whether anyone had ever seen her abuse the host.

Everyone who ever knew Martin Walre agreed that he was a cursing, swearing, drunken, abusing ogre. But those who knew the Walre family long were highly skeptical about Aldegonde's claims of incest. Only Pater Grinsel in Mechelen, who had never known Martin Walre and came to know Aldegonde quite late, believed her account and would therefore not allow her father to visit her at the hospice of St. Julian. But others did not believe—not Aldegonde's parish priest, nor the three spiritual daughters who lived right next door to the Walre family, nor especially Aldegonde's thirty-nine-year-old stepsister, Marie vande Straeten, daughter of Anna Hannar. Marie testified that though her mother was thoroughly miserable in her marriage, and though Martin was thoroughly bad, he genuinely loved Aldegonde. Once, with tears in his eyes, Martin swore that he would never have done the things being rumored, for the memory would have made him unbearably unhappy; besides, he said, he had enough women "to service him."

Witnesses reflected a similar skepticism about Aldegonde's travels as a prostitute. Yes, she had been promiscuous from an early age, said witnesses, thanks largely to neglect by her father and indifference from her stepmother. But almost none could say in how many cities she had worked. One of the most cooperative witnesses of all, Aldegonde's old crony in prostitution, named May With the Evil Eyes, was particularly skeptical.

Now respectably married (and thus now acceptable as a witness), May was sure to explain first to the interviewers that she had become a prostitute only for a time, and then only because a coupler had locked her in a room with a soldier and the soldier took her virginity by force. May also went out of her way to reveal details about the working places of most "dishonorable daughters" in Mechelen, the names of various prostitutes (many already given by Aldegonde), and which cafés in the city were, in fact, brothels—all to establish her distance from that world.*

At last May got around to the real subject. Though it was true

**Or was she trying to clear away competition? For only two years after giving this testimony, May With the Evil Eyes was issued a citation for "coupling."*

that Aldegonde had given herself "to everyone," May did not believe that Aldegonde had ever been in Holland working among sailors. Neither did she believe that Aldegonde was ever pregnant, for she was "with too many men" for no one to have noticed. Aldegonde did once care for a child, taking it along on begging trips into the countryside, where she sat in front of churches. But the child was removed from her and died in the care of Margaret Capiteyns, as Aldegonde herself had claimed. May, however, added one ominous detail: in her opinion, and contrary to Aldegonde's suggestion that the child died very soon afterward, the child died exactly one year to the day after being taken from Aldegonde. To sign-seeking May, this was no coincidence at all, but evidence of Aldegonde's sinister nature, and perhaps the direct result of a curse by her.

As for Aldegonde's administration of poison to Anna Hannar or anyone else, not a single witness had any evidence. They had all heard talk of it. Marie vande Straeten even noticed that Anna had "swollen up" and made wild claims about someone poisoning her. But Marie could not say whether Aldegonde had given any laced beer to her mother and did not believe it anyway. Aldegonde did take money from her mother's chest, but that was to buy meat, because "she liked to eat something good."

When investigators asked whether May knew that Aldegonde wished to poison her during their time together in the hospice of St. Julian, May was doubly stunned: not only was she unaware, she had never even set foot in that hospice. Neither did May know about Aldegonde's stabbing a soldier to death: a soldier named Carl had once threatened to throw Aldegonde into the river because he claimed she had given him syphilis, but May knew nothing about a stabbing. Mistress Marie of the House for Penitent Daughters offered only indirect evidence that Aldegonde was prone to violence:

when Aldegonde left the house for her current cell at the Laken gate, they found one knife in the straw of her bed and two more in her clothes chest.

May's twenty-six-year-old soldierly husband, Thomas de Langhe, an old acquaintance of Aldegonde, was able to respond in greatest detail about the soldier supposedly murdered by Aldegonde. His name was Herry, and he was indeed stabbed to death, with a short dagger in the side, on the night after Ash Wednesday in 1651, at about nine o'clock. The assailant, however, was not Aldegonde but another soldier, who had quarreled with Herry over a woman—whose name Thomas could not remember. Soon after, the attacker was imprisoned and shot outside the Neckerspoel gate for the deed, then buried in St. Peter's churchyard, next to the wall adjoining the home of the commander of the regiment. If Thomas was telling the truth, then Aldegonde at least got the place of burial right, but she had obviously conflated and embellished several other stories to make her own.

All of these events mattered much to the interviewers in weighing Aldegonde's main offense, about which they eventually asked most witnesses as well: her abuse of the host. None of the witnesses had actually seen anything in this regard but only heard, at least until the last occasion in Brussels. A woman from the hospice of St. Julian, in Mechelen, had heard Aldegonde say she could not swallow the host, and therefore threw it into the privy because "the devil must have me around the neck." But no one was able to find it.

Only Pastor Vergaelen of Mechelen, Aldegonde's one-time parish priest, could add some new information, neglected by Aldegonde, about host desecration: according to him, she did not originally leave Mechelen for St. Truiden, but Gent, where he had arranged for her to be taken into the House for Penitent Daughters of that city—thus before she ever entered the same sort of house in Brussels. Aldegonde did not stay in Gent long, however, because along with telling her frightening tales to the other girls, she claimed to have buried three hosts in the garden. A party had searched "dutifully" for the hosts, in the places where Aldegonde told them to dig, but they were never found.

Even taking into consideration that several witnesses were little more reliable than Aldegonde herself, it was clear enough that pieces of her story were falling apart, and that the investigators had serious doubts about her testimony and even stability—thus complicating how they should proceed with her desecration of the host. They therefore decided to question her again, and had her brought before them on June 25, 1652, the last of all the interviews.

What was the name of the soldier she killed? Where were his barracks? Where did Aldegonde live at the time? Why was a soldier executed outside the Neckerspoel gate? Aldegonde knew the answer to none, except her place of residence, and simply insisted again that she had stabbed a soldier in the back, with a long knife.

Why didn't Aldegonde tell them about her stay in Gent? She did not answer directly, but told them instead her version of what had occurred there—which matched closely Pastor Vergaelen's account. Where were the hosts, wondered the investigators? Aldegonde responded that they were not found because they had dissolved from moisture. How long had they been in the ground? She could not say. If she was truly worried about her misdeed, why didn't she simply keep quiet rather than boast about it? Was it because she wanted to be sent away from the house? No, Aldegonde answered bluntly, it was much worse than that: she did it because she was evil, and because she wasn't sure whether God actually was inside the host.

In addition to their many interviews, the investigators wrote to contacts in Antwerp and Gent over the next several months to follow up this point or that. A priest from Antwerp responded in July 1652 to a request for information about Aldegonde's comrade Antonette, with whom she had allegedly gathered and sold hosts: the priest knew Antonette, but hadn't been able to "fish anything" out of her, and she constantly denied "knowing her" (presumably Aldegonde). He could say only that Antonette was extremely poor, burdened with many children, and thanks to the exhortations of her good pastor had quit the brothel where she worked. Nevertheless, on account of her horrible crime (if it were true) she should surely not go unpunished.

In October they heard from another contact, who had spoken with Margaret Capiteyns about the mysterious child once watched by Aldegonde. Margaret said that she had indeed received from the city a child who "belonged" to Aldegonde, and that it was already injured and damaged and soon died. Whether Aldegonde had also borne that child was not clear to her, but the child's injuries and demise were consistent with Aldegonde's own story.

Finally, a priest familiar with the House for Penitent Daughters in Gent confirmed that Aldegonde had been expelled because she told too many unsettling stories of her past and present, including the usual claims of conversation with the devil, incest, abortions, promiscuity, poisoning, abusing the host, and so forth, instilling so much dread and fear in the residents who stood dumbstruck to listen, that discipline was ruined—but no hosts were ever found.

In the end, what the investigators could establish with certainty was much less than what Aldegonde had alleged, even if it was still enough for concern. She was indeed poorly raised, she had indeed been a prostitute, she had desecrated the host in Brussels, and she clearly did not like to confess or commune. But no one could offer proof that she had conversed with the devil, desecrated the host on other occasions, aborted her pregnancy, or committed murder—though she had perhaps contributed to a child's death through seriously neglecting it. What remained now was for the investigators to turn over their evidence to Archbishop Boonen's diocesan court, and for that court to pass judgment.

THE SEARCH FOR GUILT

As with so many legal proceedings of the time, which either did not bother to preserve the final sentence or were settled without trial, this one left no mention of either formal or informal judgment of Aldegonde. But the possibilities were apparent enough, based on current legal practices and the lines of questioning taken by the interviewers.

One possibility was that Aldegonde was simply tried and punished according to her offense. All of her genuine offenses fell clearly into the realm of "major sins," as defined by Church law, and thus deserved major punishments. Prostitution might be punished with imprisonment or public humiliation, heretical ideas with brief penance or imprisonment or banishment from the archdiocese, and stealing the host with the sort of torture, mutilation, and executions noted earlier.

But it was not likely that she was executed, because such events were highly publicized and well documented. Moreover, that Aldegonde had clearly committed crimes was *still* not enough to determine punishment. This required, again, consideration of her motives, circumstances, and state of mind, any of which might mitigate or increase guilt. Such consideration was implicit in any trial, inquiry, or sacramental confession, but in Aldegonde's case it was central.

In regard to prostitution, for instance, the investigators knew the usual mitigating circumstances. These did not include poverty (although poverty might excuse theft and murder), but they did include the assumption that women possessed a more carnal nature than men. In fact, some canon lawyers gave the impression that prostitution was practically the logical outcome for most any woman: her chastity was easily suspect and her readiness for carnal relations almost constant. Under such thinking, a prostitute would have been culpable, but not "severely culpable," because she was merely responding to her nature—in other words, she still might be punished, but not to the extreme, and not as harshly as her more responsible clients and bosses (males and older women).

Yet these assumptions about prostitution were secondary anyway in Aldegonde's case: she had already served time in two Houses for Penitent Daughters, and she had not engaged in the practice for over a year. Instead, what likely interested investigators most about her life as a prostitute (besides the intelligence she provided about other offenders) was how it might help explain her desecration of the host—namely, that it had damaged her mind.

Many jurists taught that "flagrant" devotion to a life of sin, especially sexual sin, might lead not only to the commission of still other atrocities (including murder) but to an unsound mind. This was also the case for other circumstances and events in Aldegonde's life: if such things as "terror" or a bad marriage were considered "natural" contributors to mental illness, then why not a deplorable upbringing, complete with a real or imagined wicked stepmother and incestuous father? And how much to blame were impatient or clumsy confessors who never helped Aldegonde purge herself of sin, thus aggravating her already unstable condition?

In short, a greater possibility than execution or even trial was that investigators believed something about Aldegonde's mind just wasn't right, and thus treated her in accordance with current assumptions and practices about the mentally infirm.

The relationship of one's state of mind to one's guilt had been pondered and weighed in the West since the Romans, who made intent an important part of serious crime. Thus: to be guilty, one had to understand that something was wrong and then do it anyway. This relationship was codified in Justinian's famous legal code, then embellished in the European Middle Ages, especially by canon lawyers who labored over "the interior condition of the heart." Not every judge in Europe—religious or secular—cared about the accused's state of mind, and plenty of these accused were executed or otherwise fully punished without regard for mental stability. But toward 1500 in secular courts (as Roman law became more widespread around Europe), and even earlier in church courts (whose officers were handling Aldegonde's case), sanity or wholeness was taken increasingly into consideration.

Clearly Aldegonde's investigators considered this question, even if her case never came to formal trial. It may have entered their minds even before questioning Aldegonde, thanks to the not uncommon assumption that anyone who committed an offense so grave as desecration of the host might very well be mentally unsound. But certainly it arose during her interview, as inferred from their follow-up questions, and especially during interviews with other witnesses, whom the interviewers asked explicitly about Aldegonde's sanity.

Surely they listened keenly to the judgment of Mistress Marie of the House for Penitent Daughters in Brussels, who stated that Aldegonde was of an "evil and stubborn humor" from the time of her arrival, that there was "no profit" from all the good instruction she received, and that she was of a worse disposition when taught than when left alone. Likewise to fifty-five-year-old Mertin Garzias, lay rector of the St. Julian's hostel in Mechelen, who testified that he and his wife had tried diligently to help Aldegonde, but she was of a highly changeable personality: one moment she seemed resolved to live well, then the next she was back to her former self. The investigators summed up this observation in the margin in their own words: "unsound mind."

Pastor Vergaelen, Aldegonde's girlhood priest, told investigators that Aldegonde had lied to him "many times over the years," and was even inclined to confess acts she had not committed. At one time she knew her catechism, and Ten Commandments, Creed, and prayers. But all were soon forgotten. Moreover, Aldegonde had once pretended to be possessed and asked to be exorcized—but he discovered later that she had feigned the whole thing, even putting needles in her mouth, which she spewed out during the exorcism, and which he judged reflected her unsound mind. The investigators duly noted this grim assessment as well.

The three spiritual daughters who once lived next door to Aldegonde judged similarly: once Aldegonde told them, "with tears streaming down her cheeks," about her father's crimes against her. But despite her emotion they did not believe her, mainly because they knew she had lied before: she could not have been completely sane, they concluded. Marie vande Straeten, Aldegonde's stepsister, said the same. And a priest in Gent heard from one of the city's Jesuits that Aldegonde's superiors there considered her a poor, lying girl with an "unfirm brain." Only May With the Evil Eyes judged that despite all her troubles and anger and wickedness and ability to tell "a thousand lies," Aldegonde was "sound enough" to be responsible.

Suspicion that Aldegonde wasn't sound was also reflected in the investigators' conspicuous lack of interest in her amulets and ropedancing and other activities in the dark world of magic. Hundreds besides Aldegonde were brought before the diocesan court of Mechelen for using "superstitious remedies" against sickness, for distributing cards and "superstitious papers" to protect houses from fire, for driving away evil spirits from a home by handing a consecrated candle to the mother and the son and then reading a formula that was "neither in Flemish nor French nor Spanish nor Latin" and then letting the drops fall into holy water that they were to drink for nine days, or for healing people "to the detriment of the saints and the abuse of pilgrims," or for confessing that they had sold themselves "to the devil." Aldegonde's adventures in magic were at least as serious as these, yet there was no pursuit of them, either with her or other witnesses.

Closely related was the investigators' failure to pursue the obvious: the even more serious crime of witchcraft. This even though Aldegonde practically admitted to such, even though she stated openly her fear that such an admission would increase her punishment, even though she had terrorized residents in two Houses for Penitent Daughters with her claims of conversing with the devil, and even though misuse of the host was in official minds one of the best signs that witchcraft rather than simple magic was at issue. Yet the interviewers pursued none of these, nor did they pose any questions to Aldegonde or other witnesses about the infamous pact with the devil (power over the elements in exchange for loyalty), or devil's Sabbaths where that pact was renewed, or strange bodily marks on her body where the devil took nourishment, nor did the interviewers threaten torture—all of which were regularly present in previous decades when dealing with suspected witches. Instead, when Aldegonde practically boasted of desecrating the host in the House for Penitent Daughters in Gent, the interviewers merely wondered aloud whether she hadn't done so simply to be expelled from the house—a transgression certainly, but hardly the definition of sinister.

Perhaps the investigators failed to pursue these admissions because they were less inclined than their predecessors to believe in witchcraft: the great age of witch hunts was past, with the last witch burned in Brussels in 1636 and in Mechelen in 1644. But such accusations were still around, such trials still conducted by Church courts, and such burnings still carried out—until 1685 in the Spanish Netherlands. Moreover, want of torture did not alone mean that judges—lay or clerical—had quit their beliefs, much less their violent methods of interrogation. On July 4, 1652, less than two weeks after Aldegonde's last interview, the diocesan court had a woman tortured in Brussels for two and a half hours, in the presence of the judge himself. And recall the priest tortured and executed in February of that year in Brussels for blasphemous deeds. Rather, that Aldegonde was neither accused as a witch nor tortured was more likely due to the most basic assumption about serious crime in general, and magic and witchcraft (with its demonic pact) in particular: that it required a conscious act of will. And Aldegonde, they suggested, was incapable of such.

It was not a thought they would have come to casually. Judges and lawyers were warned to be wary of defendants who feigned insanity, often by confessing the most outlandish things in order to avoid torture, execution, or other punishment. Aldegonde was certainly eager to admit her terrible crimes, and both she and her priest claimed that she once faked possession—why not her testimony as well? Laypeople knew well enough the contours of the insanity defense, and enough were suspected of employing it fraudulently in order to escape prosecution or punishment. But at some point, Aldegonde's interviewers apparently concluded that she was not faking, and that there was evidence enough of real infirmity.

This came not only from the opinions of other witnesses, but from various legal and medical considerations of the time. The most basic legal consideration, again developed by the Romans and adapted in the Middle Ages, stated that a fully responsible criminal knew what she was doing was wrong, did it anyway, spoke about it or tried to hide it, and might express remorse. There was some evidence that Aldegonde fit these requirements, and thus possibly was sane. She had spoken eagerly about her deeds with many (if erratically). And she claimed once to have expressed remorse and shame. Yet how to tell whether she really understood what she was doing, generally or specifically? Her deliberate faking of possession to her priest again suggested a certain amount of evil will. Yet this same priest concluded that her faking was itself evidence of an unsound mind!

Another legal tradition suggested that one did not have to be wholly mad in order to be insane. It wasn't always running around the streets naked or spitting nails or throwing stones that signaled insanity, but "also the one whose consciousness is obliterated by a single idea, even while he remains normal in every respect that is not related to that idea." In other words, even if Aldegonde were sane in some or even most respects, it did not mean that she was sane when she stole the host or claimed to converse with the devil.

Perhaps most instructive of all in her case were medical distinctions, which grew up in the sixteenth century as some began to question the executions of tens of thousands of accused witches. These questioners concluded, especially during the seventeenth century, that a major cause of witchcraft was melancholy, or "the abandonment of spirit, as happens frequently with women." This didn't necessarily deny witchcraft, but it could lessen one's accountability and punishment, and even give witchcraft a physical or "materialist," rather than sinister, explanation—for melancholy was simply the result of imbalanced bodily humors. As the physician Paolo Zacchia wrote, melancholy produced "an insanity that was not quite the same as furor" (outright insanity), and the groups most affected in this way were "ignorant persons and wenches," of "desperate and agitated minds," subject to vain imaginings and prone to saying "absurd and sad things." Just the sort of description that fit Aldegonde.

Taken together, the medical traditions suggested that a person was either (1) fully responsible and thus punishable, (2) melancholy mad and thus punished to a lesser degree, or (3) totally mad and thus not punished at all. The sorts of treatment recommended for each type of judgment were also familiar to Aldgonde's interviewers. The sane and responsible were subject to the sorts of humiliations, punishments, and fines already mentioned. The melancholy mad were punished, but to a lesser degree than the fully guilty—thus they might be imprisoned rather than executed. And the completely mad were not to be punished but neither could they be left free to roam: they were therefore held in custody by their family or another institution—not as punishment, but for the safety of society. Their condition was "irremediable" and the only hope for a cure was, of course, a miracle.

These were complicated by a final consideration, however: namely, that some crimes, including desecration of the host, were so heinous they had to be punished anyway—even if to a lesser degree than usual, and even if the perpetrator was completely mad. This was precisely what the priest from Antwerp suggested in regard to Antonette, and which might have been applicable to Aldegonde as well.

But again, her interviewers showed little interest in following this line of thought. Most likely they regarded Aldegonde at best as partly sound, and partly responsible. Thus, she was probably not tortured nor executed as a witch, but simply excluded from normal society.

Perhaps she stayed a long while in the tower on the Laken gate: this was an expensive option, especially if she had no family able to support her there, as was the custom, but it was possible—another offender at around the same time was sentenced to life imprisonment there. Or perhaps Aldegonde lived out her days in a closely guarded hospice, or even another House for Penitent Daughters, despite all the problems she had caused in them: such houses, accustomed to dealing with recidivism among their criminally experienced populations, took seriously the biblical injunction to forgive seventy times seven. Whether this extended to desecrators of the host was another matter, but this too was possible, for not even the most exalted sort of institution designed for reformed prostitutes—the convent—was without its ups and downs. The convent of Mary Magdalene in Brussels, also known as the White Ladies, was rampant with complaints about male visitors, accusations among the sisters of past pregnancies and other scandals, nuns sleeping together, and so forth. And finally perhaps Aldegonde was held in another hospice, such as the St. Julian hospice where she had lived for a time in Mechelen.

Aldegonde never appeared in the historical record again. A few of her old friends did, always in the least desirable sorts of records, including Marie Pantouffer, brought in to testify against one Petrus Smets, who swore that his house was not a brothel, while Marie swore otherwise for she had worked in that house! Still, for the little while that Aldegonde did appear, she was an unforgettable and tragic guide through the underworld of miracles.

FIVE

THE PERFECTLY NATURAL CURE OF WOUNDS

March 4, 1634, a Street in Brussels. Warrant in hand, entourage securely about him, the judge of the ecclesiastical court walked purposefully toward an address in the Leuven street. His very presence in this small procession signified that this was no ordinary business, which would have been left to mere prosecutors and bailiffs alone.

Suddenly, still short of their destination, the judge and his men bumped into the very man they had come to arrest: the medical doctor Jan Baptista van Helmont. Thinking quickly, the judge's chief prosecutor and a couple of sturdy bailiffs stepped forward and "exhorted" the doctor to follow them into a tavern across the street. A stunned Dr. Helmont did as he was told, though reluctantly: he resented this humiliation in plain daylight, right in his own neighborhood, and as a prominent burgher and staunch Catholic he had always avoided suspect places—as he (unlike most) considered taverns to be. And there was still more. For once inside the tavern, the prosecutor explained that the judge and the rest of the entourage were continuing on to the Helmont home, in order to search it, and that the doctor was to remain in this tavern with his guards until the search was complete.

At the head of the search party, now marching ahead, was of course the judge himself, who hoped most of all to find copies of Dr. Helmont's scandalous book on healing, published thirteen years before, which had so denigrated the church's teachings on miracles and magic—not to mention practically every physician and theologian of Catholic Europe. Though the doctor had claimed for years that no more copies of the book existed, and that he had in any event renounced the many objectionable ideas within it, the judge suspected otherwise—on both counts. Hence, upon entering the Helmont home he said to the doctor's startled wife, Margaret van Ranst, "I understand that your husband's book is still published and sold daily in town," then asked her to open every locked trunk, chest, and cupboard in the house, to see whether any copies were stashed inside.

But no luck. The judge therefore ordered his men to expand their search—to the straw in the family's beds, to the household supplies of grain and flour, to the small boxes in which Madam van Ranst kept her private things, and to "every corner" of the house, "from top to bottom," all within earshot and eyesight of the neighbors. Still no luck. But in the process of turning the house upside down, the searchers found plenty of other suspicious books and manuscripts, some fifty items in all, which the judge took away instead.

Leafing through those items several hours later, the judge grew alarmed. Though the scandalous book itself was nowhere to be found (as the doctor had claimed), there was indeed (as the judge had suspected) plenty of other incriminating evidence in its place—especially the doctor's ownership of assorted banned books of the "first class," including several by the dreaded Paracelsus. Just as troubling were a number of new suspicious manuscripts in the doctor's own hand, presumably intended for publication. Here was proof that he had hardly repented his wrongful ways. Hence, the judge ordered the doctor's detention to continue: now he was taken from the tavern to the rougher confines of the archbishop's prison tower, until a thorough investigation of the confiscated items could be accomplished.

Within that tower, a dejected Dr. Helmont was left to wonder how many times he would have to explain and renounce that cursed book, how many times he would have to proclaim his determination to live and die a faithful Catholic, how many times he would have to provide testimonials of his religious orthodoxy? Didn't the prominence of his noble family, his irreprehensible life, his long-standing aid to the poor, his conversion of Protestants to Catholicism, his inviolable right as a burgher of Brussels to be free from unreasonable searches, move his accusers at all?

Obviously not enough. Though no one was any longer executed for heresy (that ended in 1597), especially Church courts remained highly committed to rooting it out—through fines, imprisonment, and more. And the doctor's heresy was, at least to some, quite clear: his scandalous book on healing had rankled the highest authorities of Church and medicine in its insistence that various spiritual forces—both divine and demonic—long believed to be supernatural were, in fact, quite natural. In other words, there weren't as many witches and evil spirits at work in the world as people thought, and there weren't as many miracles either.

THE MAKING OF AN ADEPT

Nothing in the doctor's family or upbringing suggested that he would ever see the inside of a jail, or promote such objectionable ideas.

Jan Baptista van Helmont was baptized on January 12, 1579, in the parish of St. Goedele in Brussels. His father, Christian, of a noble Mechelen family, held office in the Exchequer of the Duchy of Brabant, while his mother, Marie van Stassart, belonged to a prominent family of Brussels.

When Christian died in 1580, Marie took over the education of young Jan, her fifth and last child, who showed great aptitude for learning. He began quite conventionally: Latin and other basics at grammar school, then the "Arts" curriculum at university (modified by this time at Leuven from the original medieval seven liberal arts to physics, metaphysics, dialectic, logic, and ethics), which provided the tools necessary to study still higher subjects. But even before finishing the Arts in 1594, Jan was disenchanted with convention.

It didn't take long to see, he wrote in later years, that learning at the university was more about fancy robes and winning arguments and citing the proper authorities than it was about the pursuit of truth: he had bitten into the apple of knowledge but came away "naked as Adam and Eve." He felt like a fool, because he knew nothing except how to argue, and merely to support a predetermined position rather than to find truth.

What then to do? For the time being, his answer was to study further in traditional subjects—perhaps he simply needed to learn more. He tried philosophy, especially stoicism, but a dream convinced him that stoicism was passive, selfish, and useless. He followed a course in demonology and magic from the author of a recent but already famous book on the subject, Martin Del Rio, but was unimpressed. He considered a career in the clergy, but recalled Saint Bernard's admonition to avoid living off the sins of the people. He tried law, but where he sought truth and certainty he found only human custom and opinion. He tried botany, but where he sought useful knowledge to improve life he discovered only the worthless classifications of ancient authorities, to be memorized rather than usefully applied. Finally he tried medicine, a subject and profession that his chagrined noble mother deemed beneath her well-born son and family.

In this too he was disappointed—at least at first. For though he devoured some six hundred authoritative works on the subject, and earned a medical degree in 1599 from the University of Leuven, he was forced to conclude that here was yet another dismal science: like all others, nothing about it was useful or certain. The professors and physicians he knew were able, on the basis of Aristotle, Galen, and other classical icons, to discuss the possible origins of every conceivable ailment, but could cure not a single one. This was because medicine, like other disciplines, was more concerned about propping up classical authorities, even when they were wrong, than with seeking to improve upon existing knowledge through personal observation and experiment. There was too much citation and not enough inspiration. There was too much logic and not enough experience. There was too much talk and not enough healing. And there was too much Aristotle and Galen and not enough Christian God.

Still, Jan would not give up on medicine altogether, because contrary to other disciplines he saw for this one a solution: Simply change authorities. If he could not trust his teachers and the classical founders, he could rely on his own observations of Nature aided by illumination from God, the author of true medical knowledge. In a dream received shortly after graduation, Jan heard the voice of God calling him to be a physician, along with the assurance that the archangel Raphael would occasionally bring him knowledge from on high.

This calling was confirmed by a second dream around 1600, in which the new doctor sat at twilight on the banks of the Schelde River. There he looked out over the ruins of the fortress of Calloo, inundated by floodwaters some years before. In his mind, Dr. Helmont saw the submerged town that lay around the fortress, the abandoned homes and wasted fields, the moss and lichen, and the massacre of humans. This melancholic state caused him to ponder yet another massacre of humans, prolonged by a conspiracy of stupidity and negligence: namely, the massacre of patients by their own physicians. The solution to this crisis in medicine came in the next part of the dream: divine illumination. Again, Jan should rely for his medical knowledge not on pagan authorities but instead the direct, sure, untainted inspiration afforded by the God of Abraham, Isaac, and Jacob. He would be a physician of another sort.

The dreams of the young Dr. Helmont reflected a growing dissatisfaction by 1600 with the science of Aristotle in general and the medicine of Galen in particular.

Despite the doctor's typical portrayal of himself battling alone against tradition, many other thinkers of the time were also fighting the old schools, from a variety of quarters. The eventual victors in the battle would be the "mechanical philosophers," who by 1650 would turn the universe into a sort of machine and whose leading lights included such enduringly famous names as Descartes and Galileo. But the *first* great challenge to Aristotle and Galen emerged from the new "Natural Philosophers,"* who saw the world as a living, spiritual organism and whose names were destined for the obscurity of defeat—such as the English Dee, Kelley, and Fludd; the Italian Campanella, Bruno, and Vanini; the German Agrippa; the Dane Severinus; or the Fleming Jan Baptista van Helmont.

Nurtured in fifteenth-century Italy by such figures as Marsilio Ficino and Giovanni Pico della Mirandola, and taken northward in the next century by especially Agrippa (d. 1534) and the controversial Swiss physician Paracelsus (d. 1541), Natural Philosophy became a genuine movement toward 1600, when more and more of its adherents were in demand at various courts of Europe—if not its universities or churches, which generally continued to promote Aristotelian science. But despite this increased presence, it was never a simple matter to identify Natural Philosophers. For one thing, all sorts of thinkers adhered to parts of various schools, old and new: though remembered best as mechanists, Johannes Kepler had his astrology and music of the stars, René Descartes his illuminations, and Isaac Newton his experiments in alchemy—just like Natural Philosophers. Moreover, no two Natural Philosophers were alike: Dr. Helmont, though an early admirer of Paracelsus, would reject many of the latter's ideas, saying that he "heard the calf bleating, but couldn't find the stall." Finally, that Natural Philoso-

**Technically, all scholars of "physica," or the natural world, could be called "natural philosophers," or what moderns would call scientists. But "Natural Philosophy" with a capital N, or perhaps better "Philosophers of Nature," is a convenient umbrella to cover all those who, like Dr. Helmont, enlarged and spiritualized Nature. There is no perfect label for these spiritualizing thinkers, who were variously called chemical philosophers, neo-Platonists, animists, and Hermeticists—the last after the mythical Hermes Trismegistus, said to have lived in the time of Moses and to have preserved the ancient secrets of the Egyptians (his writings, available in the West after 1453, were in fact, composed around the second century* A.D.*, as part of early neo-Platonism). But "Natural Philosophers" is broad enough to do.*

phers tended to work alone also made it difficult to call them a "school." Yet they read the same works and shared various assumptions—including those that led to the arrest of Dr. Helmont.

While traditional philosophers and theologians saw an irreparable rupture between heaven and earth,* so that everything above was divine and everything below was corrupt, Natural Philosophers saw the presence of God at all times and places—on earth as well as in heaven, and within not only human beings but even matter.

While traditionalists regarded matter as inherently inert, Natural Philosophers tended to regard it as alive, operating on principles of sympathy and antipathy that permeated the universe.

While traditional theologians and philosophers considered the Bible to be the book through which God revealed His Word, including on some aspects of Nature, Natural Philosophers took it even more literally, believing that the Word included both the obvious moral teachings and a host of related clues about the workings of Nature—hadn't Jesus himself tantalized that his words were obscure to the blind but offered secrets to those who would see?

While traditionalists viewed Nature as the creation of God and believed that he might certainly reveal truths through it, Natural Philosophers went further and viewed Nature as a second "book," at least equal to the Bible, through which God freely revealed a host of spiritual and physical secrets to those who would look hard enough.

While traditionalists believed that the Church was the means

**The view of theologians must be qualified, however: they agreed that the sublunar sphere was indeed fundamentally corrupt, but the principle of sacramentality meant that God could choose to be active in this sphere as it pleased Him—such as through relics, the Eucharist, or miracle-working images. But this did not go as far as the Natural Philosophers' view that God's presence was inherent both on earth and in heaven. This distinction will come out more clearly below.*

by which God revealed His will for all humanity, Natural Philosophers believed that God would also reveal His secrets directly to them, the chosen few, the Adepts, who would use those secrets—discovered through study of the physical world but in fact pregnant with spiritual truth—to benefit their fellow human beings, in body and soul.

And while traditional theologians and physicians held that truth most often emerged through rational and logical disputation and the study of indisputable religious and intellectual authorities, Natural Philosophers tended to believe that real truth came through direct illumination from God Himself and certainly not through such pagan intermediaries as Aristotle—at least not the Aristotle they saw dominating sixteenth-century education.

In short, the new Philosophers of Nature condemned the basic method and much of the substance of traditional science and medicine—and by implication traditional theology as well. They distrusted Aristotle and Galen not merely because they were pagan but especially because they were human—for among humans, quoted Dr. Helmont from Proverbs, "The number of fools is endless." And they did not so much dispute the reality of the traditional three dominant forces at work in the universe (God, the devil, and Nature) as they did change drastically the purview and workings of each: Nature was enlarged and animated, while the direct roles of God and the devil were minimized.

But this enlargement of Nature by the Natural Philosophers was not meant to remove God—far from it. While later mechanical philosophers and deists would take God (and the devil) out of everyday Nature in order to demystify it, the Natural Philosophers saturated Nature with God. It wasn't that God distanced Himself from this world, but rather that from the start He imbued Nature so thoroughly with His powers that there was practically no need for Him to intervene directly. Instead, people simply had to search out these heavenly powers, which, though often hidden, were nevertheless there for all who would only see.

Hence, in Natural Philosophy God was far closer to human beings than ever before or after. In the traditional view God created the corrupt earth, watched with great interest, and frequently intervened. In later mechanical systems God created, stood back almost indifferently to watch, and intervened only rarely if at all. But in Natural Philosophy God's presence was everywhere all the time, at creation and afterward. This enormous reduction in distance made God and humans at least neighbors, if not kindred spirits.

No wonder Natural Philosophers were more optimistic than traditionalists about the possibilities on earth for improvement and even perfection—in humans and in Nature. And no wonder Natural Philosophers were so often alchemists: in their hands, alchemy's most notorious quest, the transmutation of base metals into the noblest metal of gold, was not about greed but rather evidence of the ability to separate pure from impure matter, to change something ordinary into something perfect. If it could be done with metals, then it could be done in any sphere of life, including the human spirit.

Both traditional physicians and theologians, though bitter foes on much else, despised the new Naturalism. By 1606 physicians old and new had argued so vigorously that one scholar could compile a seventy-page list of tracts on the subject. Traditional Catholic theologians were if anything even more vehement against the new Naturalism. This was partly because they tended to be suspicious of any individual outside the formal hierarchy who made claims about illuminations from God, or stressed, as Natural Philosophers did, "man's innate knowledge of the Divinity." If eventual Catholic heroes such as Teresa of Avila and Ignatius Loyola were held briefly in suspicion by authorities for even less bold assertions than these, then it's hardly surprising that independent-minded, illumination-seeking Natural Philosophers were held in suspicion forever, right alongside such anti-heroes as Luther or Calvin.

Moreover, theologians believed that illumination seekers were too easily deceived: how could one know with certainty that supposedly divine insights were not instead the whisperings of the devil? In fact, many churchmen were sure that the insights of Natural Philosophers were in truth not "natural" at all but "magical"—and therefore inherently demonic. Put another way, to theologians the new Naturalism was based on many of the same dark assumptions and deceits as those held by Aldegonde Walre and her kind about the supernatural, yet the new sort was even more dangerous: for unlike the Aldegondes of the world, Natural Philosophers did not merely dabble in matters long considered supernatural, through trial and error with magical objects and hand-me-down spells, but rather built large, ambitious, and threatening systems to rival existing scientific and theological worldviews. The learned magician was a far more serious foe than the village wise woman or unlearned urban prostitute.

Also troublesome to most churchmen was that Natural Philosophy's divinely riddled, expanded Nature posed a distinct threat to the Church's sense of miracles. One reason traditionalists preferred the Aristotelian system (with its Christian twists) was that it emphasized the need for God's direct intervention—miracles—by distinguishing so clearly between heaven and earth, between forces natural and supernatural: the corruption of the earth made regular doses of divine grace stand out. More specifically, the powers present in shrines, relics, special images, and the Eucharist came not from any earthly source but directly from God's benevolent touch. Natural Philosophers, in contrast, blurred distinctions between this world and the other, thereby blurring miracles as well: to them, many phenomena and objects on earth held to be miraculous (including even shrines, relics, images, and the Eucharist?) worked on the same natural processes as the heavens—processes set in place by God certainly, but tapped into at the initiative of humans, and thus only indirectly from Him.

All this set traditionalists on edge, and led them to denounce such Nature-enlarging thinkers as Jan Baptista van Helmont.

Although negative sentiments against Natural Philosophy were already in the air when Dr. Helmont began his work around 1600, they would not affect him directly for more than two decades.

During these decades he investigated energetically and freely the secrets of Nature—not in the manner learned at university but instead according to the regimen advocated by his fellow adept Severinus: He sold his medical books, traveled widely (in Switzerland, Italy, France, and England), consulted with local wise men and women about their particular cures, studied the Bible for clues about Nature, and studied Nature itself—especially plants, animals, and minerals—for further clues. This latter study, of course, included buying coal and furnaces for a laboratory, where he might break things down through fire to their essences, in order to remove their "coarse cover" and discover the spiritualizing force within them (what he called the "archeus" but later scientists called "gas"), and thus understand and use Nature's gifts properly. "Fire opens the gate unto Natural Philosophy," he wrote. For however intelligent or capable the philosopher may be, however broad his knowledge, he may never be "admitted to the Root, or radical knowledge of natural things, without fire."

Dr. Helmont also served briefly as the private physician to the papal nuncio in Brussels, Ottavio Frangipani, and was invited to join the growing stable of Natural Philosophers at the court of the prince-bishop of Liège, Ernest of Bavaria, as well as that of Emperor Rudolph II of Germany. But his service to the nuncio lasted only briefly, and he refused all other offers of patronage, which he feared would endanger his soul. And though he regularly ventured out to test his cures, often for free and among the poor (including a stop in Antwerp to help battle an outbreak of the plague there), he remained dissatisfied with his knowledge and ability to cure. Thus he devoted himself more energetically than ever to the laboratory—explaining why enemies ridiculed him with the label "Doctor by Fire" or the "Pyrotechnic Physician," and why later observers ranked him among those Natural Philosophers perhaps better called chemical philosophers. Dr. Helmont responded to the insults of his contemporaries like Elijah responding to the priests of Baal: just as Elijah vanquished them with consuming fire, so with fire did he believe that he could come to greater truth than he had learned from the schools.

To pursue his laboratory investigations away from the distractions of Brussels, the doctor and his new wife, Margaret van Ranst, from a prominent local family, moved around 1607 to the nearby town of Vilvoorde, where they lived in semi-reclusiveness and where he was free to spend most of his time among flames and fumes. These solitary efforts in the laboratory would produce abundant fruit, much of it published only after 1642. Because of them

Dr. Helmont would one day be regarded as the most important chemical philosopher of the first half of the seventeenth century, a founder of modern chemistry, especially iatrochemistry (or chemistry applied to medicine), a discoverer of the workings of digestion, of conception, of disease, of fermentation, of gas, and of the thermometer. He would also be praised for his condemnation of the frequent practice of bloodletting, his rejection of the principle of contraries in curing, his use of scales and quantification in conducting experiments, other contributions to experimental method, and still more. But the larger spiritual or philosophical system of which these elements were only a part would be forgotten, even tossed aside in embarrassment.

This system included illumination from God to help the physician know how to proceed in the lab or with patients. It included as the basis for experimentation the biblical text, "by your fruits ye shall know them." It included a certainty that the physician had a divine role, on an equal footing with the priest, as intermediary between God and patient, as reflected in Ecclesiastes 38: "Honor the physician for the need thou hast of him, for the most high hath created him." It included an assumption that getting at disease was an "urgent concern of religious charity." It included liberal borrowing from the Bible, which was where, for instance, Dr. Helmont got his ideas against bloodletting—if Abel's blood "cried out from the ground" and Leviticus forbad the eating of blood, he could only conclude that blood had a special vital spirit in it and was therefore best left in the body. Finally, this system included—despite his later renunciation of it—the little book that would cost him so much trouble during the rest of his unsettled life, and even beyond.

THE LONG ARM OF MAGNETISM

In 1608 a certain Rudolph Goclenius, professor of medicine at the German University of Marburg, published a book that supported a controversial cure for gun wounds, advocated decades earlier by Paracelsus. This cure involved applying a special unguent or salve not to the wound itself, but to the gun or sword that caused it. The naturally occurring powers of magnetic attraction (or sympathy) that existed between the soothed weapon and the wound then soothed the wound as well, without the pain of traditional, direct treatments. Despite appearances, this magnetic cure was, argued the doctor, perfectly natural.

The book received little attention for several years, except from the author himself, who so fancied his ideas in print that he went to the trouble of issuing them again, in 1613. This time around, however, someone noticed: a Jesuit of Liège named Johan Roberti, who in 1615 refuted the tract and declared that the weapon salve of Paracelsus (a suspect Catholic after all) and Goclenius (an outright Calvinist) was a fine example of pure demonic magic.

Roberti did not dispute that the salve worked—in fact, like all magic it worked too well. Instead he disputed that it could possibly work by natural means. In Aristotelian Nature, matter was lifeless, and for one bit of matter to affect another there had to be direct contact. The weapon salve, to the contrary, worked over distance, and therefore outside of Nature: in other words, it was supernatural, and thus of necessity either demonic or divine. And because God would never get involved in such nonsense as a weapon salve, the force behind it was obvious to Roberti: the devil himself.

For the next decade, Roberti and Goclentius lashed out at each other in numerous works, according to the best traditions of academic disputation. They began, for instance, with dispassionate statements about the noble search for truth, moved quickly to spectacular misrepresentations and distortions of their opponent's position, then resorted at last to a hailstorm of personal attacks and name-calling. And they commenced with such dry, descriptive titles as Goclenius's *Tract on the Magnetic Cure of Wounds* (1608), and ended with Roberti's inflammatory *The Magician Goclenius Seriously Delirious* (1625).

In the middle of the fray, around 1616, the Jesuit's older brother in Brussels, Remacle Roberti, grew weary of the arguing, and even wondered whether his brother was wrong. Hence, he sought a third opinion from Dr. Helmont, who already had a local reputation as a skilled healer and disciple of Paracelsus. Would the doctor, asked the elder Roberti, like to prepare a tract on the weapon salve as well, and if necessary "make war" on little brother?

After examining the tracts from both Dr. Goclenius and Johan Roberti, Dr. Helmont agreed to do just that. Both men, he sighed, had missed the mark. Though correct that the weapon salve was natural, Goclenius had explained so "feebly" the workings of natural magnetism that he "staggered the doctrine," thus rendering it suspect: it was not the soothed weapon that promoted healing, but the blood upon it. As for the Jesuit's tract, it was "more a fine-witted censure than a solid disputation," full of prejudice and wrongful assumptions about magnetism. Dr. Helmont therefore decided to set everyone straight, and composed in 1617 his infamous *On the Magnetic Cure of Wounds*, or in its Latin original, *De magnetica vulnerum curatione*.

The doctor would always insist that he never intended the

tract for publication: it was for the combatants, and brother Remacle, only. But when Johan Roberti read it, he urged Dr. Helmont to publish it, judging it as good a defense of the subject as was likely to be written (and surely with an eye on refuting it too). A printer was arranged in Roberti's native Liège, which was perhaps no coincidence, given the numerous Natural Philosophers at the court of the prince-bishop, Ernest of Bavaria. The work was even approved by the ecclesiastical censor. Then just before publication, that approval was withdrawn. There was no explanation, though Dr. Helmont always suspected that Johan Roberti decided that he did not wish to look silly in print after all, and so used legal means to halt this devastating critique.

Unfortunately for the doctor, however, his book was not dead. For an unnamed person (most likely the mathematician Jean Gallé, supervisor of fortifications for Albert and Isabella) was so impressed with the work that he took it to Paris and arranged for publication there. It appeared at last in 1621.

Some later claimed that Dr. Helmont's tract caused a sensation. In a small circle of people, it certainly did; and many of these believed that its influence was much wider. But it was likely that only a few dozen copies were ever printed, most of these circulated by the author himself. Still, however small the print run, once in print the book was considered public, and thus in theory there for all the world to see. Which was precisely the problem.

For here was what they saw.

In some eighty pages, Dr. Helmont not only explained why the weapon salve was perfectly natural, but also labored to show that anyone who couldn't see it (specifically the Jesuit Roberti) was a pagan imbecile or worse. In fact from the start, the anti-

Aristotelian Dr. Helmont displayed a surprising flair for Aristotelian argument and contention that even the most dyspeptic traditional thinker would have envied.

The explanation for the weapon salve was simple, he began. *All* things, even things usually considered inanimate, contained within them some kind of living spirit endowed by God. For instance, philosophers often divided humans into internal (the soul) and external (flesh and blood) spheres—but contrary to prevailing opinion, the external sphere possessed spiritual force as well, if of a lesser sort. This was especially true of blood, which possessed a vital spirit, a "certain Ecstatical power," for which there was evidence enough in the Bible, most notably the already cited biblical story of Cain and Abel or the prohibition on eating blood. Indeed, the "soul of every living creature dwells in the blood of it," and certain "noble and vital powers," or spirits, were locked inside—powers so strong that they were capable of working over "vast distance," beyond the physical limits of the matter containing them.

Belief in the unusual qualities of blood was widespread. Even the doctor's Galenist foes considered blood to be "father" of all four bodily humors, a human being's "finest juice," employable as a household remedy or drug; their practice of bloodletting was due not to disdain of blood but to a belief that letting out impure blood purified what remained. Healers both learned and unlearned believed that a fleshy, ruddy, red-haired, blood-dominated person lived longer than people dominated by other humors. Observers of Nature told of a mysterious island animal whose blood possessed "marvelous virtue," so that mutilated bodies or severed hands dipped into it were "reconjoined." Cooks regarded blood as the "prime sauce" and most coveted stock. Some philosophers believed that the "soul is none other than the blood"—extreme for most traditionalists but accurately reflecting an assumption that there was "much conjunction between the blood and the soul." And theologians spoke of the special powers of Christ's blood, which figuratively or literally (in the form of the Eucharist) could snuff out disease. But Dr. Helmont and others with more literal views of scripture took things even further by attributing to blood a divinely endowed spiritual quality, and especially by insisting, based on still other biblical evidence, on its ability to transcend distance.

This worked as follows: The powerful, distance-conquering vital spirits within the soul and blood usually lay dormant, thanks to the spirit-numbing fall of Adam. But they were there. To unlock them they simply needed to be "roused and excited" to action. Ways to arouse the soul included prayers, vigils, fasts, and other acts of mortification that helped the Holy Spirit enter a person—this explained, for instance, the sudden desire of the Three Magi to visit the newborn Christ. Ways to arouse the vital spirit in blood included corrupting or spilling it, for this compelled the blood to seek wholeness—and where it sought wholeness was in the body from which it came, specifically in the healthy blood from which it had been separated.

The spilled blood, explained the doctor further, had a hidden or dormant friendship with the blood in the body, an "amity," a magnetic attraction, or natural sympathy—one of the dominant forces in Nature, according to Natural Philosophers. Traditional physicians too might follow principles of sympathy, in their use of such remedies as the application of the organs and parts of a dead person to the same organs and parts of someone ailing—but this always involved direct contact. Dr. Helmont's evidence that sympathy worked as well over distances, in blood or other substances, was, again, biblical, though of course veiled—namely in the texts "where the body is, there the vultures," also the friendship of David and Jonathan, described as a "binding of souls," and last "where your treasure is, there will your heart be also." The "treasure" of the spilled blood was the blood that remained in the body, especially at the wound, to which the spilled blood sent out "emanations."

Real as these emanations were, alone they were usually not enough to secure wholeness, presumably because there was too much foreign quality within the spilled blood and within the wound itself. That was where the weapon salve, or armary unguent, of Paracelsus came in. A basic formula for the unguent included moss from a human skull, mumy (a gum taken from an embalmed corpse), human fat, oil of linseed, oil of roses, and bole armeniac (purified earth with iron oxide). The weapon with the patient's blood was then dipped into the unguent, while the wound itself was bound with a clean cloth containing a bit of the patient's urine.

The role of the unguent was to enhance the naturally occurring magnetic attraction of the spilled blood to the wound from which it had exited: the emanations proceeding from the mixture of spilled blood and soothing unguent sucked out noxious tinctures from the "enraged lips" of the wound and soothed it as well. Soon the wound was delivered from misery, and far less painfully than if it were treated directly. In short, the "magnetical attraction, begun in the blood," was "perfected by the medical virtue of the unguent." The physician merely helped the corrupted, dazed blood find its target, by removing impediments to Nature, not by adding something outside Nature.

And there it was. Given the biblical evidence, given the almost painless cure, Dr. Helmont could only wonder in exasperation how the Jesuit Roberti could still call the weapon salve demonic?

That was the question to which he turned for the remainder of his tract, in even more scathing language.

First, on what was Roberti's judgment of demonic involvement based? Surely not any evidence, for he merely claimed the weapon salve was demonic because others said so. But it was "not agreeable to the custom of Naturalists to argue from bare authorities," or "to swear from the words of any man." They required instead "firm and convincible reasons." They subjected all things to the "touchstone of experiment." And they waited for the revelation of God, which came in "great quietude" and without the "din of words" that passed for learning. The Jesuit's reasoning was typical of the generally "profitless cunning" propagated by sons of darkness and so unsuitable for sons of light.

Most likely the Jesuit called the armary unguent "demonic" because he did not understand the natural principles on which it was based. But did his ignorance alone make the cure unnatural or demonic? When something transcended our "bleary-eyed reason," did this automatically make it evil? What Roberti "does not understand is not to be understood," and therefore could not be natural but must be demonic? What greater display of pride could there be than this, for the Jesuit to measure "all the immense works of God by the narrow extent of his own head"?

Here was the problem, explained Dr. Helmont: Humans tended to regard as natural only those things that made up the physical world. Spiritual forces they tended to regard as either directly demonic or divine. But many spiritual forces were part of divinely created Nature: in other words, God had endowed Nature with these forces, but they were not dependent on his direct intervention. Such forces were sometimes called "magical," in the pejorative sense of that term, but they were better called "natural magic," a term Natural Philosophers preferred, to distinguish it from "demonic magic." Indeed, if properly understood and used, there was no cause to "tremble" at the name of magic in general, or as it functioned in the weapon salve in particular. The forces involved in this cure did not depend on any special powers residing in the individual applying it—one typical component of "magic," including demonic magic—but were instead of divine origin and could be used by any knowledgeable person who bothered to find them out. There were no charms, incantations, spells, prayers, arrangements of stars, or bargains with the devil. Instead the weapon salve was simply about natural magnetism, one of the greatest spiritual forces in the universe, "vigorous and pregnant in everything" in the heavens and on earth. And though magnetism was a gift from God, "the devil loves getting credit for it, believe you me," just as the Jesuit Roberti was giving him.

How many examples in Nature did the Jesuit need of sympathetic or magnetic action at work, before he was convinced? The *lodestone*, a compass, and tides were all well-known examples of forces working over distance. How could the armary unguent stimulate attraction to a wound? The same way a lodestone attracted iron. Yet no one called this well-known attraction "demonic": it was wholly natural. It was also eminently demonstrable that the powers of the compass or lodestone were heightened when excited by other natural processes, especially rubbing or shaking, but it was not some special gift in the person doing the rubbing or shaking that excited these powers, it was the rubbing or shaking itself—thus again, it was perfectly natural.

Had Dr. Helmont stopped here with his explanation, he might have avoided at least some of the trouble that would soon befall him. But characteristically he pressed his case, and continued matter-of-factly citing still other examples of forces usually believed to be either demonic or divine but which in his view were merely hidden and natural. The problem was, these examples were far more controversial than lodestones and tides.

For instance, Dr. Helmont, like other Natural Philosophers, was not above learning Nature's secrets from folk healers or wise women, because their remedies often employed principles of natural magic, even if the healers didn't understand them as such. Hence, he casually cited in his tract one proven folk remedy after the next, which showed sympathy, or magnetism, at work.

1. Put the warm blood of a patient inside the shell and white of an egg, expose it to gentle heat, mix it with a bit of flesh, and give it to a hungry dog: experiment showed that this caused the disease to pass from the patient to the dog. Why did this work? It wasn't easy to explain, but it worked every time for everyone who tried it, based on the forces of natural sympathetic attraction.

2. To wean a child, a woman should simply "stroke some of her milk into a fire," causing her breasts to grow flaccid and the milk inside to dry up. Was this of the devil, since it worked for everyone?

3. To avenge yourself memorably on those who might excrete on the threshold of your door, place a red-hot iron on the excrement itself, and in very short order the offender would develop sores and scabs on his buttocks, for "dorsal magnetism" was driving "the acrimony of the burning into his impudent anus."

None of these depended on any supernatural gifts of the practitioner, much less the devil, but drew upon forces already existing in Nature, set in place by God—despite the opinions of traditional physicians and churchmen, who regarded them (if they failed) as useless superstitions or (if they succeeded) as the work of the devil.

Also sure to offend was the doctor's treatment of witchcraft, which to many churchmen was indisputably the work of the devil. Yet most so-called witches, explained Dr. Helmont, did not work by demonic power at all but by abusing the divinely planted vital spirit lying dormant within all humans—the same vital spirit that a good person might draw upon to attain piety and do good things. Rather than being aroused by the Holy Spirit, the vital spirit of the witch was aroused by fleshly desires, and hence put to evil uses. Evidence for this was that one could successfully imitate, based on natural properties, any number of deeds carried out by apparent witches, including their most notorious deeds performed over a distance (of which he offered several examples). Yet it was not the distance that was inherently evil—it was the use to which that power was put. True witchcraft at the behest of the devil was dependent on the pact between the devil and witch alone, but most so-called witchly deeds were based on natural powers—including action over distance.

And finally there were even natural forces at work in what many considered to be divinely appointed miracles—probably the doctor's riskiest assertion of all, putting him squarely in the same camp as such condemned Natural Philosophers as Paracelsus. Relics, he claimed, certainly began with a supernatural endowment of holiness from God, but that endowment could be exploited by any person, and even enhanced if one understood magnetism. In other words, relics too worked on its principles. Relics were not lifeless matter (as Aristotle said bones were) suddenly awakened by God to perform miracles (as theologians claimed they did): rather, they retained vital forces within them even after death, as did all humans—but the bones of saints were more pure and powerful still. Moreover, one could heighten or "excite" the strength of the powers in relics by natural, magnetic means—by rubbing them, transporting them, or even by mental exertion toward them (thus, by greater faith). That was why new, or rubbed, or newly transported relics tended to work better: the effects of friction and imagination, both perfectly natural, were greater.

Other sorts of relics besides bones worked the same. People bitten by mad dogs were often cured by burying within their foreheads a small lock of wool from the preserved stole of Saint Hubert: some would say that this effect came directly from God, and was thus a miracle, but in truth the wool contained within it some sacred yet still natural magic that worked for all. (Here was an example sure to infuriate Roberti, who had just published a lengthy book on his beloved Saint Hubert.) So with the sweat cloth of Saint Paul: this too worked similarly to the armary unguent of Paracelsus. True, the armary unguent worked by "a requisite conjunction and co-efficiency of corporal means, the blood and the unguent," while the sweat cloth worked because God called up a "fountain of oil, perpetually pouring forth streams of balsam." But both worked on the principle of magnetism and anyone could tap into them. Rather than lament this common ground between relics and the weapon cure, one should rejoice, for it assured one and all that God was not averse to magnetism per se—he even followed it in performing his "miracles." Why not in the weapon salve as well?

With these objections refuted, what possible reasons remained for the Jesuit to call the armary unguent demonic? Did he find suspicious the materials used to make the unguent? He probably did not know that physicians and apothecaries regularly used mumy, blood, fat, and moss of skulls in their remedies, and no one called them demonic.

Was the Jesuit still clinging to his old-fashioned Aristotelian notion that all things divine were above and all things corrupt were below? If so, this was wrong, for sublunary (below the moon) and superlunary (above the moon) powers went both ways, so that the divine was below here too—constantly, not only on those occasions when God intervened directly through miracles.

Was it perhaps the purpose to which the unguent was put that offended the Jesuit? Which was to heal without pain, danger, and consumption of the patient's purse? Disease was from the devil, cures were from God, concluded the doctor—either directly, through miracles, or more often indirectly, through the application of Nature's secrets by physicians who bothered to open their eyes. Besides, if the devil was behind the weapon salve, the cure would not last, for the devil was limited to working by delusion—any appearance of a cure would be just that, and temporary. Those cured by the armary unguent, on the other hand, remained whole. Moreover, the devil would hardly require the properties contained in the unguent—he would simply effect the appearance of a cure by his command. Attributing to the devil a cure that arose from natural causes endowed by God alienated the honor due to God and was even blasphemous.

In short, the Jesuit needed to study Nature harder, as physicians did. Here another biblical example was instructive: the parable of the Good Samaritan. Who passed by the wounded man? A priest and a Levite. The Good Samaritan, on the other hand, was a physician. From that time on, Nature "summoned not Divines to be the Interpreters of her nicer operations, but adopted Physicians only to be her darlings," the only "faithful interpreters of Nature's Oracles." Therefore, "Let the Divine enquire only concerning God, but the Naturalist concerning Nature."

To help tie together the many complex threads of this tract, an English translator appended a short poem summing up the whole (emphasis added):

> *I'm satisfied, that Sympathies combine*
> *At distance: that dispersed Mumies twine.*
> *That our Souls are able to command, when awake*
> *From that Enchantment, the first sin did make.*
> *And that this native Magic of the mind,*
> *Is the sole Devil and Witch if once refined*
> *By Ecstasy. That Reason's but the Brat*
> *Of Sensuality, and is lost with that.*
> *That . . . Magnetism extends its arm as far,*
> *And potent, as the most triumphant Star.*
> *That Earth hath Heaven in it. That Atoms may,*
> *At vast remove, their Virtual Forms display. . . .*
> *For these, like Angels, cure*
> *Only by the touch invisible, procure*
> Natural Miracles. *And easily in an hour,*
> *Cicatrize Wounds, that scorn Surgeons' power.*
> *That nice Divines, who scruple at this Art,*
> *Commit implicit Sacrilege, and impart*
> *God's honor unto Satan. While wise Zeal*
> *Calls it safe Natural Magic thus to heal.*

Only at the end of the book did Dr. Helmont briefly suppress his supremely confident tone, by stating that though convinced of his ideas he was certainly willing to submit them to the judgment of the Church for correction: "I am yours, and a Roman Catholic, who have cordially and firmly determined in myself to meditate or write nothing that may be contrary to the Word of God, or the fundamental Articles of the Church." He prayed God to forgive him any errors of understanding, due to his native human ignorance.

INTERROGATIONS

Though God may have been prepared to forgive the doctor his errors, plenty of others were not—beginning with a highly offended Johan Roberti, continuing with dozens of theologians and physicians around Europe, and ending with the local Church hierarchy.

One might have thought that Catholic churchmen, weary of so many false claims of miracles, would have welcomed a philosophy that attempted to clarify and even broaden understanding of Nature. After all, the Church had done this to some extent itself: recognizing that the heavens "had impressed many natural substances with marvelous" and hidden powers, it expanded the basic distinction between "natural" and "supernatural" to include Aquinas's special category of "preternatural," for events that seemed wondrous but were in truth natural. This preternatural sphere was precisely what Dr. Helmont and other Natural Philosophers sought to clarify, and even enlarge: could their ideas not help to curb superstition and false faith?

But it was one thing for the Church (or a physician) to say that many apparently miraculous cures were probably natural, and quite another for Dr. Helmont to suggest that various miracles already confirmed by the Church as divine were probably natural as well—for this helped bring miracles into doubt altogether. The Church might proclaim far fewer miracles than people were ready to believe, but it would never throw out miracles completely, or it would throw out as well much of its appeal and authority. Without the miracle of the resurrection of Jesus, Christianity could hardly exist. Without the miracles recorded in the gospels it was seriously weakened. And without the miracles of recent centuries and decades Catholicism was struck a staggering blow.

Moreover, the preternatural realm, where Natural Philosophers preferred to work and where Dr. Helmont had so painstakingly situated the weapon salve, was in the eyes of churchmen perilous indeed. Preternatural events were not always merely the result of hidden natural causes, but could involve the devil and his magic as well. Specifically, according to most theologians since Augustine, demons technically did not perform supernatural works at all, but were restricted to working their marvelous delusions by natural means—or, more precisely, preternatural means. In other words, one could never be sure whether demons or mere nature were behind even the most natural-looking marvelous events!

This was precisely why the word *magic*, however much Dr. Helmont and other Natural Philosophers tried to redeem it, continued to carry the negative connotation it had for centuries. To the doctor, magic was simply "a high knowledge of the real nature of things," most especially in the preternatural sphere; it was the secret knowledge of the wise, just as Christ revealed secrets to his disciples. But to traditionalists, magic was about dallying with the devil—whether done with the sophistication of a Dr. Helmont, or the ignorance of an Aldegonde Walre, did not matter. It hardly helped the cause of magic when such Natural Philosophers as Agrippa allowed the use of demons in one's natural magic so long as one's purpose was good. This wasn't quite witchcraft, which involved an explicit pact with the devil, but it was dangerously close. In fact, it was so close that many thought it better to avoid magic altogether, even if there were a good and "natural" sort. Martin Del Rio, Dr. Helmont's one-time teacher, admitted in theory that good natural magic might be possible, but it was like a host who set both poisonous and healthy dishes before his guests without saying which was which: the danger involved in trying to distinguish one from the other was simply too great, and it was better not to partake at all.

This was certainly the attitude taken by an offended Johan Roberti. And it was an attitude he thought many in the Church hierarchy would share, who generally wanted laypeople to "stay out of the sacristy" and especially out of matters the clergy considered to be supernatural. That was why within three days of receiving a copy of Dr. Helmont's "verbal tempest," the Jesuit was ready with his equally tempestuous response, which bore the characteristically unsubtle title, *The Magical Imposter of the Magnetic Cure of Wounds and the Armary Unguent, a Modest Response to the Pernicious Disputation of J. B. Van Helmont, of Brussels, Pyrotechnic Physician*. It was dedicated, not coincidentally, to Dr. Helmont's bishop, Jacob Boonen of Mechelen.

No sales figures survived, but because his goal was to humiliate and silence Dr. Helmont, sales were secondary to Roberti anyway: for even the most virulent and best-selling printed responses did not necessarily bring about tangible action. Lobbing insults and arguments was an old pastime among the learned and could go on forever without any concrete outcome—as Roberti and Dr. Goclenius had been proving for years. Hence, in addition to publishing his rebuttal, the Jesuit sought to subject Dr. Helmont to the discipline of the Church. He was no mere Calvinist or foreigner or unlearned superstitious buffoon—as a supposedly learned Catholic he had to be held to higher standards.

Roberti's strategy consisted of asking assorted prominent physicians and theologians publicly to condemn *The Magnetic Cure of Wounds* as heretical. This in turn would, he hoped, put pressure on the relevant ecclesiastical and civil authorities—most especially Archbishop Jacob Boonen—to take direct legal action. By 1624 the Jesuit had collected sixteen signatures from eminent men, attesting that at least twenty-four propositions in Dr. Helmont's tract, plus three propositions of Paracelsus that Helmont accepted, were heretical. This condemnation, almost certainly edited by Roberti, appeared that year in Liège under the title, *The Notorious Propositions of Joannes Baptista van Helmont, Physician and Philosopher by Fire*. A few of the signatories were not content merely with signing, but burst out that Helmont's tract was "monstrous," and that "no wise, Catholic, learned theologian or physician" would ever approve of its ideas.

As Roberti hoped, institutional response to the condemnation followed, beginning in October 1625. The first salvo came not from Archbishop Boonen, but the Spanish Inquisition: though it did not function directly in the Spanish Netherlands (and, in fact, was loathed by most civic institutions here), the Inquisition still presumed to exert moral authority in all Spanish domains, and its condemnation made clear that it expected punitive action. In February 1626 the Inquisition sent out another strong signal, ordering that the "instruction" of Dr. Helmont should now begin: surely he was a Lutheran or a Calvinist, because like them he relied, as his writings clearly indicated, more on his private spirit than the teachings of the Church.

Direct action against the doctor by Archbishop Boonen and his ecclesiastical court finally came the following year, without explanation. Was the archbishop finally bowing to the pressure of the Inquisition? Did he and his court take this long to act because they disliked the Inquisition's meddling, or because they were indifferent about the doctor? Or did they quite agree with the published condemnation of 1624 and the Inquisition's subsequent judgment, and only now found themselves able to act? Whatever the reason for its action, the court decided by the summer of 1627 to question Dr. Helmont closely about his book. He was ordered to appear on September 3.

The man directly in charge of the interrogation was not the archbishop himself but his judge, or "official," Jean Leroy. The precise relationship between archbishop and judge was poorly recorded, but it is safe to assume that their connection was strong: the archbishop appointed the judge, the judge passed judgment in the archbishop's name, and one could not appeal his decision to the archbishop (though the archbishop could, on his own, lighten the court's judgments or even grant full mercy). The judge had the right to excommunicate, pronounce the interdict, suspend priests from office, impose fines and imprisonment, even banish from the archdiocese. In other words, the judge's law was in practice the archbishop's.

Though few bits of evidence remain about this particular judge, these bits alone suggest that the archbishop had good reason to trust Jean Leroy: member of the cathedral chapter since 1622, judge of the ecclesiastical court from 1623 to 1638, ecclesiastical councilor to the Grand Council of Mechelen from 1638, dean of the cathedral chapter from 1643, ecclesiastical councilor to the governor-general's privy council in Brussels from 1653 until his death in 1656, Leroy was clearly a distinguished figure. It was therefore quite likely that he had the trust of the zealous and exacting Jacob Boonen and worked closely with him.

The judge's method was quite simple: He read aloud to Dr. Helmont the twenty-four condemnations published in 1624, and asked him to respond to each.

> To say that knowledge came in great quietude, through illumination rather than the din of dispute, injured every orthodox university professor.
>
> To say that logic and disputation were but profitless cunning, good for sons of darkness, caused one to wonder where that left such blessed Catholic thinkers as Bonaventure or Thomas Aquinas?
>
> To say that relics operated by means of natural virtues detracted from the honor owed relics, which clearly operated by divine means.
>
> To say that fresh or moved or rubbed relics were more powerful than other sorts meant that miraculous healings were no longer attributable to pious prayers or the entreaties of saints or the will of God, but to rubbing.
>
> To say that the sweat of Saint Paul was some kind of magnetic ointment, rather than a medium touched directly by God, was impious irreverence and mixed the sacred with the profane.

> To say that all things entailed the presence of the Creator or a vital spirit was to commit the pantheistic error that all things had spirits.
>
> To say that man's own vital spirit could be awakened through pious exercises, as if these exercises were some kind of natural force, slighted God and committed the Pelagian heresy (which emphasized human will and downplayed grace) that God's power was there for the taking by an act of will.
>
> To say that witches worked through natural powers endowed by God, rather than through demons, was blasphemy, and to give examples of those works in print was to teach the arts of the devil—it was as blasphemous to deny devils as it was miracles!
>
> To say that "where your treasure is" referred to magnetism was a blatant corruption of scripture, as it was to say that Abel's blood literally cried out, and as certainly it was to say that the Good Samaritan was a physician and the passersby priests (with this last point Doctor Helmont's fellow physicians, however much they despised him, might have happily agreed).
>
> To say that the friendship of David and Jonathan was produced by sympathetic magnetism ascribed the pure love of these heroes to enchantment.

And so on.

What did the doctor have to say to these charges? Since this was his first interrogation, he naively believed that the best approach was to answer the condemnations fully in an attempt to clarify things. Thus, he did not retract any of the condemned propositions as erroneous but instead tried simply to refine his original words and ideas. If the judge understood what the tract was actually saying, supposed the doctor, surely there would be no objections and the condemnations would wither away.

Hence, explained Dr. Helmont, he did not mean to denounce all human learning, but simply to emphasize the greater certitude that came with divine illumination. Or: the purity and incorruptibility of relics gave them power, but these came by virtue of the saint's holiness while alive, and were gifts from God. Just as natural magnets could be shown to work better after friction, so with supernatural magnetism, even with relics. Saint Paul's sweat cloth was simply a metaphor to explain that natural magnetism worked on the same principle as supernatural magnetism, and was thus not inherently evil. He did not mean to convey the impression that God was in all things; rather, a divine spirit planted by God was in all things. Nor did he mean to suggest that pious exercises were somehow natural means to awaken one's dormant spirit—this came by divine grace. The examples of witchcraft were meant to show that the powers placed within us were dormant and could be awakened either to evil or to good. And the assertion about the spiritual binding of David and Jonathan's spirit came from the respected Albert the Great (Albertus Magnus), teacher of Thomas Aquinas. And so on.

The doctor's responses gave rise to several new questions by the obviously suspicious judge. The most relevant of these for miracles was as follows: When saints performed miracles through their relics, did they work by virtue of this natural and awakened power within them, or by God? The doctor answered that "miracles come from God"—a vague answer, but also truthful: it did not deny miracles, or God's direct intervention, yet allowed the doctor to retain his belief that much of what passed for "miracles" were poorly understood natural processes, and that God usually worked indirectly through Nature.

Further: The judge also asked whether a man awakened in spirit could through his own will and words, like God, raise the dead and perform miracles of himself? To this the doctor answered at length (shallowly, wrote the clerk, further reflecting that all the interviewers had already adopted a negative attitude toward the accused): Man could do a number of things by his will to harness existing spiritual forces, such as washing pepper in cold water to heal an ulcer, or building a compass, or applying the armary unguent, but in all such cases he was merely using his will to manipulate forces already present, placed there by God.

By the end of the interview the doctor seemed already to have regretted his decision to answer fully, which he realized only gave his critics more to work with. He therefore took care to volunteer to the judge that he was prepared to submit the book to the judgment of the "Roman Catholic Orthodox Church" and to recant whatever precept was found to be in error, and would personally consign the book to the flames if the Church so required.

There is good reason to believe the doctor was sincere, out of genuine respect for his Church or deep anxiety about his fate. Surely examples of condemned Natural Philosophers weighed on his mind. Thomas Fienus, one of the signatories of the 1624 condemnations and the doctor's former teacher at the University of Leuven, had recently criticized Paracelsus and Pietro Pomponazzi (d. 1525) for saying that relics acted solely by virtue of the imagination and confidence of the patient, rather than at the initiative of God. Pomponazzi had been condemned in his own lifetime for denying the existence of angels and demons, and for eliminating miracles from scripture. The Italian Vanini was put to death in 1619 for his work on natural magic, which claimed among other things that holy water healed the possessed more because it was cold than because it was blessed. In 1623 the walls of Paris were covered with denunciations of the Rosicrucians, a secret society whose members could be numbered among the Natural Philosophers and to which Dr. Helmont was rumored to belong. And the following year Vitaud, De Clave, and Villon in France published fourteen theses against Aristotle, which the Sorbonne decided to ban, and which got them thrown out of Paris. Indeed a later author termed these early decades of the seventeenth century a time of "*libertinage flamboyant*," full of freethinkers whose God was Nature, rather than God himself—precisely what some local churchmen suspected of Dr. Helmont.

That Judge Leroy of the diocesan court of Mechelen was one of these churchmen was likely, if not entirely clear.

On the one hand, even before this interrogation of 1627 began there was a plan in place to arrest the doctor immediately when it was over—his answers were expected to make little difference. The plan was foiled when the doctor's servant, waiting outside, overheard bailiffs talking among themselves about the impending arrest, and ran inside to tell his master. The embarrassed judge let the doctor go free. But the doctor was truly unnerved, and immediately wrote the archbishop to inform him of certain shady dealings at his diocesan court, and to remind the noble archbishop how odious prison would be to him and his noble family—indeed the very act of a trial would be an unbearable humiliation, so that he would rather live abroad in exile than submit to such agony. He also could not bear being suspected of heresy, and explained to the archbishop that he never intended to publish *The Magnetic Cure of Wounds* and that no copies had been seen for years—truly did he regret its publication, truly was he orthodox, truly could he produce numerous witnesses who would say so, and truly was he prepared to submit to the judgment of the Church.

On the other hand, the judge decided three days after the interrogation to let the doctor be, to delay any decision, and to seek other opinions. He sent the doctor's book, along with the doctor's responses during the interrogation of 1627, to Leuven in order to be examined by theologians and physicians from the university. Was this the judge's way of avoiding punitive actions, stalling for time, or even hoping that the case would simply fade away through inattention? Possibly, but since these same men of Leuven had already signed their names to the condemnation of Dr. Helmont's propositions, there was little chance that the matter would be forgotten, and little doubt what their conclusions would be. The judge's action can therefore hardly be interpreted as sympathetic.

And so though it took three years for the opinions to come back from Leuven, it was almost certain that they would come back, and that they would be steadfastly against the doctor. Moreover, whatever the judge's precise intent or disposition may have been in seeking those opinions, once they arrived he took action again. In accordance with them, the judge had a bailiff deliver a summons to Dr. Helmont on October 17, 1630, ordering him to appear one week later at the diocesan court for further questioning about *The Magnetic Cure of Wounds*, a work "abounding" with assertions perhaps not quite heretical but clearly superstitious, and which the theologians of Leuven called "pernicious to the greatest degree," making it impossible to distinguish among the workings of Nature, the devil, or God.

This time around, the experienced and disillusioned doctor took an entirely different approach to the interrogation: namely, that of the penitent. He defended himself only on certain claims of how the book came to be published, but regarding its substance he threw himself prostrate at the feet of the Church. Hence, he still insisted that the book was no longer available, that he had given away no copies beyond the original twenty-three sent to him (ten of which he gave to churchmen), that he was not preparing a second edition, and that he never intended the book for public consumption. But as to whether his book was teeming with heresy and opened the door to diabolical magic, he simply said that the theologians of Leuven had thus judged and thus he would accept. And so forth: On illumination, on the value of disputation, on the qualities of relics, on rubbing relics, on Saint Paul's sweat, on man's will, on witches, on blood, on healing at a distance, on every point he submitted to the judgment of the Church, and "now believed the way the Church believed." God performed miracles through ways known only to Him rather than through natural properties, rubbing relics was useless, and the Good Samaritan may indeed have been a priest rather than a physician, agreed the doctor.

Still, these answers were not good enough for the judge, nor for the dean of Brussels, Henri Calenus, the same man who would be involved in the battle for the Jesus Oak some years later, and who participated in this interrogation of 1630 as well. Both men suspected that the doctor hadn't really changed his beliefs but merely his answers—that was the way of heretics, warned theologians. And so the questioners asked him frequently, when he expressed his submission to the teachings of the Church, what it was precisely "that the Church believes and teaches" on this point or that? Only to have the doctor respond that he was prepared to think whatever his superiors required him to think and he was willing to be instructed on whatever the Church mandated, for he was an obedient son.

After much of this, all the judge could do was declare at last that such a book as *The Magnetic Cure of Wounds* should not be tolerated in a Christian state, that the doctor should make a formal declaration of his faith, admit his error, make reparation, and promise to abstain from all such works in the future. In the meantime, the court would await still further judgment, from the theologians at Leuven, of the doctor's latest answers. Dr. Helmont of course concurred: he was prepared to do all these things. And would the judge please remember, reminded the doctor once more, that no copies of the book had been seen in years? It truly was suppressed, and he truly had renounced it.

To be sure that everyone knew of his penance, Dr. Helmont wrote to the archbishop's vicariate to submit himself, and to the archbishop as well, whom he asked to treat him "as a father might, or a shepherd, who seeks not to scatter his sheep or household. From your reverence's sheep-stall, one of your humble, submissive sheep, Jan Baptista van Helmont."

ARREST

Given his submission and what he thought was his absolute renunciation of *The Magnetic Cure of Wounds*, and given the several years in between interrogations, which led him to believe that prosecution might cease after all, no wonder Dr. Helmont was surprised when Judge Leroy arrested him on the street in Brussels in March 1634, and seized so many books and manuscripts from his home.

It did not help the doctor that he apparently never made a formal recantation of his work—as he said he was willing to make and as the more famous Galileo had made the year before. One recantation was prepared for Dr. Helmont after the interrogation of 1630, by the theologian Schinkelius from Leuven, as follows: "The theologians of Leuven have concluded that my tract is not so much magnetic as diabolical, and that the guidance of the universe is taken away from God and granted partly to the devil under the name of the spirit of the world, and partly to Nature under the name of magical power . . . and I now agree with them." But this statement was never signed, and perhaps never presented to the doctor. Though the diocesan court wanted a recantation, perhaps it wished to prepare its own version rather than be seen as merely doing the bidding of theologians from Leuven. The doctor provided the court in 1630 with testimonies of orthodoxy from his pastors, and expressed willingness to recant, but these were not enough for anyone.

It also did not help the doctor's cause that men such as Schinkelius held the common attitude that "atheists and magicians" (including natural magicians) had no conscience but only pretended to have one, hence their penance was never sincere. Or, in public they cursed the devil but in private honored him. Obviously the doctor's brain had been "possessed and penetrated deeply and widely by the darkness of diabolical mania against God." If the doctor got away now, he would only be more careful in the future of how he said things but no less convinced of his dangerous ideas, and thus he would spread his infection subtly but still surely.

None of these, however, were the reasons stated by Judge Leroy for arresting the doctor in 1634. The only explanation given, after so many years of apparent peace, was this: By now there were so many people condemning *The Magnetic Cure of Wounds* that he and the archbishop had little choice but to take action against it again, this time conclusively.

Specifically, since 1630 Johan Roberti had been busy gathering more signatures to add to the original condemnation of 1624. Although logistical problems dragged the process out, getting signatures was not hard in the current climate: Galileo was condemned in 1633, if for very different substantive reasons from Dr. Helmont, but in large part for likewise presuming to interpret the Bible in private, untraditional ways. Hence, in 1634 a new condemnation of *The Magnetic Cure of Wounds* appeared, this time boasting the signatures of forty-nine theologians, thirty physicians, and four philosophers from all around Catholic Europe, making it a truly international scandal, and once again putting pressure on the local diocesan court to do something meaningful.

Still, it wasn't merely the new signatures that made Leroy act, he explained further. Rather, it was that the new published condemnation necessarily repeated the doctor's dangerous ideas in order to denounce them, and might prove tempting for the simple. In other words, the ecclesiastical court moved against Dr. Helmont in 1634 because of the irony that this latest condemnation had made his ideas more public than ever before! The doctor's lawyer complained that his client could not be rearrested simply because his enemies had multiplied; what mattered were his ideas, and he had already explained and renounced those in 1627 and 1630. But this did not deter the judge—especially not when new rumors surfaced that the doctor's book remained in print: the theologian Schinkelius of Leuven, for instance, was certain that *The Magnetic Cure of Wounds* was being worn out with use in the households of France and the Spanish Netherlands.

In any event, concluded the judge, the only way to determine with certainty the doctor's current sentiments or the rumors about extant copies of the book was to search the doctor's home and arrest him. And so it was done.

After a long night in the archbishop's tower, the doctor wrote his host to plead his case, on March 5, 1634. He had always conducted himself as an honest Catholic, always appeared in court when summoned, acknowledged his errors, and stood prepared to revoke the entire book—which, he reminded the archbishop once again, had been published thirteen years ago without his knowledge, as a disputation rather than an assertion of truth, and for which he had been apologizing for the last four years. Would the archbishop not release him on the usual condition that he would appear again when called? For this business of imprisonment was too much humiliation for himself, his wife, and children.

The archbishop and judge approved the doctor's request to be moved—but not immediately to his home. On March 6, after two nights in the tower, the doctor was released to a room among the local Franciscans, on an enormous bond of six thousand florins (paid by his wife's brother), and on his noble word that he would not go out nor receive any visitors besides his family. In return for this relaxation, the doctor made a formal profession of faith, and promised to renounce all objectionable ideas not only in *The Mag-*

netic Cure of Wounds but in whatever might be found among his recently seized papers and books: here at last was a signed recantation. So good was his behavior among the Franciscans, and so influential the voices of those who intervened on behalf of his family, that on March 18, 1634, he was granted the even lighter condition of house arrest, agreeing again neither to go out nor to receive guests.

Still, house arrest was arrest, and it was compounded by yet another round of interrogation by Judge Jean Leroy, this one even more severe than the last. It occurred over at least three different days—March 17, 21, and 27 of 1634—and this time the focus was not the old news of *The Magnetic Cure of Wounds* but instead the new items seized from his home.

The first day was devoted to a fairly simple summation by the judge of Dr. Helmont's copy of Goclenius's old tract on magnetic healing, as if to suggest that by still possessing it Dr. Helmont remained a devotee of the subject. The other two days, however, involved far more aggressive questioning over just how sincerely the doctor had renounced his dubious ideas.

The questioning focused especially on the contents of eleven books and manuscripts found in the doctor's home, all of which touched on magnetism or magic. These did not include the doctor's two commentaries on Hippocrates, or a unique, 176-page manuscript summing up his medical knowledge, or his "Collectanea" of notes on various works, and many other items seized, in which investigators found nothing objectionable. Instead the court was interested most in these eleven, beginning with a manuscript in the doctor's hand, entitled the "Philadelphus," which supported the magnetic cure of wounds.

This manuscript was, argued the court, written after 1621—or the year *The Magnetic Cure of Wounds* was published, proving that the doctor had not quit his dangerous ideas. But Dr. Helmont explained that he began the "Philadelphus" in 1618, against another work on magnetism by Roberti. The judge: Then how could the "Philadelphus" cite *The Magnetic Cure of Wounds*, which was published only in 1621? Because the latter, said the doctor, was actually completed in manuscript by 1617, and thus available to him when working on the "Philadelphus." Then how did the doctor explain the notation at the top, in his own hand, that Roberti had "exposed me to all the bishops," when such exposure didn't occur until at the earliest 1624? Because he made the notation on a later occasion when he was rereading the tract. Why didn't he throw the "Philadelphus" away after *The Magnetic Cure of Wounds* was condemned? Because he supposed he was allowed to keep his private writings.

Why did he call it "Philadelphus," implying a secret brotherhood? Because he was simply defending the brotherhood of chemists from the slanders of Johan Roberti, who called them "fumivendulous," or smoky, trifling men, good for nothing. By brotherhood, did he mean the secret brotherhood of Rosicrucians? No, he was unaware of such a group and believed it was pure fancy. Suspicion about the doctor's involvement in this group was not unfounded. He practiced, after all, one of their chief tenets, which was to serve the sick for free. Moreover, the society was notorious for its secretiveness—would the doctor have admitted association even if it were true?

Then came various substantive questions about the "Philadelphus," especially regarding magnetism and blood, and the revelations that would come by way of the archangel Raphael. All of these Dr. Helmont explained that he "used to believe" but no longer did; further, when formulating those ideas, he supposed as a believing Catholic that it was acceptable to try them out without necessarily asserting them as truth.

Also curious to the court were propositions 51 to 67 of the "Philadelphus," which explained that the mysteries of "our orthodox faith" contained within them the secrets of chemistry, or, as outsiders knew it, alchemy. For instance, chemists believed that "Christ the Lord" was the mercury of the philosopher: just as Christ was "not able to sin neither to be sick," so was mercury able to remain free from contamination. "Original sin" gave a clue to the "sordidness" of the first earthly matter. "Regeneration of the total man" signified the possibility of the perfection of metals. That "Christ was born of a virgin who was liable to neither pollution nor sin" was another clue to the purity of mercury and the matter whence it was extracted. "Purgatory" was a concept of faith vital to the process of purifying metal. And so forth. All these mysteries were true in and of themselves but also were metaphors for chemists, and provided the keys to their chemical knowledge, explained the doctor.

But wasn't it blasphemous to apply these mysteries of the faith to chemical matters? No, because all chemists used them—and chemists who were pagans or heretics thereby indirectly learned the mysteries of the true faith in addition to chemistry, and hence were better off for it. In fact, he was sure that plenty of heretical (Protestant) chemists actually believed Catholic mysteries, even if they denied them in public, because they relied upon them in their chemical work. Nevertheless, he wished not to assert anything contrary to the Church and thus yielded to its censure on these points. When warned to give more complete satisfaction to questions about heresy and blasphemy, the doctor insisted he had answered already as best he could.

Did he stand by his praise of Paracelsus, which appeared at the end of the tract? No longer, since much of Paracelsus truly deserved censure. Most important, when asked once again and at last whether he affirmed that magnetic healing was a natural process, he likewise said that he once believed it in good faith, but now did not.

Then it was on to other papers and books. Why was he interested in an English tract called the "Asterburden," which discussed healing people by means of sheets of paper containing special markings? He wasn't that interested; in fact, he had hardly read it because it was of little importance. How could he make that judgment without having read it, or how did he then explain all the marginal notations? He wasn't sure.

What about this horoscope of Cardinal Richelieu, in the doctor's own hand? He had copied it from a nobleman who served Marie de Medici, queen of France. And this horoscope of Clementine van Helmont, his sister? Trifles, explained the doctor: he found astrology but a big spiderweb, and misleading, for Clementine was told she would live until seventy and she died at forty.

Did he not write the manuscript entitled "God, Father of the Fecundity of the Sexes?" No, he had copied it at age eighteen from a work by Agrippa on males, females, and creation, but he hadn't looked at it in years. The judge read various heretical propositions from that work, and Helmont responded that they were of little account. But then the judge got to his real point: He insisted that Helmont himself had written the work, for it was all in his hand and it had too many changes and deletions to be someone else's.

The doctor responded that he probably wrote it out while someone dictated to him, then afterward redid various passages. Yet, said the judge, Archbishop Boonen had read all of Agrippa, and when these passages were shown to him in recent days he recognized none of them. Again the doctor insisted he got the manuscript from someone else, one Peter Papius, a law student at Leuven fourteen years ago, but now dead. Papius was also the source for another manuscript in the doctor's hand, also from Agrippa, called "Concerning Original Sin." He couldn't remember what the tract contained, but the Judge reminded him of one note: "Original sin was in our opinion the carnal copulation of Adam and Eve."

Why did he own Alchindus's "Concerning the Influences of the Lower World"? This was not his own, but loaned to him by a Canon Steensel of St. Goedele's, who tutored a young girl and found in her deceased grandfather's rooms a copy of this tract, then asked Dr. Helmont's opinion of it.

What of "External Man," also in his own hand? This was but a copy of a work sent by Marin Mersenne, the well-known Minim from Paris, who would later be a proponent of the mechanical philosophy that so condemned Natural Philosophy, but who was friendly with Dr. Helmont and wanted his judgment.

Did he know that his copy of "Understanding German Theology" was a condemned work? He did not, for he had heard many Capuchins praise it.

What about "Mercury Triumphant"? This he had read: it concerned the making of gold, and he ignored the heretical passages and strictly concerned himself with the passages on the physical process.

Then, after a few final questions on astrology, including

"French Works on Critical Days and Horoscopes," which the doctor explained was a gift from a French friend, the interview ended.

As a final act, one of the prosecutors added to the nineteen folios of interview summary a three-page list of "theological errors" found in these writings, which could be summed up in three points: Dr. Helmont repeatedly committed the anthropomorphic sin of making God into man and vice versa; he committed the error of the Manichees in claiming that all things were alive; and he interpreted scripture against the unanimous sentiment of the Church Fathers. Not to mention other "absurd falsities" as well.

The message was clear: The Church and not Dr. Helmont would determine what was magical, what miraculous, what demonic, and what natural.

THE BITTER END

For a week, then two weeks, then four, the doctor and his family awaited the judge's decision. Would it all proceed to a formal trial and sentence? But nothing happened. Then the doctor's mother-in-law, Isabella van Halmale, decided to take matters into her hands.

It was thanks to her previous interventions with the archbishop, and her persuasion of various friends to do the same, that Dr. Helmont had been released to house arrest back on March 18, 1634. But here, in early May, she went even further and tried to end this embarrassing matter altogether. Specifically, from this point until October she appealed to the Council of Brabant, the highest secular court in the duchy, for protection from the diocesan court: The latter court had acted improperly, she alleged, and thus forfeited jurisdiction—if indeed it ever held jurisdiction at all.

Hence, Madam Halmale pointed out that her son-in-law wrote his tract under explicit submission to the Church, that it was printed without his knowledge, that his enemies had used it unfairly and interpreted it against "the sense of the words," that he had renounced it anyway, that no copies of it remained, that he had been dragged before the Church's court more than once (and on occasion without counsel or adequate time to prepare), that he had always appeared willingly when summoned, that he was currently not even allowed to leave his home for Easter services (to the great chagrin of his family), and that he had been detained without trial or judgment longer than the three days allowed in this duchy of Brabant. These were all reason enough to remove him from the hands of the diocesan court.

Just as in the case of the Jesus Oak, the Council of Brabant proceeded carefully in this tussle over jurisdiction. Rather than moving immediately to take over the case, it asked the diocesan court to respond to the claims of Madam Halmale. Not surprisingly, this court's view was much different: Archbishop Boonen had decided to let the doctor be in 1630, in the hope that the book had disappeared, but the new condemnation of 1634 and all the clamoring of respectable people for judgment made inaction impossible, explained the judge. Moreover, the doctor's true demeanor could not be determined from his interviews alone, necessitating a search, and as feared this had uncovered plenty of heresy. Finally, the legal privileges of Brabant hardly prohibited action against heretics, and the doctor's claim of submission to the Church were the first words out of any heretic's mouth, starting with Martin Luther.

And so the exchanges continued for several months, with the Council of Brabant acting as mediator between the doctor and diocesan court, and with new and longer variations on the basic themes and increasingly torturous legalese over jurisdiction and privileges and precedent—none of it doing much to promote goodwill between the parties. Madam Halmale asked the Council of Brabant to compel the diocesan court to live up to its oath to administer true justice, "without mental reservations." The court responded that it was ready to do just that if the doctor's family would stop these delaying tactics: everyone knew that he should stand trial now, and that he was stalling only because he had a guilty conscience. How, by the way, did the family suppose the doctor would have fared in Spain, where anyone even suspected of heresy was held for long in prison? And the court would be obliged if Mother Halmale would cease implying that somehow all clergymen took oaths only with mental reservations.

If the doctor had truly felt guilty, countered Mother Halmale, he could have fled long ago, for he had no guards. Moreover, genuine heretics kept defending their mistakes, while Dr. Helmont had admitted his. As for mental reservations among the clergy, Mother Halmale referred the council to the writings of Leonard Lessius, the famous and recently deceased local Jesuit, who suggested that just such a thing was at times perfectly acceptable.

The doctor's guilt would gnaw at him soon enough, responded the diocesan court, and he would try to escape; what besides guilt would have caused Mother Halmale to state in her last brief that the doctor feared imprisonment each time he was summoned to testify? And what besides guilt motivated him to hide his new writing, the "Philadelphus," in his wife's linen cupboard? And might the court add that it was terribly presumptuous of Isabella Halmale to assume that she could say whatever she pleased against her ecclesiastical superiors?

The doctor was not a heretic, repeated Mother Halmale. He was a good child of the holy Church, as good as the "most principal" bishop of the land. He had even reconverted two heretics to the true religion; he never swore or wished anyone harm (not even during these miserable years); he often treated the poor for free; and he was never insolent during his interrogations by the judge. As for his "Philadelphus," she repeated that he wrote this years ago and that it was not hidden at all but was deemed so inconsequential that it was kept among the pattern scraps used by his wife for sewing.

Finally the court used its last and longest brief (135 pages) to dispute Madam Halmale's claim that her son-in-law was not a heretic. However much he tried to cover his evil intentions with legal niceties, every barrel's aroma eventually gave away what was inside. Or, another metaphor would do: The devil might disguise himself, but one of his claws always stuck out. In this case, the claw was obvious: Those who misused scripture against common understanding were clearly heretics, and *The Magnetic Cure of Wounds* and other books and manuscripts found in the doctor's home were rampant with such misuse, as witnessed by his ideas on relics and miracles—as if they were from rubbing rather than from God! Or by his suggestion that the mysteries of the faith may be demonstrated by fire and chemistry! Just because he said he was Catholic did not make him so. The theology faculty of Leuven considered him a devil, he interpreted scripture privately, and he consistently refused to recant when given the chance. As for converting others, the court wouldn't be surprised if he hadn't done that just for appearances during his current troubles. He still deserved strict incarceration, and public punishment. Look at Germany, the Netherlands, France, and Switzerland, where heretics had been allowed to run free, and the chaos there; then look at orthodox Spain, where the Inquisition reigned. It was obvious which was better. He was merely trying to escape the court's judgment and to wound its jurisdiction. And by the way, how could he have cited passages from *The Magnetic Cure of Wounds* in his last brief, if he didn't still have a copy in his possession?

Madam Halmale, or the Council of Brabant for her, decided not to respond further, so that the exchanges ended there. The council made its decision slowly, but finally in March 1636 concluded that jurisdiction did indeed reside with the diocesan court and that the case could proceed. At the same time, however, the council ordered that until a formal trial was again under way, or a judgment rendered, the doctor was at last to be released from house arrest; the previous bond of six thousand florins would still apply. But with jurisdiction now settled, it looked as if things would once again get moving and that a decision would be reached.

To the doctor's frustration, this statement of 1636 was the last official action taken in the case, until his death on December 30, 1644. There came from the diocesan court during his remaining years neither a formal sentence nor exoneration. To the end he was left in limbo.

Given the court's many efforts over the years, how is this lack of finality to be explained? Some later concluded from the lack of a sentence, from the long years between interrogations, from the three years it took for the diocesan court to swing into action after the initial public condemnation of 1624, and even from the absence of the sorts of severe penalties that befell other Natural

Philosophers in Europe around the same time, that perhaps the court really wasn't as offended by the doctor as it seemed—and was in a way protecting him from worse. The true movers behind the prosecutions were instead his rival physicians, and had the Church's court surrendered jurisdiction to some other entity, those physicians would have used that entity to tear him apart.

Such a scenario was possible: after all, Dr. Helmont had been offending rival physicians for decades, with, for example, a treatise published in 1624 on the waters of Spa—not a terribly controversial subject at first glance, yet his tract condemned more than one established physician, including a certain Henri de Heer, who had worked with the waters for some twenty-five years! Not surprisingly, de Heer added his name in 1624 to the list of signatories condeming *The Magnetic Cure of Wounds*. He also took to calling Dr. Helmont "Hell-mouth," a play on the Dutch approximation of his name, "Helle-mond." And Dr. Helmont's former professors at Leuven, Fienus and Villers, could have been no more pleased with their onetime student's recent condemnation of their tracts—they too signed the condemnation of *The Magnetic Cure of Wounds*.

It was also true that Dr. Helmont was punished less strictly than his contemporary, Galileo: the latter was confined to house arrest for the rest of his life, while Dr. Helmont for only two or three years. Moreover, Galileo suffered a conclusive and heartbreaking judgment of "vehement suspicion of heresy," while Dr. Helmont was never formally condemned.

But both the very act and the tone of the appeals made by Isabella van Halmale to the Council of Brabant in 1634 belie the notion that the doctor's chief foes were physicians and that the Church mainly sought to protect him. So did the diocesan court's responses to those appeals, and the judge's sharpness during the three interrogations. So did the fact that many more theologians than physicians signed the condemnations of 1624 and 1634.

This did not mean that one could speak as if Church leaders acted unitedly against Dr. Helmont, just as one could not speak of them acting unitedly against Galileo: three of the ten cardinals who tried Galileo refused to sign the condemnation, and one invited Galileo to his house as a long-term guest. And just as clergymen were interested in Galileo's work, so were they in Helmont's: Remember that he sent ten precious author's copies—nearly half the total—of *The Magnetic Cure of Wounds* to clergymen, who presumably were not known enemies. Moreover, several pastors testified to his orthodoxy. Indeed it wasn't that "the Church" usually condemned someone unanimously, but that certain elements within the Church won or lost a particular internal battle.

Accordingly, some have wondered whether Archbishop Boonen was not the crucial protector of Dr. Helmont—and not only from physicians but from theologians. In fact, Judge Leroy stated in justifying his actions that had the doctor been subject to the formal judgment of theologians alone, he would have suffered even greater censure. Perhaps this knowledge explained the lack of a final condemnation by the diocesan court. And perhaps the archbishop, despite his necessarily close relationship with the judge, was even more sympathetic to the doctor than was his own court. After all, Leroy left this office around 1638—just about the time when aggressive action against the doctor ceased.

In fact the archbishop was a worldly wise and learned man, in demand for various diplomatic delegations, and interested enough in Natural Philosophy (or appalled) that he bothered to read Agrippa; was he among those churchmen who did not find natural magic wholly objectionable? Moreover, based on Judge Leroy's explanation for the doctor's arrest in 1634, it was apparently the archbishop who ordered prosecution to cease in 1630, in the hope that the affair would die out. It was also the archbishop who released the doctor to milder house arrest in March 1634, who allowed Dr. Helmont to make several medical visits during his house arrest (to the great displeasure of the archbishop's friend, Dean Henri Calenus of Brussels, who thought it terribly dangerous to let the doctor out in public), and who would eventually exonerate the doctor from all suspicion of heresy (though posthumously).

These certainly are clues that the archbishop bore some sympathy for Dr. Helmont, and in relative terms perhaps they were a form of protection—all the archbishop might have been able to offer in the climate of the time. Yet from the perspective of Dr. Helmont, such treatment was hardly "protection" at all. This was evident in a 1638 letter to Archbishop Boonen, in which the doctor complained bitterly. For besides asking for the return of numerous valuable books confiscated at his arrest in 1634, and reiterating for the tenth time that there were no more copies of *The Magnetic Cure* to be found, he also made sure the archbishop knew the sorrows and grave inconveniences that the interrogations and arrests had caused him.

Most onerous were the deaths of two of his children while he was under house arrest. They were quarantined in the care of some nuns who applied treatments much different from his own, and therefore died needlessly. That broke his heart, and he would regret it his entire life. This was not to mention his loss of reputation and income, his legal expenses, the tedium of imprisonment, the wasting of his best years. Yet "these disadvantages, which in this life you'll never be able to repay, I have borne willingly."

Moreover, if his books were so hideous, why hadn't the Council of Brabant acted against him as well, as they usually did in cases of grave heresy and banned books? It seemed to the doctor that the ecclesiastical judge, unable to find a copy of *The Magnetic Cure*, was determined to find something in his home and thus invent a transgression, so that he might offer the doctor to the theologians, and especially to the Jesuits, as a sacrificial lamb. Thanks to the judge, concluded the doctor, "the Jesuits got their way": namely, the doctor's humiliation and silencing. Though it was true that no sentence had been passed against him, for which he was grateful, he reminded the archbishop that it had cost him more than a third of his possessions to win his freedom. Moreover, he bluntly told the archbishop that he thought it the latter's task to deal with him more as a shepherd than as a murderer. "My enemies will rejoice that they've taken a leg from me, as they had hoped. But I will rejoice in this: comfort in the Almighty which I knew in my difficult time." Clearly the doctor felt no debt of gratitude to Archbishop Boonen for his "light" punishment. Twenty years of arbitrary interrogations, public arrests, embarrassing imprisonment, and nagging uncertainty must have seemed to him strange and heartless ways to show concern or protection, even in the current atmosphere.

Nevertheless, all these were not quite formal punishment, and despite the doctor's resentment it is worth pondering how he at least escaped that. Perhaps the best explanation was offered by one of his enemies, the Parisian physician Guy Patin: He claimed that Marie de Medici, queen of France, had benefited from the advice of Natural Philosophers generally and Dr. Helmont in particular, and thus intervened with Archbishop Boonen to save him from prison or worse. Dr. Helmont once alluded himself to an indirect connection to the queen, but there is no other evidence to support this claim. Still, it is perhaps the most convincing explanation of why he was spared the greater humiliation of a formal trial and condemnation for heresy.

The doctor's last years were filled not only with uncertainty but more study and writing—more than ever before. He avoided the specific subject of the weapon salve, but continued to write about sympathetic attraction generally as if it were a basic truth—suggesting that his questioners were right to suspect he still held to his beliefs. He wrote even more on safer subjects such as fever and digestion. Then, just before dying of pleurisy, in December 1644, he told his aptly named son, Franciscus Mercurius, that he had pondered destroying his mushrooming writings, but in a dream he was instructed to have his son publish them. The obedient son did so. Thus the doctor began his career with a dream and ended it with a dream as well. And thus the universe was filled with far more writings by Jan Baptista van Helmont in death than in life.

His last years were also filled with more criticisms from his enemies, including the physician Plempius, the leading light of the Leuven medical faculty, who criticized not only Helmont but also the latest supporters of magnetism, such as Erycius Mohy, insisting that "the devil himself with his own hand effects the secret processes" which Mohy called "natural." They could not be natural, insisted the dean, because Catholic academics had for long said so. It was an old argument by now and it wasn't finished yet: the debate over magnetism and the weapon salve raged perhaps most furiously in England after the 1630s, thanks in no small way to the controversy around Dr. Helmont.

And finally the last years were filled with still more attempts to clear his name. Even while lying in bed from the illness that would kill him, Dr. Helmont sent his son to Archbishop Boonen to ask once again for purgation. But it was not until after the doctor's death, when it was safer, that the archbishop finally granted the wish. On October 23, 1646, sixteen years to the day after the doctor's second unpleasant interrogation, Archbishop Boonen proclaimed that, yes, Dr. Helmont had written *The Magnetic Cure of Wounds*, and other manuscripts seized in his home, and was briefly imprisoned, but he nevertheless recanted and repudiated the contents of the book and all other writings that offended the Holy Roman Church, even if he never did this in formal legal terms. Because he understood that the doctor died piously and Catholicly, fortified by the sacraments of the Church, and that many learned men still thought well of this man's life, he was found by the archbishop to be undeserving of censure. Instead, he was now to be regarded as a man who stood firm in the faith. "We therefore declare that he should not be considered a heretic, but that it ought to be thought he lived piously and died a Catholic, even an obedient son of the Holy Roman Church."

Did this comfort the doctor's wife, Margaret van Ranst, who died herself on December 31, 1654, ten years after the demise of her husband? For it was little, and it was late, and it would hardly be surprising if she received the news with some bitterness. Certainly the letter of purgation did little to mollify the doctor's foes, such as Guy Patin, who judged the doctor a "wicked rogue Fleming" who did nothing valuable for medicine. (Patin, incidentally, was hardly a fan of the saints, or miracles, and concluded that most were counterfeit, or natural.)

Yet there were others who continued to be inspired by the doctor and his kind. Into the eighteenth century plenty of thinkers still believed that the universe "bonded magnetically and that the tides could be explained by the magnetic attraction between the earth and the moon," and that "magnetic forces stretched mysteriously through space," even beyond iron and lodestone, as in the simultaneous maturation of wine and the harvesting of grapes. Plenty still were investigating the effects of "twisting, filing, hitting, heating, and rubbing iron bars and wires," like Dr. Helmont rubbing his relics and lodestones. Thomas Sprat was still arguing in 1667 that "God seldom or never chooses to perform miracles in times when natural knowledge prevails, but only in dark and ignorant ages: for the experimental philosopher is clearly in no need of miracles since he cannot fail to see the impressions of God's footsteps in His creatures." And Isaac Newton was likely influenced by the idea of sympathetic magnetism as he developed his theory of gravity, and spoke of "the most subtle spirit which pervades and lies hid in all gross bodies"—precisely the sort of thinking that caused some to condemn gravity as an "occult" force. Then there were mesmerism and magnetism in the eighteenth and nineteenth centuries, not to mention the unsophisticated practices of more ordinary believers that depended, if they did not know it, on what used to be called Natural Philosophy.

Even the mechanical philosophers, prophets of modern science, learned from the precepts of Dr. Helmont and other Natural Philosophers, especially in regard to gas, personal observation, and the use of fire—though they condemned or ignored his larger system. In fact, the rival system of mechanical philosophy would triumph among most thinkers, if not most churchmen, by 1700. This was in part for social reasons: there were too many undesirable social elements among Natural Philosophers, too close an association with the hocus pocus, vulgar beliefs, and superstitions of ordinary people, too much chance that public order would succumb to "an innumerable company of croaking Enthusiasts," too close a resemblance between Jan Baptista van Helmont and the village wise woman. But it was also for intellectual and religious reasons that the mechanical philosophy prevailed: it was convincing and even comforting for many to reestablish the clear line between God and Nature that had been blurred by the Natural Philosophers. In fact, despite its eventual troubles with the Church, in its first incarnation the mechanical philosophy was meant to reverence God, to rescue Him from the messiness and indignity of the Natural Philosophers' magical universe, and was promoted by such churchmen as the monk Mersenne or the priest Gassendi, and the arguably devout Descartes.

Hence, it was hardly surprising that even if the early mechanical philosophers and later secular scientists praised Dr. Helmont for certain details, they were forever stupefied by his "extreme naivete," dismissive of his larger system, and most especially embarrassed by *The Magnetic Cure of Wounds*. Why would he promote such ideas, they asked incredulously, or write such a thing?

Because he knew a different world, alive with God.

EPILOGUE

Leuven, Belgium, Another Summer. After spending so much time in the archives and merely imagining places and characters, I want to see what is left of them. I start, like millions before me, with the most famous choice, the Sharp Hill, still thriving today.

Though I've visited the shrine before, my Belgian friend Jan, a fellow historian, has insisted I go there on foot, "the way pilgrims experienced it." Hence on a lovely Sunday morning made for pilgrims, five of us set out on the seventeen-mile walk from Leuven. Jan wears his usual suit and dress shoes, though he has forgone this once a tie. The other three are in such various stages of health and age that upon seeing them and Jan's shoes I doubt that anyone will arrive at our destination except me.

The walking is pleasant and the scenery charming, even though there is no longer any organized footpath to the Hill. Through sunlit, peaceful villages and (thanks to Jan's army ordnance map) various glimmering, picturesque fields, we make good, direct progress, at least until we come to a field not found on the map. Puzzled, we finally learn that Jan's map was printed in 1954: as a big-picture sort of historian, it was a detail he hadn't considered important. We take a few detours, and add a couple of miles to our journey, but he assures us that this will only reinforce the discipline required of pilgrimage.

Jan also allows us one stop, at a café in a rural castle. It worries me that I seem to need the rest more than anyone. In fact, around mile thirteen while everyone else is as fresh as the cut hay we often pass, my right foot has begun to ache so painfully that after another mile I can put no weight on it at all and am forced to sit down on the side of a country road. Without the slightest hint of weariness, my companions all have a look at me. Calmly, they suggest a walking stick. Privately, I wish they would call me a cab, but I am too embarrassed to say so. Hence I hop along a bit until finding a suitable stick, and continue on, straining with every step.

After another mile or so I find a rhythm, but the last three miles are exhausting. Around each bend I keep hoping that the domed basilica of the Sharp Hill, with its waving flags, will come into view. At last it does, and we arrive at the main street, quite a sight—a group of pilgrims straight out of Chaucer, and at least one of them seriously in need of a cure. I want to sit down immediately at one of the many crowded restaurants surrounding the church, but Jan insists that we go a few hundred yards farther, "just briefly" inside the shrine first, according to pilgrim protocol. I struggle on, long enough to see a silent multitude of faces staring intently at the image of the virgin above the altar; it's a moving scene, but I feel too much pain to pray or linger.

My companions seem completely fresh—no blisters from hard shoes, no discomfort from suits, no aching backs or legs from age or infirmity. They eat calmly and are unfazed when we discover halfway through the meal that there is no bus service from the Sharp Hill on Sundays: we'll simply walk another three miles to the nearest train station, they declare. But I am completely fazed, and announce that I'll have to take a taxi. One of them replies, with a smile: "You've actually had a reverse miracle. You started whole and ended lame." The next day a doctor declares that my foot is not broken, but I must stay off it for a while. Obviously the Sharp Hill, for all its magnificence, is not the shrine for me.

Like Maria Caroens I keep looking. A more suitable place turns out to be, fittingly, the humble Jesus Oak, where I should have gone in the first place.

I don't walk from Leuven this time, given my foot, but I do want to walk at least the mile or two through the woods from the middle of Tervuren, the way by which Dimpna Gillis and thousands of others passed. The Soniën Woods, still owned by the royal family, look just as deep and dark as they must have centuries before. I park my car nearby and begin walking.

Here, in the vast stillness of the woods, I sense, much as I do in the abbey of Park, that connection to the otherworldly past. I feel the equal parts of calm and foreboding experienced by Peter van Kerckhoven and other travelers in these woods. Harsh light and distant noises are blocked so that objects appear sharper and nearby sounds louder. This quiet and the unusual lighting make it easier to envision the mothers and fathers who desperately carried their children in search of cures. By the time I reach the church of the Jesus Oak, only a couple of miles away, I feel as if I've come through another world. And is it just my imagination that my foot feels so much better?

The spell is broken by the fact that the modern village of the Jesus Oak is not so otherworldly at all. A street of Tervuren runs right up to the church now, lined on one side with woods certainly, but houses full of diplomats and the wealthy on the other. A busy freeway is not far away, and the road to Overijse is hardly rural at all anymore, but full of stores. The spire of the church rises modestly above the "skyline" of the tiny town, where the main activity revolves not around the church but the popular cluster of restaurants facing it, heirs of the original and long-forbidden vendors. Still, the church is charming, and several restaurants offer a fine view of its well-restored Baroque facade. The interior is equally charming—more than twenty eighteenth-century portraits-of-thanks still hang on the walls, and the sacred, rather dark, heavily clothed image of the Virgin holding the child Jesus is still visible above the altar. The tiled floor is the same one installed in 1672. The stained glass windows recall the founding of the shrine, including the raising of the image by Philip van Kerckhoven.

But all the ex-votos, the waxen arms and legs and feet and breasts and hands, the silver tongues, the trusses and crutches, the medallions, have been taken away, as has every sign of the Oak itself. Until several years ago there was displayed a reduced, sprawling facsimile of the old tree, to recall the forestly origins of the place, yet even this is gone, probably considered tacky or not religious enough. There are three masses each weekend, with decent attendance, and the parish organizes short walks from the woods to the church, but otherwise the church is rarely busy and contains no pilgrims besides me. Most striking of all is the irony that in the efficiency-driven fusion of Belgian communities in the 1970s, when smaller villages were merged with larger, the Jesus Oak was annexed to Overijse, not Tervuren, with very little fuss.

I then set out to see Gent, where the Jesuit church in which Maria Caroens overflowed with milk was ruined during the French Revolution and all the statues and paintings destroyed or scattered—save the Rubens altarpiece, now displayed elsewhere. In place of the church now stands the main hall of the University of Gent. The Savaan street, where Maria and her family had their home, waffle shop, and pilgrimage business, still runs near the same foul-smelling canal, but the old houses are gone. The Bagatten street around the corner, where Maria's friend Margaret Doosens once lived, and various other streets in the neighborhood where Maria once walked, bear the same names today, if very different buildings.

The chapel of the tailors and its houses for the poor are nowhere to be seen, replaced by a single large building in a state of modern crumble. The place where the convent of Groenebriel once stood has mutated into a large mental hospital, with only traces of the original buildings still present, while the surrounding neighborhood is dominated by high-rise, low-aesthetic apartments. The Augustinian convent, famous for its library, still stands.

The prison chapel in Brussels where Aldegonde Walre could not swallow the host is, like most of the other sites, gone, while the Jesuit church in Mechelen where she tried once more was replaced by a new model in 1660, whose walls are adorned with an impressive unbroken line of wooden confessionals, which would have made her uneasy. Her home, her barracks, her places of work, more poorly built than the home of Maria Caroens, have all surely vanished in Mechelen, or Antwerp, or wherever else she may have been—or claimed she had been.

The monuments to Jan Baptista van Helmont are more numerous and lasting. In Vilvoorde a house blackened by pollution boasts a plaque near its front door stating that the good doctor once lived there. In Brussels a statue of the doctor stands rather inconspicuously on the new Grain Market, overshadowed by an asphalt basketball court, and a hospital bears his name. His writings, far more numerous than those left by the rectors of the Jesus Oak or Maria Caroens or the nuns of Groenebriel or Aldegonde Walre, began receiving great attention in the nineteenth century, from historians of science, and are undergoing a new revival, so that his name will be even greater.

But aside from the volumes left by the prolific doctor, the concrete landmarks of my stories still feel scattered and overwhelmingly vanished.

Or are they? For during my searches, and especially when I have completed them, I am more aware than ever of events in my own world that I had hardly noticed before but now seem very familiar. These go beyond our age's quasi-miracles, such as "miracles of science"—a phrase that may suggest merely a different understanding of miracles, but that may also imply a harsh judgment on past miracles—to include those of an old-fashioned sort.

There are still over six thousand Catholic shrines in Western Europe, visited by sixty to seventy million people a year, and many more elsewhere in the world.

There are still events whose only explanation seems otherworldly. Nuns of a convent in New Mexico report the building of a miraculous unsupported staircase in their convent by someone they believe was Saint Joseph himself, and modern engineers struggle to explain what holds it up. Books and dramas called *Miraculous World*, *It's a Miracle*, and *Expect Miracles* document thousands of rationally unexplainable incidents. A Pennsylvania girl diagnosed with incurable deafness begins to hear after praying for intercession from Katharine Drexel, who soon afterward is officially declared a saint of the Catholic Church. A newborn boy in Michigan, presumed dead, comes to life after his parents hold him close for three hours, and no one can explain why. The reliquary holding the shroud of Turin is trapped in a fire in the church of Turin, Italy (under four layers of bulletproof glass), but the linen itself remains intact: "It's a miracle" says the archbishop.

There are still, despite all the ecumenical efforts of our day and renewed interest among many Protestants in faith healing or speaking in tongues, strong differences in belief about miracles between Christians, including a Protestant preacher in Brazil who publicly shatters a Catholic holy image, to denounce it as superstition.

There are still events that some call otherworldly and others coincidence, such as a beguine (a quasi-religious woman) in Belgium who in the 1930s lost a favorite needle while sewing in the thick grass of the garden, prayed nine days to Saint Anthony but could not find it, angrily threw her image of Anthony out the bedroom window into the garden, felt guilty about her action and thus went to retrieve the image—and found the needle lying right next to it, to her delight and renewed faith.

There are still struggles within Catholicism over control of the holy. Nuns in Massachusetts shut down a holy site because it is overwhelmed by pilgrims and the nuns wish to discourage it. Some priests refer to miracles and shrines as "monks' work." The Church stifles the cult of Yvonne-Aimée de Malestroit (1902–1952), mother superior of a French convent decorated by General de Gaulle for heroic resistance, because the reports of miracles and visions associated with her sound suspicious to Church officials. Similarly, the Church discourages promoting what in official circles were the dubiously miraculous deeds of a Brazilian priest named

Cicero Batista (1884–1934), while Brazilian politicians eager to gain popular support encourage circulation of the tales. Perhaps the most visited Catholic shrine today, Medjugorje, has still not been recognized by the official Church. And though two and a half million sick people have visited Lourdes, and doctors have declared at least thirty-five hundred cures there to be supernatural, the Church has confirmed only sixty-five as miraculous—enough to admit the existence of miracles, enough to keep large streams of the hopeful coming, but far fewer than people are ready to believe.

There are still those in the West who promote supernatural systems meant especially to rival Christianity, or which are reactions to it, as in the many unchurched and anti-church alternatives today.

There are still scientists who deal with mysterious forces. Some posit the existence of a "dark energy" that pervades empty space and though difficult to measure may "dominate the universe." A Belgian physician, who works fittingly at the Helmont hospital in Brussels, describes a special process at his in-vitro fertilization center that features rubbing a glass rod over the surface of a frozen embryo—somehow, but for reasons not entirely clear, the rubbing "increases the likelihood that a fertilized egg will attach itself to a woman's womb."

These occurrences are not from some past "age of faith" but from now, and they cause me to reflect that there is a stronger connection to that older world of miracles, and even Nature, than I once supposed or recognized. The contexts and specific forms and debates of that other world are indeed modified today, but these recent examples help me to feel even more confident that we may enter that world, however briefly and partially, with more sympathy than I had imagined.

I feel the sense of that world most especially as I rise to leave the archive of the abbey of Park, perhaps forever, because it is rumored that after 850 years it will soon become a cultural center and its few monks allowed to die out. Looking out over the lakes, then walking on mended foot through echoing halls to the main entry, past the portrait of Abbot Jan Masius with the small chapel of the Jesus Oak in the background, I imagine myself for a last time in the world of Anna Eregiers and Maria Caroens and the others, until the smiling porter nods good-bye and closes the door behind me.

SOURCES

Abbreviations:

AAP	Archive of the Abbey of Park, Belgium
AAM	Archive of the Archdiocese of Mechelen-Brussels, Belgium
BAG	Archive of the Diocese of Gent, Belgium
BIHBR	*Bulletin de l'Institut historique belge de Rome*
BN	*Biographie Nationale*
KB	Royal Library Albert I, Brussels
ARA	National Archives of Belgium, Brussels
NBW	*Nationaal Biografisch Woordenboek*
RAG	Provincial Archive of Gent, Belgium

Sources are cited in full the first time they are mentioned in a chapter note: thereafter they are cited within the same note in abbreviated form.

PROLOGUE

Park is still an abbey, but its current superior is called prior (usually second-in-command) rather than abbot, as numbers dwindle. At the time of this writing, about eight members still live there. Signs of new life have emerged—a new lay archivist, student boarders, a center for religious studies, renovations of the garden and possibly the buildings—but not from within the religious community itself.

The manuscript that inspired my curiosity in miracles lies in the Provincial Archive of Kortrijk, OSAK, Enkwest 858. This was also the basis for a licentiate thesis by C. Bruneel, "Een onderzoek naar de mirakelen van Onze-Lieve-Vrouw van Groeninge te Kortrijk (1634–1660)" (Leuven, 1987). Another excellent miracle register, dating from the fifteenth century, is in the Parish Archive of Lier, 126/13, which includes a section for the seventeenth century.

MODELS: Apologetic works became especially popular after the Reformation; numerous titles of this sort are cited below, especially in Chapters 1 and 2, but an example is F. Costerus, *Waerachtige historien, stichtighe exempelen ende sekere miraculen in verscheyden landen ende tijden geschiedt van de H. Moeder Godts Maria* (Antwerp, 1615). Any number of bookstores today features title after title of inspirational miracles, with little discussion beyond the story itself.

Naturalistic and theological explanations are equally old and common, beginning with Protestant ridicule of Catholic miracles, such as the *Heylige Maghet van Halle. . . . tot bespottinghe der pauselicke Roomsche afgoderije* (Delft, 1605), which ridicules Catholics for believing in spurious events and implies that even if the events happened there were surely other causes behind them; these continue with seventeenth- and eighteenth-century philosophers and scientists, discussed by H. C. Kee, *Miracle in the Early Christian World: A Study in Sociohistorical Method* (New Haven, 1983), and ending with such recent examples as "The Religious Context of Crisis Resolution in the Votive Painting of Catholic Europe," *Journal of Social History* 23/4 (Summer 1990): 755, which reviews research on the link between the brain and the immune system, or E. Fales, "The Case of St. Teresa: Scientific Explanations of Mystical Experiences, Part One," *Religious Studies* 32/2 (June 1996): 143. R. van Dam, *Saints and Their Miracles in Late Antique Gaul* (Princeton, 1993), 84, also discusses such approaches.

Trying to define miracles began especially with Augustine, was continued in such famous works as Aquinas's *Summa Theologica*, questions 43, 104, 105, 110, 114, 117, and 178, Montaigne, *The Essays* (London, 1991), especially "On the Lame," 351–68, M. Cline Horowitz, "Montaigne's Doubts on the Miraculous and the Demonic in Cases of His Own Day," in R. Schnucker, ed., *Regnum, Religio et Ratio: Essays Presented to Robert M. Kingdon* (Kirksville, MO, 1987), 81–91, and continues today in E. Dhanis, "Que'est-ce qu'un miracle?" *Gregorianum* 40/2 (1959): 201–41, and R. M. Grant, *Miracle and Natural Law* (Amsterdam, 1952).

The model of the lab coat is from a review of one of my earlier books, which in pointing out (quite rightly) my overdone statistical analysis of the genre of pamphlets, repeated Richard Cobb's quip that soon dreary historians in white coats will solemnly declare that bread shortages cause riots; see *Renaissance Quarterly* 62/1 (Spring 1989): 105–07.

An interesting example of using miracle accounts to focus primarily on something else is M. Goodich, *Violence and Miracle in the Fourteenth Century: Private Grief and Public Salvation* (Chicago, 1995).

Some of the most useful models for approaching past religious worlds generally I found to be, by precept or example, B. Gregory, *Salvation at Stake: Christian Martyrdom in Early Modern Europe* (Cambridge, MA, 1999), especially Chapter 1; N. Davis, "Some Tasks and Themes in the Study of Popular Religion," in *The Pursuit of Holiness in Late Medieval and Renaissance Religion* (Leiden, 1974): 307–36; N. Davis, "From 'Popular Religion' to Religious Cultures," in *Reformation Europe: A Guide to Research* (St. Louis, 1982): 321–41; E. Duffy, *The Stripping of the Altars* (New Haven, 1992); and especially J. H. Van den Berg, *Metabletica, of leer der veranderingen: beginselen van een historische psychologie*, 17th edition (Nijkerk, 1956), translated into English as *The Changing Nature of Man: Introduction to Historical*

Psychology, Metabletica (New York, 1961). This work studies not the history of psychology but the history of human psychology itself, including a brilliant chapter on miracles. Unlike those who have controlled official definitions of miracles and who insist on the scientific approach to testing them (thus that to be genuine miracles must be observable to all and measured by some kind of objective criteria), Van den Berg, a Catholic psychologist, argues instead that miracles could be both subjective and real at the same time—the major role played by one's perspective did nothing to detract from the reality of the miracle. To make this concrete, he cites the example from André Gide, who as a boy saw a girl in a meadow and suddenly the meadow was alive and full of light and wonder for the boy, while someone else passing at the same time might have seen the meadow as merely a geological cleft in a geographical landscape. Also compelling is Van den Berg's discussion of the biblical text that Jesus himself *could not* perform any miracles when people did not believe; it wasn't that he would not perform miracles, nor that people could not see them, but that he literally could not perform them. The reality of a miracle began therefore in people's hearts and minds, not in external events, just as by viewing a valley as a geological phenomenon one misses the presence of wonder. A similar pattern is true in other phenomena: H. C. E. Midelfort, in *A History of Madness in Sixteenth-Century Germany* (Stanford, 1999), 14, concludes that ". . . however socially or culturally 'constructed' a mental disorder might be, the condition is nonetheless 'real.' Patients are not necessarily 'faking it' when they 'remember' things that never happened: the suffering is often all too real."

Other helpful models for approaching and thinking about miracles were B. Cousin, "Deux cents miracles en Provence sous Louis XIV," *Revue d'histoire de la spiritualité* 52 (1976): 225–44, and *Le miracle et le quotidien: les ex-voto provençaux, images d'une société* (Aix, 1983); H. Platelle, *Les Chrétiens face au miracle, Lille au XVIIe siècle* (Paris, 1968); R. B. Mullin, *Miracles and the Modern Religious Imagination* (New Haven, 1996); A. Dierkens, ed., *Apparitions et Miracles* (Brussels, 1991); V. Flint, *The Rise of Magic in Early Medieval Europe* (Princeton, 1994); W. Giraldo, *Duizend Jaar Mirakels in Vlaanderen* (Brussels, 1995); T. Kselman, *Belief in History* (Notre Dame, 1991); L. C. B. M. van Liebergen, G. Rooijakkers, *Volksdevotie. Beelden van religieuze volkscultuur in Noord-Brabant* (Uden 1990); J. Massant, ed., *Les Signes de Dieu aux XVIe et XVIIe siècles* (1993); H. Barbin, J. P. Duteil, "Miracle et Pèlerinage au XVIIe siècle," *Revue d'Histoire de l'Eglise en France* 61 (1975): 246–56; G. Rooijakkers, M. Monteiro, J. Rosendaal, eds., *De dynamiek van religie en cultuur. Geschiedenis van het Nederlands katholicisme* (Kampen 1993); Van Dam, *Saints and Their Miracles*; B. Ward, *Miracles and the Medieval Mind: Theory, Record and Event, 1100–1215* (Philadelphia, 1982), plus numerous works cited in the chapters below.

GOLDEN AGES OF MIRACLES: P. Soergel, *Wondrous in His Saints* (Berkeley, 1993), 103, notes that in the two-hundred-year period after 1575 there were

12,000 miracles at one shrine in Bavaria and 16,500 at another. Also J. Delumeau, *Rassurer et protéger: Le sentiment de sécurité dans l'Occident d'autrefois* (Paris, 1989), 202, 207, pinpoints in France the years 1620–70 as critical; and H. Platelle, "Mirakels in de Zuidelijke Nederlanden," *Spieghel Historiael* (1973): 175–77, on the resurgence of interest after 1600 in the Low Countries, but also noting the importance of the period 1400–1500; M. Therry, *De religieuze beleving bij de leken in het 17de-eeuwse bisdom Brugge* (1609–1706) (Brussels, 1988), especially Part III; M. Nolan and S. Nolan, *Christian Pilgrimage in Modern Western Europe* (Chapel Hill, 1989), 85, shows the seventeenth as the biggest shrine-establishing century ever; P. Geary, *Furta Sacra: Thefts of Relics in the Central Middle Ages* (Princeton, 1990), 18–19, points to the eighth and ninth centuries as a dynamic time as well. Midelfort, *A History of Madness*, 291, notes that in the bishopric of Passau 53 shrines were founded before the Reformation, and 127 after; he also notes the numerous miracles before the Reformation, including five thousand or more from 1444 to 1518 at St. Rasso's in Grafrath, 1,748 at St. Leonard's in Inchenhofen from 1506 to 1512, and 2,109 at St. Richildis' in Hohenwart from 1486 to 1520.

DISAGREEMENT AMONG CATHOLICS: One example is I. Backus, *Le miracle de Laon* (Paris, 1994), which examines four elites disagreeing among themselves on the meaning of a single miracle. That Protestants had miracles of their own, if usually more subtly, in R. Scribner, "Incombustible Luther," in his *Popular Culture and Popular Movements in Reformation Germany* (London, 1987), or Gregory, *Salvation at Stake*, which suggests miracle-type occurrences among Protestant or Anabaptist martyrs.

All of the stories in this book were generated by legal proceedings; on the value and limits of using criminal records or trials for cultural and social history, see E. Muir and G. Ruggiero, eds., *History from Crime* (Baltimore and London, 1994).

CHAPTER ONE

A Holy Place

PETER VAN KERCKHOVEN AND THE ORIGINS OF THE JESUS OAK: My narrative account is built from a variety of sources, including numerous briefs and letters from the lawsuit over the Jesus Oak, in AAP, Losse Stukken, Corpus VII, Kastje XXIX, lias 3, Jezus Eik; AAP, Kastje XLIII, lias 1, Tervuren; AAP, Registers, VII, 45 and 50; AAP, Registers, X, 153; AAM, Parochialia, Jezus Eik. Also the first chronicle of the Jesus Oak, Bartholomeus Segers, *Den Pelgrim van Sonien-Bosche naere O.L. Vrauw van Iesukens-eyck* (Brussels, 1661), and the main secondary sources, L. Hoefnagels, *Notre-Dame-au-Bois: essai historique* (Brussels, 1924), F. Maes, "De bouw van de kapel van Onze-Lieve-Vrouw van Jezus-Eik," *Eigen Schoon en de Brabander* (1971): 218–36, G. Vande Putte, "Jezus Eik ou Notre-

Dame-au-Bois?" *Le Folklore Brabançon* 200 (1973): 391–404, M. Loones, "De beginjaren van het Mariaoord," *Zonien* 20/3 (1996): 119–64, and R. Denayer, "Nieuwe gegevens over het prille begin van de devotie," *Zonien* 20/3 (1996): 185–216. The last article is important because it offers details from primary sources of Overijse's contentions about the Oak (including evidence that Anna Eregiers' claims upon the Jesus Oak began even before 1642), while most of the sources listed above in the abbey of Park reflect Tervuren's point of view only; some of Overijse's sources are in AAM, Parochialia, Jezus Eik. See also AAM, Dekenale Visitatieverslagen, Brussel, 5, for the dean's reports on the two parishes and their pastors during the 1630s and 1640s. For shrines that began similarly, thanks to merchants who traveled often through nearby woods, see M. Wingens, *Over de grens: de bedevaart van katholieke Nederlanders in de zeventiende en achttiende eeuw* (Nijmegen, 1994), 71.

TRADITIONS OF SHRINES, RELICS, PILGRIMAGE, VOWS, AND MIRACLES: I have relied especially on P. Brown, *The Cult of the Saints* (Chicago, 1981); S. MacCormack, "The Organization of Sacred Topography," in R. Ousterhout, ed., *The Blessings of Pilgrimage* (Urbana, 1990), 20–27; J. Wilkinson, "Jewish Holy Places," 52, in the same volume; C. Hahn, "Loca Sancta Souvenirs," 86–87, the same volume; P. Geary, *Furta Sacra: Thefts of Relics in the Central Middle Ages* (Princeton, 1990); A. Vauchez, *Sainthood in the Later Middle Ages* (Cambridge, 1997); P. Soergel, *Wondrous in His Saints* (Berkeley, 1993); J. M. Sallmann, *Naples et ses saints (XVI–XVIII siècles)* (Paris, 1994); W. Christian, *Local Religion in Sixteenth-Century Spain* (Princeton, 1981); J. Sumption, *Pilgrimage* (London, 1975); J. Delumeau, *Rassurer et protéger: Le sentiment de sécurité dans l'Occident d'autrefois* (Paris, 1989), especially chapters 5–7; E. Muir, "The Virgin on the Street Corner: The Place of the Sacred in Italian Cities," in S. Ozment, ed., *Religion and Culture in the Renaissance and Reformation* (Kirskville, 1989): 25–40; J. Sanders, "De heilige eik tussen Den Dungen en Schijnel: van kerstening tot reformatie," *Tijdschrift van de Heemkundevereniging Den Dungen* 4 (1979): 2–10; B. Cousin, *Le miracle et le quotidien* (Aix, 1983); A. Thijs, "Over Bedevaarten in Vlaanderen: van Stichtelijke Propaganda naar Wetenschappelijke Interesse," *Volkskunde* 97/3 (1996): 272–349. For a long review of literature from the fifteenth century to the present, H. Platelle, *Les Chrétiens face au miracle. Lille au XVIIe siècle* (Paris, 1968), and R. Finucane, *Miracles and Pilgrims: Popular Beliefs in Medieval England* (London, 1977). M. Carroll, *Madonnas That Maim: Popular Catholicism in Italy Since the Fifteenth Century* (Baltimore, 1992), 37, stresses the importance of protection from danger, while B. Ward, *Miracles and the Medieval Mind* (Philadelphia, 1982), 117, the importance of prayer, penance, absolution, and protection. Especially good on the instrumental quality of shrines is Wingens, *Over de grens*. On unfulfilled vows, L. Smoller, "Miracle, Memory and Meaning in the Canonization of Vincent Ferrer 1453–1454," *Speculum* 73/2 (April 1993): 430, and "Defining the Boundaries of the Natural in Fifteenth-Century Brittany: the Inquest into the Miracles of Saint Vincent Ferrer (d. 1419)," *Viator* 28 (1997): 357, plus R. Finucane, *The Rescue of the Innocents: Endangered Children in Medieval Miracles* (New York, 2000), 33.

IMAGES: The respective importance of images and relics changed over time, especially in periods when relics were rare. Geary, *Furta Sacra*, 37, notes that one ninth-century author argued relics deserved greater veneration than images, which could serve only a didactic function. But such a view began changing a few centuries later, and by the early modern period images might be regarded as just as powerful as any relics.

CHRONICLES OF SHRINES: Besides the work by Segers on the Jesus Oak, also J. Bueckelius, *Historien ende mirakelen gheschiet tot Aerlen by Helmont door het aanroepen van Ons L. Vrou . . .* (Den Bosch, 1614); F. Costerus, *Waerachtige historien, stichtighe exempelen ende sekere miraculen in verscheyden landen ende tijden geschiedt van de H. Moeder Godts Maria* (Antwerp, 1615); *De historie van de H. Keerse van de H. Moeder Godts, miraculeuselyck ghebrocht ende bewaert in de stede van Atrecht sedert het jaar 1105* (Kortrijk, 1636); plus the titles listed for the Sharp Hill, or Scherpenheuvel, below. An example of a manuscript chronicle, kept only at the shrine itself, may be found in the Parish Archive of Lier, 126/13, treating miracles from 1475–1499, which is continued for the seventeenth century in 126/22.

THE SHRINE AT LORETO: Among others, see B. Hamilton, "The Ottomans, the Humanists, and the Holy House of Loreto," *Renaissance and Modern Studies* 31 (1987): 1–19.

WORLDLY INFLUENCES: the politics of declaring miracles is explored more in the next chapter, but I mention here two recent studies, G. T. Ahlgren, *Teresa of Avila and the Politics of Sanctity* (Ithaca, 1996), or B. R. Kreiser, *Miracles, Convulsions, and Ecclesiastical Politics in Early Eighteenth-Century Paris* (Princeton, 1978). M. Nolan and S. Nolan, *Christian Pilgrimage in Modern Western Europe* (Chapel Hill, 1989), 337, note that shrines and miracles depend on a combination of "political, economic, and social-psychological" factors; in this study I have naturally been influenced by such approaches to ask this-worldly questions, but I try to see them as much as possible through contemporary eyes. Nolan and Nolan, 306, successfully sum up the thinking of believers then and now with the statement that "wondrous events have their own logic."

The Battle for the Holy

INTERACTION OF CLERGY AND LAITY ON MATTERS SUPERNATURAL: P. Hoffmann, *Church and Community in the Diocese of Lyon* (New Haven, 1984), chapters 2–3; S. Nalle, *God in La Mancha* (Baltimore, 1992); Christian, *Local Re-*

ligion, and Sumption, *Pilgrimage*, 53, for examples of lay initiative around the holy. L. Rothkrug, "Popular Religion and Holy Shrines," in J. Obelkevich, ed., *Religion and the People, 800–1700* (Chapel Hill, 1979), 21, stresses that the history of shrines reveals much about the beliefs of all social groups, reflecting that they had plenty in common. Vauchez, *Sainthood*, 99, 100, 245, notes that both clergy and laity thought it their right to pronounce upon holiness.

TERVUREN'S MOTIVES: AAM, Parochialia, Jezus Eik, letter from Abbot Masius of Park to Jacob Boonen, undated, but during the hearings before the commission, which began in 1642; in this the abbot notes how little income the pastor of Tervuren had, or for that matter parishioners, especially after the massive fire and invasion of 1635. For more on Tervuren itself, J. E. Davidts, *Geschiedenis van de Parochie Tervuren en de Sint-Janskerken* (n.p., 1965).

PILGRIMAGE AND PROCESSIONS: Sumption, *Pilgrimage;* Christian, *Local Religion;* D. Gentilcore, *From Bishop to Witch* (Manchester, 1992), 116. On clashes of neighboring parishes at bordering shrines, K. Luria, *Territories of Grace: Cultural Change in the Seventeenth-Century Diocese of Grenoble* (Berkeley, 1991), 93–94.

JACOB BOONEN AND THE DEAN OF BRUSSELS, HENRI CALENUS: These two friends, and later Jansenist allies, play major roles as well in Chapter 5. For more on them see M. Lemmens, "Hendrik Calenus, 1583–1653: Contrareformist en Jansenist," *Ascania* 23 (1985): 31–84, and P. Claessens, "Jacques Boonen," in *Histoire des archevêques de Malines*, vol. 1 (Leuven, 1881); J. Lefèvre, "La Nomination des Archevêques de Malines sous l'Ancien Régime," *Handelingen en Mededelingen van de Koninklijke Kring van Mechelen* 63 (1959): 75–92; L. Ceyssens, "Jacobus Boonen," in *NBW*, vol. 2 (Brussels, 1966), columns 74–89; L. Jadin, "Procès d'information pour la nomination des évêques et abbés des Pays-Bas, de Liège et de Franche-Comté d'après les Archives de la Congrégation Consistoriale (1637–1709)," *BIHBR* (1929): 133–38, 148–55.

The Blind See

DIMPNA GILLIS: Segers, *Den Pelgrim*, 38–41, AAP; Registers VII, 50, f. 103; and original testimonies from witnesses to her miracle in AAM, Parochialia, Jezus Eik.

A Gaggle of Lawyers

CHURCH-STATE RELATIONS IN THE COURTS: Especially H. J. Elias, *Kerk en Staat in de Zuidelijke Nederlanden onder Albertus en Isabella* (Leuven, 1931). The expectation of fairness, despite personal connections, is inferred from numerous sources, including C. Harline and E. Put, *A Bishop's Tale* (New Haven, 2000), 128, 272–73, in which measures are taken to ensure that Archbishop Mathias Hovius would act from integrity, not passion, against a man who had publicly offended the archbishop, plus a second case in which the archbishop's good friend Jacob Janssonius does not fear to disagree with him, even sharply, despite their close relationship.

Staking Claims

BUILDING THE SHRINE: Financial records that reveal the rector's purchases and activities in AAP, Registers, VII, 45; the accounts from various years are summarized on f. 229. Folios 204 and 229 make clear that Piccaert was working for the Jesus Oak by July 18, 1642; also Registers, VII, 50, f. 100, October 12, 1642.

INVESTIGATIONS INTO THE MIRACLES: AAM, Parochialia, Jezus Eik, beginning September 4, 1642. More on the definition and criteria of miracles in the next chapter.

REQUESTS FOR A LARGER CHAPEL: AAP, Registers, VII, 50, fols. 87, 89, 93, contain several appeals from Tervuren to the central government in Brussels.

THE VALUE OF PHYSICAL PRESENCE: In September 1642 various persons from Overijse also tried to assert a presence by seeking to build some permanent benches around the chapel, and some tents from which they wished to sell food and drink to pilgrims. Tervuren argued to the governor-general that this would turn the holy place into a circus, with beer, violins, drums, and other instruments which "awaken a drunken man to do evil." The governor-general accepted Tervuren's argument, and ended Overijse's plan but this would come back to haunt Tervuren when it later insisted that vendors were badly needed to sustain the shrine; AAP, Registers VII, 50, f. 97, the pastor and mayor of Tervuren to chancellor of Brabant; response on September 5, 1642.

OAKS, IMAGES, AND SHRINES: The problems of stripping the bark and worries about pagan beliefs appear repeatedly at shrines featuring trees, especially oaks, as for example in A. Boni, *Scherpenheuvel. Basiliek en gemeente in het kader van de vaderlandse geschiedenis* (Antwerp 1953), and T. Morren, "Bastion op de 'scherpenheuvel,' " in A. F. Manning and M. de Vroede, eds., *Spectrum Atlas van Historische Plaatsen in de Lage Landen* (Utrecht and Antwerp, 1981). W. Christian, *Apparitions in Late Medieval and Renaissance Spain* (Princeton, 1981), 20, believes that the numerous rural oak stories of the seventeenth century reflect a "paganization of Christianity," that in order to "deal with nature they must go to it." Also Wingens, *Over de grens*, 67–68, 101, Soergel, *Wondrous in His Saints*, 224, Nolan and Nolan, *Christian Pilgrimage*, 328–29, and J. Sanders, "De heilige eik tussen Den Dungen en Schijnel: van kerstening tot reformatie," *Tijdschrift van de Heemkundevereniging Den Dungen* 4 (1979): 2, 6–10.

COST AND TERMINATION OF THE LAWSUIT: AAP, Registers, X, 153, f. 185 (not all folios are in order) details the expenses, including 124 separate payments for various things. The specific date of the suit's conclusion is not mentioned, but all evidence points to 1647, when the new chapel was begun.

THE ABBOTS OF PARK: Among others, see *Monasticon Belge*, Tome IV, vol. 3 (Liège, 1969), 773–821; E. H. J. Reusens, "Jean Maes (Masius)," in *BN*, v. 13 (Brussels, 1894–95), cols. 136–38; N. J. Weyns, "Joannes Masius (Maes)," in *NBW*, v. 3 (Brussels, 1968), cols. 552–56; Ed. van Even, "Libert de Pape," *BN*, v. 5 (Brussels, 1876), cols. 615–18; "Libert de Pape," *NBW*, v. 4 (Brussels, 1970), cols. 641–52.

A Modest Shrine

COMPARISON TO OTHER SHRINES: Shrines came and went, so that it is difficult to say exactly how many disappeared. On the Sharp Hill, see Boni and Morren, above, plus materials in AAM, Parochialia, Scherpenheuvel, 8, including the first accounting January 9, 1604, and the inventory of jewelry, December 22, 1603. Printed chronicles of the Sharp Hill include P. Numan, *Historie vande Miraculen die onlancx In grooten getale ghebeurt zyn, door die intercessie ende voorbidden van die Heylighe Maget* (Leuven, 1604), J. David, *Beweeringhe van de eere ende mirakelen der hoogh-verheven Moeder Godts Maria, tot Scherpenheuvel* (Antwerp, 1607), and J. Lipsius, *Diva Sichemiensis sive aspricollis nova eius beneficia et admiranda* (Antwerp, 1605)—plus a handwritten account by the shrine's first promoter, G. Tienwinkel, KB, Handschriftenkabinet, 3549, "Het belt met een cort verhael van onze Lieven Vrouwe ten Scherpenheuvel." On the shrines of Rome, Sumption, *Pilgrimage*, 162–66, including his conclusion that what shrine keepers wanted most was prestige. For a later period, the nineteenth century, D. Blackbourn, *Marpingen* (New York, 1994), 367, notes that villagers who provided food and lodging probably profited most, but this does not mean they were cynical about the miracles; even those who doubted might still take pride in their village's fame.

ON "LOCAL" AND "REGIONAL" SHRINES: Wingens, *Over de grens*, 111, and others point out that as time went by very few people healed at shrines came from the host town, but neither did they come from far away. Hence, "local" meant less the immediate town and more concentric circles of surrounding villages—presumably far enough away to make the shrine attractive as a special destination. Wingens distinguishes among local, regional, and supra-regional shrines, 149. Numerous sources discuss the rapid growth, big hopes, and early decline of many shrines, including Finucane, *Miracles and Pilgrims*, 181–84, who notes that the cult for Saint Cantilupe declined precisely when papal commissioners at last met to discuss that saint's case. Also Christian, *Local Religion*, 112–13 concludes that most shrines probably made enough from alms to maintain themselves, if that, though the few larger ones may have done better; more systematic study of the financial side of shrines would be useful. He also notes, 121, that only one in forty shrines in Spain was visited by more than the surrounding communities; Finucane, *Mira-*

cles and Pilgrims, 169, found a similar pattern in England. Kreiser, *Miracles*, 165, notes however that communities certainly believed there were monetary benefits to be had from hosting shrines; again this is a subject that needs to be studied more carefully.

THE ABBOTS OF PARK TRYING TO COMPLETE THE CHURCH: Abbot of Park to the Chamber of Finance, February 10, 1665, AAP, Losse Stukken, Corpus VII, Kastje XXIX, lias 3, no. 26.

SUPERIORITY OF MIRACLES AND EXPLANATIONS OF STATURE: Sumption, *Pilgrimage*, 150, on the view that old shrines gracefully made way for new; also Ward, *Miracles*, 127. Christian, *Local Religion*, 247, for the explanation of greed, quoting a source from 1622. On God's will explaining the site of a shrine, see A. de Soto, *Twee T'samensprekingen, Behandelende de leeringe ende materie vande mirakelen* . . . (Brussels, 1614), dialogue two, also confirming the idea that God elevates a lesser saint to help a new one get attention. The historian Segers's views on the quality of his shrine's miracles in *Den Pelgrim*, 28. He includes over thirty-two miracles, but adds that many more have occurred and people were simply too modest to report them. Lipsius in "Heilige Maagd van Leuven," Leiden University Library, Ms. Lips. 12, in preparation for publication by Jeanine Delandtsheer; he is also responsible for "the lord scatters them and divides them" phrase. For impressive miracles at other shrines, see the chronicles noted above, plus E. V. Dom, *De Geschiedenis van O. L. Vrouw van Goeden Wil te Duffel* (Tongerloo, 1936), C. Bruneel, "Een Onderzoek naar de mirakelen van Onze-Lieve-Vrouw van Groeninge te Kortrijk (1634–1660)" (licentiate thesis, Leuven, 1987), and the primary source on which it is based, Provincial Archive of Kortrijk, OSAK 858 (Enkwest), or P. Croon, *Onse Lieve Vrauwe van Hanswyck* . . . (Mechelen, 1670), and *Diversche nieuw liedekens tot eere ende Lof van de H. Maghedt en moeder Gods Maria ende haer H. miraculeuse beelde tot Groeninghe* . . . (Gent, 1645). For numbers of miracles at German shrines, see Midelfort, *A History of Madness*, 284, 290, including an astounding 23,050 miracles at the Holy Mountain of Andechs, near Munich, from 1454 to 1657.

COST OF THE CHURCH: The abbots of Park estimated that they spent thirty thousand florins on the new church; the governors-general donated various amounts of wood, stone, and sand. They did therefore contribute, but always with conditions and limits. My total figure of forty thousand is an estimate.

LIMITING THE JESUS OAK: Some of the many exchanges on this topic, and the reluctance of the governors-general, in AAP, Losse Stukken, Corpus VII, Kastje XXIX, lias 3, no. 19, response to abbot of Park from governor-general and *rekenkamer*, plus no. 5, request by Bartholomeus Segers to the governor-general.

Also AAP, Registers, VII, 50, f. 11 (no date, from the abbot of Park), request to Governor-General Melo, including the statement that if vendors aren't allowed then the shrine will die, and Melo's refusal to allow more vendors in AAP, Losse Stukken, Corpus VII, Kastje XXIX, lias 3, June 8, 1654. The letter referring to the privileges promised by Archduke Leopold in the same lias, no. 37. Our Dear Lady of Lovely Fragrance in J. Vervaeke, "De Kapel van OLV van Welriekende," *De Brabander* 3 (1923): 67–69.

PATRONS: Governor Melo visited the Jesus Oak more than once with his entire family during the 1640s and left it gifts in thanks for his daughter's cure from a fever, while Archduke Leopold once prayed before the image for thirty minutes, besides laying the first stone of the new church; AAP, Registers, VII, 45, account book, April 11, 1643 and May 19, 1644 for Melo; Leopold on April 11, 1647. But again such great patrons as these went more often to the Sharp Hill; AAM, Mechliniensia, 10, the journal of Archbishop Mathias Hovius, mentions visits on September 1, 1618 by the archbishop of Cambrai, on October 16, 1618 by the nuncio, and on October 6, 1619, by Archbishop Hovius himself. Boni, *Scherpenheuvel*, 107–08, notes the presence of Abbot Libertus de Pape, of Park, at the Sharp Hill. In AAM, Kloosters, Scherpenheuvel, 8, November 3, 1603, the archdukes sent a circular letter to magistrates near the Sharp Hill, ordering them to provide men and supplies to help build immediately a fort to protect the Sharp Hill. An argument over sponsoring windows at the Sharp Hill in AAM, Parochialia, Scherpenheuvel, the first accounting, which mentions a certain Captain Brouchorst, whose request for a window was denied because "various great lords" had already reserved ahead of him, and there was no more room. On August 8, 1644, the rector of the Jesus Oak mentions waiting in antechambers, in AAP, Registers, VII, 45. Soergel, *Wondrous in His Saints*, 46, 190, cites the examples of a shrine to Saint Benno and a shrine at Wilsnack that were popular without official support; these weren't the only such cases, but lack of official support made long-term popularity more difficult; Nolan and Nolan, *Christian Pilgrimage*, 309–10, argue the same, though Vauchez, *Sainthood*, distinguishes between northern and southern Europe, arguing that in the latter shrines of popular origin could flourish while in the north popular shrines would stay that way only if official. Also on unofficial saints or shrines, P. Burke, "How to Be a Counter-Reformation Saint," in K. Von Greyerz, ed., *Religion and Society in Early Modern Europe* (London 1984): 47. Wingens, *Over de grens*, 149, on the efforts of clerical and secular patrons in increasing the stature of the shrines of Handel, Uden, and Kevelaer. Ward, *Miracles*, 128–29, on the importance of patrons in building prestige.

"A LITTLE SHARP HILL": The phrase is from Franciscus Duriux, the twenty-sixth pastor of the Jesus Oak, from 1864 to 1884; AAP, Kastje XXIX, lias 3, no. 51.

Final Glimpses

1702 LETTER: AAP, Losse Stukken, Corpus VII, Kastje XXIX, lias 3, no. 36, 37.

1766 CONDITIONS AND PORTRAITS: L. Everaert, "De glasramen, schilderijen en biechtstoelen," *Zonien* 20 (1996): 165–84.

1797 FLIGHT: AAP, Losse Stukken, Corpus VII, Kastje XXIX, lias 3, no. 45, November 12, 1797; attestation of the pastor of Jesus Oak about the image.

1951 CELEBRATION: Crownings of images discussed in T. Kselman, *Miracles and Prophecies in Nineteenth-Century France* (New Brunswick, NJ, 1983), 33. The playwright for the celebration was Pastor Frans Eykans, and the play was performed on August 5, 9, 12, and 15 at 8:30 each evening.

THOMAS THE BEGGAR: Mentioned in AAP, Registers, VII, 45, in an account beginning "Register vanden uuytgheeft des offers," for 1643. It reads, "for 50 nails dug out of the filth, to Thomas a beggar, one-half stiver."

DOWNPLAYING CONFLICT IN OFFICIAL CHRONICLES: Also U. Strasser, "Bones of Contention: Cloistered Nuns, Decorated Relics, and the Contest over Women's Place in the Public Sphere of Counter-Reformation Munich," *Archive for Reformation History* 90 (1999): 260–61.

CHAPTER TWO

The Milk Flows

MARIA CAROENS: Primary sources are in RAG, Bisdom, B3035, which contains the documents into the 1658 investigation of Maria's cure as well as the 1655 investigation into the image. Much of my account is drawn from her testimony before the vicariate, on August 19, 1658, her testimony to a notary in February 1658, the summaries of the vicariate in BAG, Acta, 1657–1660, 101r–117v, as well as consultation of old maps and drawings of Gent in the Gent City Archives, Collection Goetghebuer. Incidentally, Maria never mentions the gender of her child, but this wasn't unusual in miracle accounts—R. Finucane, *The Rescue of the Innocents: Endangered Children in Medieval Miracles* (New York, 2000), 121, shows that three in ten accounts of healed children failed to specify gender.

INFANT MORTALITY: Finucane, *Innocents*, synthesizes much of the literature on this subject; see also M. Lindemann, *Medicine and Society in Early Modern Europe* (Cambridge, 1999), 23, who notes that generally speaking the most dangerous ages were, until the mid-eighteenth century, infancy and early childhood, as one out of every four or five children didn't survive their first year; 50 percent of all deaths in the premodern west occurred before age ten.

ANTONY DE WITTE AND THE GUILDS OF GENT: On the economic situation in Gent, J. Decavele, ed., *Gent: Apologie van een Rebelsestad* (Antwerp, 1989), 128–29, and J. Dambruyne, "De Gentse bouwvakambachten in sociaal-economisch perspectief (1540–1795)," in C. Lis and H. Soly, eds., *Werken volgens de regels: Ambachten in Brabant en Vlaanderen, 1500–1800* (Brussels, 1994), 51–66. Like most smiths, Antony never became a master; if he was a "free" laborer, then he belonged to the guild and might have had fairly regular work, while "unfree" laborers did not belong to the guild and were allowed to work when a "free" laborer was not a member—hence the work of the latter was sporadic, and their wages lower, which sounds more like the situation of Antony. Also H. van Werveke, *Gent: Schets van een Sociale Geschiedenis* (Gent, 1947), 7, 8.

PROXY PILGRIMS: J. Sumption, *Pilgrimage* (London, 1975), 296–99; W. Christian, *Apparitions in Late Medieval and Renaissance Spain* (Princeton, 1981), 112; R. Finucane, *Miracles and Pilgrims: Popular Beliefs in Medieval England* (London, 1977), 46–47; a female proxy appears in ARA, SJ, FB, L 1042, January 2, 1631, story of Maria Ambrois.

WOMEN AND WORK: M. Wiesner, *Women and Gender in Early Modern Europe* (Cambridge, 1993), 83–85, 94–96.

WET NURSES AND BREAST-FEEDING: Wiesner, *Women and Gender*, 71–72; Finucane, *Rescue of the Innocents*, 40, notes the practice of feeding beer to hungry infants. Maria speaks of the methods applied by her friend Margaret as if they were very common. Also R. Trubowitz, " 'But Blood Whitened': Nursing Mothers and Others in Early Modern Britain," in N. Miller and N. Yavneh, eds., *Maternal Measures: Figuring Caregiving in the Early Modern Period* (Aldershot, 2000), 82–103, and in the same collection, E. Bergmann, "Language and 'Mothers' Milk': Maternal Roles and the Nurturing Body in Early Modern Spanish Texts," 105–20.

AFFECTION BETWEEN PARENTS AND CHILDREN: Finucane, *Rescue of the Innocents*, is one of many to refute the old idea that frequent death caused parents to avoid close emotional bonds with children; see also C. Harline and E. Put, *A Bishop's Tale* (New Haven, 2000), 202–06, for a specific example of miraculous resuscitation of dead infants so that they might be baptized.

SPELLS, REMEDIES: D. Gentilcore, *From Bishop to Witch* (Manchester, 1992), 138, 145, 146; on 107 he notes a trend in Italy of going to a priest first for cures and then, if unsuccessful, to a wise woman; Finucane, *Rescue of the Innocents*, 40, and *Miracles and Pilgrims*, 62, 63; H. G. Hechtermans, "Mirakelen te Scherpenheuvel," *Vlaamse Stam* 8 (1972): 621 for a 1593 case that mentions other marginal remedies tried first; and K. Thomas, *Religion and the Decline of Magic* (New York, 1971).

SIMILARITY OF SOME METHODS BETWEEN CLERGY AND LAITY: Among many others, Finucane, *Miracles and Pilgrims*, 54, 63, and Thomas, *Decline of Magic*, especially Chapter 2, "The Magic of the Medieval Church."

CHOOSING SHRINES: Finucane, *Miracles and Pilgrims*, 85, 162–63; Sumption, *Pilgrimage*, 148–51, notes the "tendency of the laity was always to visit . . . the most recently established"; M. Wingens, *Over de grens: de bedevaart van katholieke Nederlanders in de zeventiende en achttiende eeuw* (Nijmegen, 1994), 213; C. Bruneel, "Een Onderzoek naar de mirakelen van Onze-Lieve-Vrouw van Groeninge te Kortrijk (1634–1660)," (licentiate thesis, Leuven, 1987), 128, shows that most people healed at this shrine were from Kortrijk itself, so that great distance was not always a high priority. The contractual nature of the vow in H. C. E. Midelfort, *A History of Madness in Sixteenth-Century Germany* (Stanford, 1999), 283.

DANGER OF HOUSEHOLD FIRES AND BOILING CAULDRONS: Lindemann, *Medicine and Society*, 27; Finucane, *Innocents*, 143.

CHURCH OF THE RECOLLECTS: F. De Potter, *Gent, van den oudsten tijd tot heden: geschiedkundige beschrijving der stad*, 9 vols. (Gent, 1882–1933) vol. IV, 232–55.

EX-VOTOS: Sumption, *Pilgrimage*, 157; Finucane, *Miracles and Pilgrims*, 97–99, names waxen ships, images of people, wax images of many body parts, plus objects made of many other materials, including silver.

RESPONSES TO NOT RECEIVING A MIRACLE: J. Beuckelius, *Historien ende mirakelen gheschiet tot Aerlen by Helmont door het aenroepen van Ons L. Vrou* (Den Bosch, 1614), on how to deal with a shrine not working—perhaps it wasn't right for one's salvation to receive a miracle, or one wasn't worthy. See also the counsel by Jacob Janssonius, confessor of a convent in Leuven, to a miracle-seeking nun that she should instead endure her maladies in faith, in Harline and Put, *A Bishop's Tale*, 94.

WOMEN TAKING INITIATIVE: Wingens, *Over de grens*, 191; Finucane, *Innocents*, 161–62, and Chapter 3.

CORRESPONDENCE AND SPECIALTIES: P. Burke, *Culture and Society in Renaissance Italy* (New York, 1972); A. Vauchez, *Sainthood in the Later Middle Ages* (Cambridge, 1997), and J. Delumeau, *Rassurer et protéger* (Paris, 1989), 218–19, for a list of saints and their specialties.

MARY BREAST-FEEDING: C. W. Bynum, *Jesus as Mother: Studies in the Spirituality of the High Middle Ages* (Berkeley and Los Angeles, 1982); Bynum, *Holy Feast and Holy Fast: The Religious Significance of Food to Medieval Women* (Berkeley, 1987), plates 21–25; N. Yavneh, "To Bare or Not To Bare: Sofonisba Anguissola's Nursing Madonna and the Womanly Art of Breastfeeding," in Miller, Yavneh, eds., *Maternal Measures*, 65–81; W. Christian, *Local Religion in Sixteenth Century Spain* (Princeton, 1981), on the popularity of Mary for womanly problems.

DESCRIPTION OF THE JESUIT CHURCH: De Potter, *Geschiedenis van Gent*, v. IV, 168; L. Brouwers, *De Jezuieten te Gent* (Gent, 1980), 39–56; and the original sources from the house histories in ARA, SJ, FB, 981.

OFFICIAL VIEWS OF IMAGES: Trent, Session 25, as well as P. F. X. de Ram, J. F. Van de Velde, eds., *Synodicon belgicum, sive acta omnium ecclesiarum belgii a celebrato concilio tridentino usque ad concordatum anni 1801. I and II. Nova et absoluta collectio synodorum tam provincialium quam dioecesanarum archiepiscopatus mechliniensis* (Mechelen, 1828–1829), 387, Titulus XIV, De Imaginibus et Sanctorum Reliquiis.

MARIA'S VOW: The exact phrase she used was, "Heylighe Maria indien ick vertroost worde ick belove, soo langhe als ick in dese stadt ben, dat ick u alhier daeghel[ijks] sal komen besoeken, met een kort ofte lanck ghebbedt, ten alderminste van een misse." That last clause can be translated as "at least the length of a mass," or, "at least one mass," but I find the former makes more sense in this context. The latter might be right, especially since Maria told her Jesuit confessor later that she wished to sponsor a mass.

BREAST-FEEDING GUIDELINES: J. Sherwood, "The Ideology of Breast-feeding: Deconstructing Spanish Medical Texts Concerning Nursing Women at the End of the Eighteenth Century," in A. Saint-Saëns, *Religion, Body, and Gender in Early Modern Spain* (San Francisco, 1991), 94–107, which includes long-standing assumptions and views.

Jesuits

MARIA'S VISITS TO THE JESUIT CHURCH: In her testimony of August 1658, Maria claims that since the time of her healing she had continued "her devotions." This probably refers to her vow to visit the church daily and pray.

PATER VAN LIERE: A. Jansen, "Contritionisme tegen attritionisme. Strijd tusschen de pastoors van Gent en de Jezuieten (1661–1670)," in *Miscellanea historica in honorem Alberti De Meyer*, 2 vols. (Leuven, 1946), v. 2, 1107–29; A. Poncelet, *Nécrologe des Jésuites de la Province Flandro-Belge* (Wetteren, 1931), 95.

RELIGIOUS ORDERS AND MIRACLES: Sumption, *Pilgrimage*, 13, 152–53; H. Platelle, *Les Chrétiens face au miracle, Lille au XVIIe siècle* (Paris, 1968), 41; Wingens, *Over de grens*, 25, 61, on the Jesuits' promotion of instrumentality; Vauchez, *Sainthood*, 94, 123; Delumeau, *Rassurer*, 207; on similar sensibilities of religious and laity, G. Hanlon, "Piété populaire et intervention des moines dans les miracles et les sanctuaires miraculeux en Agenais-Condomois au XVIIe siècle," *Annales du Midi* 97 (1985): 115–27; T. Johnson, "Blood, Tears, and Xavier-Water: Jesuit Missionaries and Popular Religion in the Eighteenth-Century Upper Palatinate," in B. Scribner and T. Johnson, eds., *Popular Religion in Germany and Central Europe, 1400–1800* (London, 1996), 183–202; also on Jesuits, H. de Waardt, "Van exorcisten tot doctores medicinae: geestelijken als gidsen naar genezing in de Republiek, met name in Holland, in de zestiende en de zeventiende eeuw," in W. de Blécourt, W. Frijhoff, M. Gijswijt-Hofstra, eds., *Grenzen van genezing: Gezondheid, ziekte en genezen in Nederland, zestiende tot begin twintigste eeuw* (Hilversum, 1993), 98–105.

RIVALRIES AND SELF-PROMOTION OF ORDERS: Sumption, *Pilgrimage*, 87; Vauchez, *Sainthood*, 5, 454, two of many examples; also R. Pillorget, "Les miracles de Bérulle," *Histoire des miracles* (Angers, 1983); Finucane, *Miracles and Pilgrims*, 77; Wingens, " 'Van de handt des heeren geraeckt.' Miraculeuze genezingen in bedevaartsplaatsen nabij de grenzen van de Republiek, 1600–1800," in De Blécourt, et al., *Grenzen van genezing*, 78; Wingens, *Over de grens*, 22–26 on Jesuits; on competition, J.-M. Sallmann, *Naples et ses saints (XVI–XVIII siècles)* (Paris, 1994), 93; P. Geary, *Furta Sacra: Thefts of Relics in the Central Middle Ages* (Princeton, 1990), 130; H. Platelle, "Mirakels in de Zuidelijke Nederlanden," *Spieghel Historiael* (1973): 172–177, 228–37; for the name-calling ("black crows") see ARA, SJ, FB, L 197 and L 192, August 1659, February 1659; torrential sweats in Sumption, *Pilgrimage*, 48, 87; resentment of parish clergy in A. Sedgwick, *Jansenism in Seventeenth-Century France* (Charlottesville, 1977), 205; V. Arickx, " 'Mirakelen' in en rond de jezuietenkerk van Kortrijk (1623–1643)," *Biekorf* 87 (1987): 113–20.

REGULAR-SECULAR COMPETITION: Wingens, *Over de grens*, 61; U. Strasser, "Bones of Contention: Cloistered Nuns, Decorated Relics, and the Contest over Women's Place in the Public Sphere of Counter-Reformation Munich," *Archive for Reformation History* 90 (1999): 255–88, includes nuns among the regulars in this competition; Vauchez, *Sainthood*, 128–29, points out that the secular clergy was not as indifferent as supposed to miracles, as does Finucane, *Miracles and Pilgrims*, 157, so that this distinction is a matter of emphasis only.

LIMITS TO SELF-INTEREST: Vauchez, *Sainthood*, 5, and Finucane, *Rescue of the Innocents*, 2, on Becket and Clare of Montefalco.

JESUIT MILK MIRACLE: Arickx, " 'Mirakelen' in en rond de Jezuieten Kerk van Kortrijk, 1623–1643," *Biekorf* 87 (1987): 119; for a medieval example of a similar cure, Finucane, *Innocents*, 40.

PATER VAN DELFT: Little is known of him except his death in Gent in 1669; Poncelet, *Nécrologe*.

ANTONY'S PILGRIMAGE: It's not clear exactly when this happened or why it was noted. The document of August 1658 states that Pater van Delft hired Antony "before" the session with the notary. Was this also before his taking of testimony in February, or during? The business relationship of the two men in the August document may have been a way for the vicariate to question how much it affected Maria's testimony.

PRELIMINARY PROCEDURES IN MIRACLE INQUIRIES: Platelle, "Mirakels," 173; B. R. Kreiser, *Miracles, Convulsions, and Ecclesiastical Politics in Early Eighteenth-Century Paris* (Princeton, 1978), 152.

GETTING STORIES RIGHT: Christian, *Apparitions*, 208; G. T. Ahlgren, *Teresa of Avila and the Politics of Sanctity* (Ithaca, 1996), 148–49; L. Smoller, "Miracle, Memory and Meaning in the Canonization of Vincent Ferrer 1453–1454," *Speculum* 73/2 (April 1993): 438–40; N. Davis, *Fiction in the Archives: Pardon Tales and Their Tellers in Sixteenth-Century France* (Cambridge, 1988); Wingens, *Over de grens*, 78–84.

DOCTORS IN MIRACLE INVESTIGATIONS: Vauchez, *Sainthood*, 467–70; Wingens, *Over de grens*, 66; Finucane, *Miracles and Pilgrims*, 61; T. Kselman, *Miracles and Prophecies in Nineteenth-Century France* (New Brunswick, NJ, 1983), 42; ARA, SJ, FB, L 1042, undated document (ca. 1646), healing of Barbara Mari Goubau, mentions medical cures attempted but is careful to make clear that they failed; also February 11, 1676, testimony of Johan de Cocx, MD; April 5, 1664, Guilielmus Marcquis Lazari filius, MD, November 20, 1663, Maria Anna van Leyen and many others in the same file, showing the doctors' futile attempts; and testimony for AAM, Parochialia, Jezus Eik, October 10, 1642, regarding Dimpna Gillis's blindness; especially D. Gentilcore, "Contesting Illness in Early Modern Naples," *Miracolati*, Physicians and the Congregation of Rites," *Past & Present* 148 (1995): 117–32, on the significant but potentially embarrassing role of doctors.

EXPLANATION OF MARIA'S SUPERNATURAL CURE: Unlike the physicians later enlisted by the vicariate, those employed by the Jesuits explained their conclusion in some detail. First, despite her obvious fertility, Maria rarely had menstrual "purgations" outside her pregnancies as well as little milk—she was never especially abundant in any bodily fluids; second, she had always been in good health, "of sufficiently solid and dense flesh"—suggesting that the sudden flow of milk was not part of a pattern of erratic health; and third, this time no physical remedies had worked at all yet she had more milk than ever. The doctors were William Thijs, Joannes de Eijckere (June 2, 1658), J. Stalins (June 8, 1658); Joannes de Lau, Joannes Dustrici, J. de Lespiere, P. Dorlix, and J. B. de Leeuw (May 19, 1658). The first three were from Gent and the rest from Brussels.

The Bishop's Men

IMPOTENCE TRIALS: P. Darmon, *Damning the Innocent, A History of the Persecution of the Impotent in pre-Revolutionary France* (New York, 1986), 141–86.

PERSONAL QUESTIONS INTO ONE'S PHYSICAL CONDITION: See testimonies cited in the Jesuit miracles above, in ARA, SJ, FB, L1042, among many other examples.

SLEEP AND MIRACULOUS CURES: Vauchez, *Sainthood*, 444–45; Finucane, *Innocents*, 12.

BISHOPS' FAMILIARITY WITH MIRACLES: That miracles formed a common theme in their lives may be concluded from a glance through the agenda and acta of most any bishop, such as Mathias Hovius's Manuale, in AAM, Mechliniensia 10, November 8, 1617; January 1, 10, 1618; May 21, 1619; July 30, 1619; November 22, 1619; December 18, 1619; January 16, 1620; February 26, 1620; March 20, 1620. The bishop's right to pronounce on miracles was handled at Trent in session 25. That cures dominated miracles from Vauchez, *Sainthood*, 467–69, who also notes they declined in percentage over time but still were overwhelming.

NO SINGLE VIEW OF MIRACLES: I. Backus, *Le miracle de Laon* (Paris, 1994) shows how four churchmen interpreted the same set of miracles under review; Finucane, *Miracles and Pilgrims*, 10; L. Chatellier, "Le miracle baroque," in *L'histoire des miracles* (Angers, 1983), 90–91. That the greatest scholar in Europe, Justus Lipsius, would not deny miracles suggests again how ingrained they were among almost all—Lipsius recommended that the printer Jean Moretus send his son to the Sharp Hill to be cured, "for truly there are lovely miracles there daily, and what harm in trying? At least he'll do his devotions," in A. Gerlo, ed., *La correspondance inedite de Juste Lipse conservée au Musée Plantin-Moretus*, vol. 1 (Antwerp, 1964), 199; Lipsius also wrote two miracle books for shrines, an activity for which many scholars berated him, especially in Protestant countries, as he himself suggested in "Heilige Maagd van Leuven," a manuscript in the library of the University of Leiden (Ms. Lips. 12), about to be published in English by Jeanine Delandtsheer.

OFFICIAL DEFENSES OF MIRACLES AND CONVERGENCE WITH LAITY: Kselman, *Miracles*, 141, 152; Finucane, *Miracles and Pilgrims*, 22; J. Paul, "La perception du caractère populaire du fait religieux au début du XIVe siècle d'après l'enquête sur les miracles de Louis d'Anjou," in *La Religion Populaire* (Paris, 1979): 77–84, emphasizes different views of laity and clergy, while Vauchez, *Sainthood*, xx, Delumeau, *Rassurer*, 189, 195, Sallman, *Naples*, 371, and G. Hanlon, "Piété populaire et intervention des moines dans les miracles et les sanctuaires miraculeux en Agenais-Condomois au XVII siècle," *Annales du Midi* 97 (1985): 115–27, argue for strong beliefs and similar sensibilities among both. Vauchez, 459, recognizes attempts by church leaders, after the thirteenth century, to distance themselves from popular beliefs, but attitudes toward the saints remained basically similar. Delumeau, *Rassurer*, 199, notes one churchman's lament that instrumental miracles were preferred by most, but even these, he conceded, were not all bad, because they prompted devotions of commemoration, with spiritual benefits. That only the true church had miracles is cited in nearly every apology on the subject, such as Beuckelius, *Historien*, 4–5. Denouncing unbelievers within the church in Sumption, *Pilgrimage*, 41, 61, or H. Kamen, *The Phoenix and the Flame* (New Haven, 1993), 90. Bishops approving relics in AAM, Mechliniensia, 5:131, January 14, 1616; 6:244v, March 4, 1609; AAM, Vicariaat, III, a whole box of relic approbations from bishops, and a host of others. Bernard of Clairvaux, in D. Menozzi, *Les Images: L'Eglise et les arts visuels* (Paris, 1991), 118. Torrentius example in a letter to Mathias Hovius, June 27, 1594, M. Delcourt, J. Hoyoux, *Laevinus Torrentius Correspondance*, 3 vols. (Paris, 1950–54), III, 575–75. Examples of defenses include Thomas More, in J. Shinners, ed., *Medieval Popular Religion, 1000–1500* (Peterborough, Canada, 1997), 201; A. De Soto, *Twee T'samensprekingen, Behandelende de leeringe ende materie vande mirakelen . . .* (Brussels, 1614); *Antwoorde op een Valsche Leugenachtich Verhael . . .* (Leuven, 1604); the polemicist Johannes Molanus, who despite his many criticisms of practices within the faith still defended miracles, in G. Rooijakkers, *Rituele repertoires. Volkscultuur in oostelijk Noord-Brabant (1559–1853)* (Nijmegen, 1994), 577–79; and D. Freedberg, *Iconoclasm and Painting in the Revolt of the Netherlands, 1566–1609* (New York, 1988), chapter 5. These defenses were not written by bishops, but they were approved before publication. More examples of miracle books for shrines include H. Sedulius, OFM, *t'Boeck van Ons Lieve Vrouwe van Maestricht* (Leuven, 1612), *Corte Verhael van die Myrakelen die welcke in dese voorleden Jaeren, door die Intercessie ende voorbidden der heyligher maghet ende moeder godts Maria, zijn gheschiet inder Capellen van Omel* (Den Bosch, 1612); F.M.V.B, *Den Devoten Pelgrim reysende naer diversche Miraculeuse Beelden van de H. Maghet Maria, Soo in Brabandt, als andere omligghende Plaetsen* (Brussel, n.d.); P. Boville, *Den Oorspronck ende Mirakelen van Onse Lieve Vrouwe van Foye by Dinant* (Leuven, 1624); and the two works by Lipsius, which earned him so much criticism from especially Dutch scholars, *Iusti Lipsii Diva Sichemiensis sive Aspricollis* (Brussels, 1605), and *Die Heylighe Maghet van Halle* (Brussels, 1607). The majority of stories in these books bishops allowed to be published as "edifying" or "marvelous," rather than officially approved miracles. Wingens, *Over de grens*, 184, notes that of fifty-nine miracle stories in one shrine chronicle, only five were officially approved miracles, but the rest were approved for publication. The propaganda value of miracles, including Dutch Catholic identity, German Catholic identity, and so forth, in X. van Eck, "From Doubt to Conviction: Clandestine 'Catholic' Churches as Patrons of Dutch Caravaggesque Painting," *Simiolus* 22/4 (1993–94): 217–34; D. B. Moody, "Healing Power in the Marian Miracle Books of Bavarian Healing Shrines, 1489–1523," *Journal of the History of Medicine and Allied Sciences* 47/1 (1992): 68–90; Platelle, "Mirakels," 228–37; Beuckelius, *Historien*, 1–5, 13; Soergel, *Wondrous*, 159; during the French Revolution, M. Cattaneo, "Fonti per lo studio dei 'miracoli' del 1796–97 nello stato della chiesa: i verbali del processo canonico," *Dimensioni e Problemi della Ricerca Storica* 1 (1991): 269–83; or for Jansenism, see below. On the hope that miracles will convert Protestants, De Soto, *Twee T'samensprekingen*, and P. Numan, *Historie vande Miraculen die onlancx In grooten getale ghebeurt zyn, door die intercessie ende voorbidden van die Heylighe Maget* (Leuven, 1604).

BISHOPS' CAUTION TOWARD MIRACLES, ESPECIALLY AMONG WOMEN: "all novelty . . ." from J. Brown, *Immodest Acts: The Life of a Lesbian Nun in Renaissance Italy* (Oxford, 1986), 105; also Soergel, *Wondrous*, 50, 167; Vauchez, *Sainthood*, 11, 269; R. Kagan, *Lucrecia's Dreams: Politics and Prophecy in Sixteenth-Century Spain* (Berkeley and Los Angeles, 1990), 4, 115; Christian, *Apparitions*, 197; Ahlgren, *Teresa*, 14, 21, 62, 98; Kreiser, *Miracles*, 141; More's scenario from Sumption, *Pilgrimage*, 55; Delumeau, *Rassurer*, 214; Finucane, *Miracles and Pilgrims*, 10, 38, 58; and J. Pelikan, *The Christian Tradition: A History of the Development of Doctrine. Vol. III. The Growth of Medieval Theology (600–1300)* (Chicago, 1978), 179–81.

PROTESTANT UNBELIEF IN MIRACLES: A. van Oosterwijck, *Heylige Maghet van Halle. Hare weldaden ende miraculen wt de Latijnsche in onse Nederlantsche tale overgheset, deur eenen lief-hebber der eere syns eenigen salichmakers, tot bespottinghe der pauselicke Roomsche afgoderije* (Delft, 1605); J. Biemans, "De Paapse Poppecraam: Rituelen en gebruiken van katholieken in de classis Hertogenbosch in gereformeerde ogen, 1677–1795," *Brabants Heem* 43 (1991): 20–31; B. Mangrum, G. Scavizzi, *A Reformation Debate: Karlstadt, Emser, and Eck on Sacred Images. Three Treatises in Translation* (Toronto, 1991); S. MacCormack, "The Organization of Sacred Topography," in R. Ousterhout, ed., *The Blessings of Pilgrimage* (Urbana, 1990), 9; Thomas, *Decline of Magic*, 51; Soergel, *Wondrous*, chapter 5, among other places; Calvin's comments from C. Eire, *War Against the Idols: The Reformation of Worship from Erasmus to Calvin* (Cambridge, 1986); and H. Beveridge, ed., *Tracts and Treatises on the Reformation of the Church, by John Calvin* (Grand Rapids, 1958), vol. 1, 93–99. Luther from J. Pelikan and D. Poellot, eds., *Luther's Works* (St. Louis, 1958), vol. 24, 74–75, 272, 275, 278–79, 368–69; W. Hazlitt, *Table Talk* (London, 1995), 20; Soergel, *Wondrous*, 63, points out that Luther could be "reasonable" toward the saints. Also D. P. Walker, "The Cessation of Miracles," in I. Merkel and

A. G. Debus, eds., *Hermeticism and the Renaissance: Intellectual History and the Occult in Early Modern Europe* (Washington, 1988), 111–24. Examples, however, of possible Protestant miracles and relics would include fireproof portraits of Luther, George Fox's healing power, Johan van Oldenbarnevelt's eyeglasses and cane or the sword that beheaded him, and Hugo Grotius's cloak and chest, in B. Scribner, "Incombustible Luther," Finucane, *Miracles and Pilgrims*, 215, and W. Vroom, *In Tumultu Gosico: Over relieken en geuzen in woelilge tijden* (Nijmegen, 1992), 33. That Protestants had little to match Catholic miracles in Soergel, *Wondrous*, 159. Marnix van Aldegonde's distorted sense that Catholic leaders were behind the spate of miracles in Delumeau, *Rassurer*, 216–17.

INVESTIGATION PROCEDURES: Wingens, *Over de grens*, 182–3; AAM, Vicariaat, I.5, Inquest into Anna of Saint Bartholomew; M. Goodich, *Violence and Miracle in the Fourteenth Century* (Chicago, 1995), 6–13; Paul, "La perception"; and Sumption, *Pilgrimage*, 64.

PRECONCEIVED NOTIONS, DEFINITIONS, AND ORTHODOXY ABOUT MIRACLES: Vauchez, *Sainthood*, 2–3, 491, 496; L. Daston and K. Park, *Wonders and the Order of Nature, 1150–1750* (New York, 1998), 121, on the desire to distinguish nature and miracles more sharply; B. Ward, *Miracles and the Medieval Mind: Theory, Record and Event, 1000–1215* (Philadelphia, 1982), especially chapters 1 and 2; Kagan, *Lucrecia*, 61, on investigators' notions of "how a divinely inspired dream should sound"; Geary, *Furta Sacra*, 113–15; L. Chatellier, "Le miracle baroque," in *L'histoire des miracles* (Angers, 1983), 86–87; Gentilcore, *From Bishop to Witch*, 169; Kreiser, *Miracles*, 128; Lipsius, *Die Heylighe Maghet*, 22; Goodich, *Violence and Miracle*, 147; Kselman, *Miracles*, 152; Soergel, *Wondrous*, 140. Some questioned how important "suddenness" really was, including Numan, *Historie vande Miraculen*, 2v–4v. One contemporary definition that held for long, before and after, was repeated by Beuckelius, *Historien*, 74: miracles were nothing but works against or above nature, "like that sticking of the fingers by Christ in the ears of the deaf, and making him hear," which was no natural remedy "or we could do it also." These definitions were quite similar to those of ordinary people, who also stressed incurable, sudden, lasting, and above nature, as discussed in L. Smoller, "Defining Boundaries of the Natural in Fifteenth-Century Brittany: the Inquest into the Miracles of Saint Vincent Ferrer (d. 1419)," *Viator* 28 (1997): 333–59. Kreiser, *Miracles*, is among many who stresses the importance of preconceptions as one judged whether an event was miraculous, as on ix; see more below under "Neighbors."

LEGAL CONSIDERATIONS: Paul, "La perception," 81–84; Goodich, *Violence and Miracle*, 6; Sumption, *Pilgrimage*, 64; AAM, Vicariaat, III (relic approbations and what passed as good evidence), Vauchez, *Sainthood*, 50; but Smoller, "Miracle, Memory, and Meaning," 432, shows that evidence didn't have to be perfect, just consistent enough.

THEOLOGICAL CONSIDERATIONS: These are countless, but those used here are from Soergel, *Wondrous*, 140; Lipsius, *Die Heylighe Maghet;* Goodich, *Violence and Miracle*, 13; Vauchez, *Sainthood*, 498. The difficulties of distinguishing between especially preternatural and supernatural in A. Kazhdan, "Holy and Unholy Miracle Workers," in H. Maguire, ed., *Byzantine Magic* (Harvard, 1995), 76, 82, reflecting the difficulty in the Byzantine church as well; L. Daston, "Marvelous Facts and Miraculous Evidence in Early Modern Europe," *Critical Inquiry* 18 (Autumn 1991): 95–97, 99, 101, 106–07, 121–23.

EXAMPLES OF OFFICIALLY APPROVED MIRACLES, RELICS, IMAGES: AAM, Mechliniensia, 6, f. 244v, March 4, 1609, Hovius proclaims events in Volkegem miraculous.

END OF PROCESS: Bronckhorst, the former rector, is named in the Acta as the Jesuit responsible for pushing Maria's case forward; BAG, Acta, 1657–60, 101r, September 2, 1658. The opinion of the medical doctors is merely summed up in the acta; perhaps they submitted other documents as well, but these were not preserved. Efforts of the Jesuits to get their documents back are noted in the Acta as well, 1657–60, 117v. The possibility of bringing the case before the ecclesiastical court noted in L. Ceyssens, *Fin de la première période de Jansenisme, v. II, 1657–1660* (Brussels, 1965), 310, which quotes the house history for 1658, in ARA, SJ, FB, 981. That the case of Maria Caroens is filed in Gent with the papers of the ecclesiastical court suggests that the case was at least considered there.

Neighbors

PAOLO ZACCHIA: Gentilcore, "Contesting Illness," 132.

OTHER EXPLANATIONS, INCLUDING POLITICS: Ken Woodward, *Making Saints* (New York, 1990); P. Burke, "How to Be a Counter-Reformation Saint," in *Religion and Society in Early Modern Europe, 1500–1800*, ed. K. Von Greyerz (London, 1984); L. Villalon, "San Diego de Alcalá and the Politics of Saint-Making in Counter-Reformation Europe," *Catholic Historical Review* 83/4 (1997): 701. Vauchez, *Sainthood*, 76–84, notes in regard to politics and religion that the existence of pressure groups within a religion should hardly surprise, since this was the pattern of larger society as well.

ABILITY TO RESIST FIRE: G. J. Snoek, *Medieval Piety: From Relics to the Eucharist* (Leiden, 1995), 330–32.

ELEVATION: "From one cosmic world to another," Geary, *Furta Sacra*, 126, quoting the anthropologist Van Gennep; the comments of P. Marchant, in RAG, Bisdom, B3035, in the papers of the 1655 investigation; Nolan and Nolan, *Christian Pilgrimage*, 164, and Sumption, *Pilgrimage*, 147.

ANTOON TRIEST AND THE JESUITS: L. Ceyssens, "Triest et les rigueurs romaines," *BIHBR* (1958), 207–80; "Les dernières années de Triest," *Jansenistica Minora*, v. VI (Mechelen, 1962), 1–17; and *Fin de la première période*, vols. 1, 2. That Triest allowed the Jesuits to go through with their elevation is inferred from the date of the expert testimony, dated October 1, 1655, the very day of the elevation, but not arriving in Gent until later. Also, a copy of the poster was included in the investigation file. See also BAG, Acta, 1645–57, 206–217v, mainly on Jansenism, then the investigation into the image on 294r–302r.

JESUITS AND JANSENISTS: "Colluding in the ignorance of the peasantry" from Johnson, "Blood, Tears," 200, refers to a later period but the sentiment was apt; also Kreiser, *Miracles*, 4–5, 99, showing that Jansenists could disagree among themselves on miracles and could use them freely when necessary, but many downplayed them; also D. Van Kley, *The Jesuits and the Expulsion of the Jesuits from France, 1757–1765* (New Haven, 1975), chapter 1; and more specifically on the situation in Gent, which some thought was the most heated spot of all, Jansen, "Contritionisme tegen Attritionisme," and the Ceyssens articles above. Wingens, "Miraculous Cures," 61, on the Jansenists' focus on internal religion; R. Taveneaux, *La vie quotidienne des jansénistes aux XVIIe et XVIIIe siècles* (Paris, 1985), chapter 10, showing Jansenist belief in miracles, but limits, and also W. Frijhoff, "La fonction du miracle dans une minorité catholique: Les Provinces-Unie au 17e siècle," *Revue d'histoire de la spiritualité* 48 (1972): 151–77. Vauchez, *Sainthood*, 96, gives examples enough to show that the Jesuits were hardly the only order to act first then ask permission later.

TRIEST MAKING AMENDS WITH JESUITS: For example, in BAG, Acta, 1646–56, 190v–191r, Triest gives approbation and permission to the Jesuits for the public veneration of the relics of Saints Cornelius, Eusebius, Hypolitus, Caelestinus, Benignus, and Valentinus, December 31, 1650; Acta, 1633–45, 331r, Triest consecrates in 1631 the altar of Our Lady of Mercy in the Jesuit church, the very altar where the later disputed image is placed; Brouwers, *Jezuieten te Gent*, 114–15 cites other examples, including after Triest's condemnation by Rome.

EXPERT THEOLOGIANS: These were Bartholomew D'Astroy and H. Du Monte from Liège; Christopher Mauritus, SJ, Joannes Erardus Fullomus(?), SJ, and another Jesuit who simply added his name to the opinion of the last; Peter Marchant, a Franciscan Recollect; Joannes Anthonius D'Aubermont, a Dominican; and the Augustinians Alipius Reylof, Ignatius Dijckerus, Petrus de Vos, and Cornelius Dickman. For more on Peter Marchant, *Den Reghel der Derder Orden van S. Fransoys* (Gent, 1626), S. Schoutens, OFM, *Martyrologium Minoritico-Belgicum sive Breves Biographiae Virorum Illustrum Qui in Ordine Minorum ex Belgio et Hollandia oriundi vel in Belgio et Hollandia floruerunt* (Hoogstraten, 1901), 191, which lists his many achievements and offices in the order.

PATER VAN LIERE AND THE AUGUSTINIANS: BAG, Acta, 1645–57, 216r–217v, August 31, 1653.

L'HERMITE AND TRIEST: Ceyssens, *Fin de la première période*, II, 503, March 16, 1654, mentions L'Hermite's letter condemning Triest.

WORRIES ABOUT DUTCH PROTESTANTS: Wingens, *Over de grens*, 34. Marionettes in ARA, Raad van State en Audiëntie, Briefwisseling, 1947/2, letters from Joost Bouckaert to the Council of State, July 1613. The pregnant Jesuit and others in Soergel, *Wondrous*, 45, 151–58. "Stupid images" in W. Oostenhof, *Niet door stomme beelden* (Gorinchem, 1991); also Menozzi, *Les Images*. Martin's boots and other objects in Rooijakkers, *Rituele repertoires*, 149, quoting the preacher Abraham Magyrus in *The Almanac of Saints*. Also Freedberg, *Iconoclasm and Painting;* J. Friedman, *The Battle of the Frogs and Fairford's Flies: Miracles and the Pulp Press During the English Revolution* (New York, 1993), 140–41; MacCormack, "Sacred Topography," 9; A. van de Sande, "Decadente Monniken en Nonnen: Aard en functie van een antipapistisch motief (ca. 1500–1853)," in M. Monteiro, G. Rooijakkers, J. Rosendaal, eds., *De dynamiek van religie en cultuur* (Kampen, 1993), 239–60; L. Palmer Wandel, *Voracious Idols and Violent Hands: Iconoclasm in Reformation Zurich, Strasbourg, and Basel* (Cambridge, 1995); and such sarcastic tracts as *Historie van de wonderlijcke Mirakelen, die in menichte ghebeurt zijn, ende noch dagelijcx ghebeuren, binnen de vermaerde coop-staat Aemstelredam: in een plaets ghenaempt het tucht-huys, gheleghen op de heylighe-wegh* (Amsterdam, 1612). On shifting resources from ritual to feeding the poor, see E. Muir, *Ritual in Early Modern Europe* (Cambridge, 1997).

CATHOLIC DEFENSES OF IMAGES: Beuckelius, *Historien*, Part Five especially; Menozzi, *Les Images*, 129, who could deny that Saint Francis was spoken to by a crucifix? Vauchez, *Sainthood*, 448–49 on the ancient use of images. P. Geary, "The Ninth-Century Relic Trade," in J. Obelkevich, ed., *Religion and the People, 800–1700* (Chapel Hill, 1979), 13, notes that images were seen as aesthetic or instructional objects in that period still, but this would change in a couple of centuries when images would become miracle-working objects too, as suggested in Nolan and Nolan, *Christian Pilgrimage*, 167, 171, and Snoek, *Medieval Piety*. Freedberg, *Iconoclasm and Painting*, 76–95, cites Benoist arguing that "the same honour was due to the image as to that which it represented," which probably went further than most learned Catholics would have gone, but was probably how many lay believers saw it. See also Eire, *War Against the Idols*, 19–20; Kamen, *Phoenix and Flame*, 139; Numan, *Historie vande Miraculen;* Smoller, "Miracle, Memory, and Meaning," 429, cites an example of a priest praying to Saint Vincent that Vincent might restore a sick person to life, rather than the more theologically correct approach that Vincent would intervene. Further background in R. Ousterhout and L. Brubaker, eds., *The Sacred Image: East and West* (Urbana, 1995). Teresa's sentiment is from her *Life*, chapter 9, paragraph 6.

ARGUING AND CRITICISM WITHIN CATHOLICISM: Sumption, *Pilgrimage*, 22–23, 211, including Paulinus van Nola quote; Catholics destroying some of their own images as false in G. P. Marchal, "Bilderstürm im Mittelalter," *Historisches Jahrbuch* 113 (1993): 255–82, and "Jalons pour une histoire de l'iconoclasme aux Moyen Age," *Annales* 50/5 (1995): 1135–56; also N. L. Brann, "The Proto-Protestant Assault upon Church Magic: The 'Errores Bohemanorum' According to the Abbot Trithemius (1462–1516)," *Journal of Religious History* 12/1 (1982): 9–22; Mangrum, Scavizzi, *Reformation Debate;* Menozzi, *Les Images*, 44–48; Freedberg, *Iconoclasm and Painting*, chapter 5; Eire, *War Against the Idols;* and such famous critics as Pascal or Erasmus, in C. Kegan Paul, ed., *The Thoughts of Blaise Pascal* (London, 1885), 267, where after defending the reality of miracles he argues that "miracles are no longer needful, because they have already been," yet still there may be conditions under which they might occur; less nuanced is Erasmus, especially in "A Pilgrimage for Religion's Sake," in C. Thompson, ed., *Ten Colloquies* (Indianapolis, 1957).

REDUCING INTEREST IN THE IMAGE, THE PROBLEM OF TOLERATION, AND LAY INITIATIVE: Ecclesiastical authorities avoiding "violent confrontation" in Vauchez, *Sainthood*, 413, also 157. As Thomas, *Decline of Magic*, 48–49, points out, official concepts of superstition "had a certain elasticity" about them." Examples of accommodation by Triest in M. Cloet, ed., *Het Bisdom Gent* (Gent, 1992), 197, in France, K. Luria, *Territories of Grace: Cultural Change in the Seventeenth Century Diocese of Grenoble* (Berkeley and Los Angeles, 1991), and Spain, Kagan, *Lucrecia's Dreams*, 99. The Holy Blood Procession in Sumption, *Pilgrimage*, 48. Stillborn babies among other places in Harline and Put, *A Bishop's Tale*, chapter 11, "The Women of Limal." Cultural negotiation and interaction in Burke, "How to Be," 45, and Wingens, *Over de grens*, 13. The church's official stamp mattered not necessarily for the short term, because people would continue to believe, but more for the long term, in Kreiser, *Miracles*, 96–97; moreover, official condemnation could easily cause trouble, as in W. Christian, *Visionaries* (Berkeley and Los Angeles, 1996). On people doing as they pleased, or taking initiative, B. Cousin, *Le miracle et le quotidien: Les ex-voto provençaux, images d'une société* (Aix, 1983); Soergel, *Wondrous*, 45–51; Vauchez, *Sainthood*, 139–40; Sumption, *Pilgrimage*, 44, 71; Christian, *Local Religion*, 174, citing leaders' complaints that people were celebrating their own saints and feast days more than those of the Church.

TRIEST'S MEETING WITH THE RECTOR: RAG, Bisdom, B3035, Triest undated memo, and BAG, Acta, 1647–57, November 17, 1655 meeting. L'Hermite is not named specifically in these documents, merely "the rector," but he was rector at this time, according to Brouwers, *Jezuieten te Gent*, 254.

COMPOSITION OF VICARIATE IN 1658: From BAG, Acta, while information about the members of the vicariate is from E. Hellin, *Histoire chronologique des évêques, et du chapitre exempt de l'église cathédrale S. Bavon à Gand* (Gent, 1772), and Ceyssens, *Fin de la première période*, 264, 462, and many other citations here (see that work's index). They were as follows: Jacob Roose, provost of the cathedral chapter, of unclear allegiance; Maximilian van de Woestyne, dean of the chapter, not a Jansenist, and recommended to a bishopric by Karel Van den Bosch, a well-known anti-Jansenist; Andreas Guyard, archdeacon of the chapter, who opposed Jesuits in a later dispute with the city's pastors; Nicholas Breydel, cantor of the chapter, of unclear allegiance, and the vicar-general sede vacante at the time and thus administrative head of the vicariate; and Joannes le Monier, treasurer, an anti-Jansenist. Villalon, "San Diego," 702, notes an example of violent disagreement among physicians over the miraculous or natural quality of a cure, and the huge political implications involved that may or may not have influenced their respective positions. But even if no politics were involved, doctors would not necessarily agree, making it hard to separate politics from science; for one of many examples, Finucane, *Innocents*, 95, where some doctors called an ailment paralysis, while others blamed an evil spirit.

COULD NOT BE TRUE, OR HAD TO BE TRUE, AND PRECONCEIVED NOTIONS: Hans Behem in R. Wunderli, *Peasant Fires: The Drummer of Niklashausen* (Bloomington, 1992), 113, 125, 134; Jansenists in Kreiser, *Miracles*, ix, x, 68, 76, 95, 398; the critical role played by doctors in that controversy on 127, 205; on 14, he notes that so blindly did the Church sometimes proceed against Jansenism that in condemning their articles the Church unwittingly condemned even those passages taken straight from the New Testament; on Joan of Arc, Vauchez, *Sainthood*, 539; for Spain, see Christian, *Visionaries*, 127, 151, 157.

JESUITS KEEP WORKING: Brouwers, *Jezuieten te Gent*, 55, 75; the Xavier miracle, in *Mirakelen ende Wel-daden ver-kreghen door het aen-roepen vanden H. P. Franciscus Xaverius* . . . (Antwerp, 1660), 78; the Jesuits had been denied before, as the whole impressive dossier of alleged miracles through the deceased Leonard Lessius attests, in ARA, SJ, FB, L 197—his case was turned down.

MARGARET DOOSENS: Maria mentions in her testimony of August 1658 the "widow" Margaret Doosens, while in February 1658 Margaret's husband had testified in Maria's behalf.

CHAPTER THREE

Unholy Diversions

Core documents are in RAG, Bisdom, B4623–29, and the archive of the Diocese of Gent itself, BAG, Acta Episcopatus, 1657–60, hereafter cited as Acta. The first testimonies cited here are from a memo summarizing the different documents presented by the convent in the legal case that ensued, in RAG, B4629, beginning "Inventaris Advertissement ende Applicat omme d'Eerwde. Vrauwe Abdesse vande clooster ende Abdys Sta. Margriet, gheseyt Groenenbriele."

ORIGINS AND USES OF SAINTS: G. J. C. Snoek, *Medieval Piety: From Relics to the Eucharist* (Leiden, 1995), 9, 252, 328, 334; R. Finucane, *Miracles and Pilgrims: Popular Beliefs in Medieval England* (London, 1977), 25, 26, 50; J. Delumeau, *Rassurer et protéger* (Paris, 1979), 191, 216–19, 225 on Fiacre; J. Toussaert, *Le sentiment religieux en Flandre á la fin du Moyen-Age* (Paris, 1963), 279–94; and especially P. Brown, *The Cult of the Saints* (Chicago, 1981).

CHILDREN AND MIRACLES: R. Finucane, *The Rescue of the Innocents: Endangered Children in Medieval Miracles* (New York, 2000), especially 42–44, 95–99, 141–49, 159–67; Delumeau, *Rassurer*, 209.

POPULARITY AND NUMBER OF SAINTS, ESPECIALLY FIACRE: Delumeau, *Rassurer*, 180, 219; J. Van Haver, *Nederlandse Incantatieliteratuur* (Gent, 1964), 483–87; *La Vie de Saint Fiacre* (Troyes, 1752); *Het wonderlyck ende miraculeus leven vanden glorieusen belyder den H. Fiacrus . . .* (Gent, 1661), more on this below; *Encyclopédie Théologique* (Paris, 1850), v. 14, 1009–10, *Oxford Dictionary of Saints*, 2nd ed. (Oxford, 1987), 159; C. Jökle, *Encyclopedia of Saints* (London, 1995), 152, and a tract entitled *Sur l'enlèvement des reliques de sainct Fiacre, apportées de la ville de Meaux, pour la guerison du cul de Mr. le Cardinal de Richelieu* (Antwerp, 1643), a rhymed satire, but Richelieu does appear to have called upon Fiacre, an event also recounted by A. Huxley in his novel *Grey Eminence* (London, 1942).

RITUALS SURROUNDING THE SAINTS: A. Vauchez, *Sainthood in the Later Middle Ages* (Cambridge, 1997), 430, 446; Snoek, *Medieval Piety*, 159, 236, 237, 344–45; Finucane, *Miracles and Pilgrims*, 27; Finucane, *Innocents*, 12–15; Delumeau, *Rassurer*, 229; J. Sumption, *Pilgrimage: An Image of Mediaeval Religion* (London, 1975), 82; P. Soergel, *Wondrous in His Saints* (Berkeley, 1993), 24; G. Vikan, "Pilgrims in Magi's Clothing: The Impact of Mimesis on Early Byzantine Pilgrimage Art," in R. Ousterhout, ed., *The Blessings of Pilgrimage* (Urbana, 1990), 97–107.

CRITICISMS OF SAINTS AND RESPONSES: Finucane, *Miracles and Pilgrims*, chapter 1; Vauchez, *Sainthood*, 49, 499–508; Aquinas in J.-M. Sallmann, *Naples et ses saints (XVI–XVIII siècles)* (Paris, 1994), 333; Sumption, *Pilgrimage*, 22–24; J. Beuckelius, *Historien ende mirakelen gheschiet tot Aerlen by Helmont door het aenroepen van Ons L. Vrou* (Den Bosch, 1614), 79; Soergel, *Wondrous*, 108, S. Ditchfield, "Sanctity in Early Modern Italy," *Journal of Ecclesiastical History* 47/1 (January

1996): 98–112. On Protestants continuing old ways, R. A. Mentzer, "The Persistence of Superstition and Idolatry Among Rural French Calvinists," *Church History* 65 (1996): 220–33.

CONTINUING VALUE PLACED ON SAINTS: Snoek, *Medieval Piety*, 23–25 on subdividing, and 74 on cutting up Elizabeth of Thuringen in 1231; C. Eire, *War Against the Idols: The Reformation of Worship from Erasmus to Calvin* (Cambridge, 1986), 16, on the monks of Fossanovo boiling and decapitating Thomas Aquinas, and quoting Jacques Toussaert's reference to furious subdividing as "découpage millimetrique"; or A. Poncelet, "Documents inédits sur Saint Jean Berchmans," *Analecta Bollandiana* 34–35 (1915–1916): 26–31, on the tearing asunder of that presumed saint's body; Sumption, *Pilgrimage*, 28, on subdividing, and 214–16 on rules about reliquaries; W. H. Vroom, *In Tumultu Gosico: over relieken en geuzen in woelilge tijden* (Nijmegen, 1992), 10, 17, on Philip's relics; on stealing and traders, P. Geary, *Furta Sacra: Thefts of Relics in the Central Middle Ages* (Princeton, 1990).

Unsmiling Nuns

ANNA MARIA VAN HAMME: She emerges not only in the core documents, cited at the beginning of this chapter, but especially in the convent's other records, collected in RAG, Groenebriel, a separate inventory authored by G. Marechal (Brussels, 1975), which also includes a brief history of the convent. Other general sources on the convent include V. van der Haeghen, *Het klooster Ten Walle en de abdij van den Groenen Briel* (Gent, 1888), which provides a survey but also transcribes large portions of a seventeenth-century chronicle, among other sources. Anna Maria's initial letters to the vicariate in RAG, Bisdom, B4629, March 11 and 23, 1660. Her claims about the tailors' greed are in the memo containing the list of documents submitted to the ecclesiastical court, cited above.

ECONOMIC STATE OF CONVENTS: For a review of general conditions see C. Harline, *The Burdens of Sister Margaret: Inside a Seventeenth-Century Convent* (New Haven, 2000), especially chapter 11, which also summarizes much literature on the subject; also Harline, "Actives and Contemplatives: the Female Religious of the Low Countries before and after Trent," *Catholic Historical Review* 81/4 (1995): 541–67.

ECONOMIC STATE OF GROENEBRIEL AND CONVENTS IN GENT: J. Decavele, ed., *Gent: Apologie van een Rebelsestad* (Antwerp, 1989), 118, 130; Van der Haeghen, *Groenen Briel*, 290, contains a 1663 quote about the convent being "rich," while 272 contains an abbess's complaint of their meager annual income of three thousand florins. One clue to their status is that the nuns called each other "Juffrouw," connoting Madam, rather than the less dignified "Sister," a practice followed in only more prestigious monasteries. The accounts of the convent, almost always in the red, in RAG, Groenebriel, 46, 47, 48. Anna Maria's efforts to manage the convent's goods well are all over the convent's records, including the convent's manufacture of aloe pills, to the outrage of local apothecaries, in RAG, Groenebriel, 134; other contemplative nuns were also (in)famous for their medical efforts, as in E. Arenal and S. Schlau, *Untold Sisters: Hispanic Nuns in Their Own Words* (Albuquerque, 1989), 75–76. See also the many documents numbered 24–84 in Marechal to get a bigger sense of the convent's temporal life.

ENTERTAINMENTS AND REPUTATION: Hosting friends is inferred from the usual comments and concerns about outsiders in the bishop's visitation reports, RAG, Bisdom, B4623, B4628 especially, and from Harline, *Burdens*, chapters 11 and 12, which includes accounts of recreations and plays; no record remains of the nuns of Groenebriel putting on plays, but such was not uncommon in well-heeled convents, as reviewed by E. Weaver in "Spiritual Fun: A Study of Sixteenth-Century Tuscan Convent Theater," in *Women in the Middle Ages and the Renaissance*, ed. M. B. Rose (Syracuse, 1986), 173–206. The possession of Groenebriel's previous abbess, Francis Thevelin, in RAG, Bisdom, B4624/1, but especially BAG, Acta, 1646–57, f. 74r, February 5, 1648, when Gabriel Jaecquemijns is given permission to enter the convent and exorcize the abbess. The convent's routine, and singing of the Office, can be assessed in the bishop's visitation reports, in RAG, Bisdom, B4623, B4624, B4628.

THE CHURCH OF GROENEBRIEL: A drawing of the original church, from 1580, in Decavele, *Gent*, 118; the history of the church especially in Van der Haeghen, *Groenen Briel*, citing the seventeenth-century chronicle at length, from 292 on. RAG, Groenebriel, 72, is an account book devoted exclusively to expenses for the church.

THE RELICS OF FIACRE: These are also discussed in Van der Haeghen, *Groenen Briel*, but original documents are in RAG, Groenebriel, 20a, which include various attestations of authenticity, including the earliest of November 22, 1592, and those on the newest acquisitions from November 5, 1658, one from 1659, and August 12, 1660; other saints in the monstrance of the church included Victor, Margaret, Sebastian, Polycarpus, Jerome, Anthony, Lucia, Agnes, Monica, and still more. Bishop Triest's indulgence is included in this file and also in RAG, Bisdom, B4624/1, August 17, 1648. Approbations of the Fiacre relics in BAG, Acta, 1647–60, March 26, 1659; 1660–64, October 24, 1660.

THE NEW WALL: A special account book is devoted to this expense, in RAG, Groenebriel, 73. It receives special mention in the chronicle of the anonymous seventeenth-century sister, quoted at length by Van der Haeghen, *Groenen Briel*.

OPINIONS OF ANNA MARIA VAN HAMME: The praise is contained in the interviews for the election of a new abbess, in 1646, when she did not win, and in 1648, when she did, both in RAG, Bisdom, B4624/1. Criticism is from later visitation reports, also in RAG, Bisdom, B4628/1 and 2.

FURTHER GLIMPSES OF THE CONVENT: BAG, Acta, 1622–33, visitation by Bishop Triest, June 8, 1622, and February 1, 1624; Acta, 1646–57, March 23, 1649, installation of Anna Maria van Hamme as abbess.

Defiance

JAN BAPTIST LE MONIER AND THE VICARIATE OF GENT: His seat on the vicariate noted in BAG, Acta, 1657–60, and E. Hellin, *Histoire chronologique des évêques, et du chapitre exempt de l'église cathédrale S. Bavon à Gand* (Gent, 1772); his identity as an extraordinary confessor of Groenebriel (thus that he visited regularly but was not the regular confessor) in RAG, Groenebriel, 46 and 47, the accounts from 1653 on. The workload of the vicariate is inferred from their Acta, and that of many other bishops and diocesan councils, such as in AAM, Mechliniensia, 2–9. Their actions on March 23 and 26, 1660 in BAG, Acta, 1657–60. The new diversions are recorded in loose testimonies in the bundle RAG, Bisdom, B4629, including Catharina Cottensies and François Asseliels. The identity of Paulo Saleere and Francis Sateau is not perfectly straightforward, because elsewhere there are mentioned two men named Paul de Sadeleere and François Sorii or Sotii. The spelling of especially the first seems merely a variant to me, while the second is trickier. But given the context and the practice of irregular spelling, these seem to be the same men.

CHURCHMEN AND HOLY FRAUD: Pascal in his *Pensées* (Paris, 1952), 407, 408, among other editions. More in slightly different form in his *Dialogue on Heresies*, book II. On the belief of churchmen in relics, see the many indulgences and approbations they granted, and their own trips to holy sites, such as in the journal of Archbishop Mathias Hovius, in AAM, Mechliniensia, 10, or again Vauchez, *Sainthood*, 245. Examples of fraud include P. Marshall, "The rood of Boxley, the blood of Hailes and the defence of the Henrician church," *Journal of Ecclesiastical History* 46/4 (1995): 689, also discussed in Finucane, *Miracles and Pilgrims*, 208–10, and other cases on 33, 70, 258–60. Some consequences of fraud in Soergel, *Wondrous*, 133, 151, 157, and J. Friedman, *The Battle of the Frogs and Fairford's Flies: Miracles and the Pulp Press During the English Revolution* (New York, 1993), 140, and Sumption, *Pilgrimage*, 37. The problem of authenticity in H. Kamen, *The Phoenix and the Flame* (New Haven, 1993), 138; Snoek, *Medieval Piety*, 18; G. Gray de Cristoforia Dosi-Delfini, "Oratorie 'Reliquie' Pontremolesi in una lettera a Cosimo III," *Archivio Storico per le Province Parmensi* 35 (1983): 101–09; H. Platelle, "Reliques circulant sous un faux nom: formalisme et religion populaire," in *La religion populaire* (Paris, 1979), 96; W. Christian, *Local Religion in Sixteenth-Century Spain*

(Princeton, 1981), 171. The fraudulent priest in Brussels was Henri Costerius, recounted in C. Harline and E. Put, *A Bishop's Tale* (New Haven, 2000), chapter 7. A dispute in AAM, Mechliniensia, 6, f. 9, March 27, 1601, specifically states that an argument between a parish and an abbey over which had the authentic relics of Saint Helena was dividing the faithful and giving Protestants great opportunity for ridicule. Defenders of supernatural explanations for apparently impossible problems with relics from Snoek, *Medieval Piety*, 356, or Erasmus's repeating, satirically, the notion that God multiplied relics as he pleased, *Ten Colloquies*, 70.

EFFORTS TO PREVENT FRAUD: Snoek, *Medieval Piety*, 23, on prohibiting division; Sumption, *Pilgrimage*, 214–16, on displaying regularly; Vauchez, *Sainthood*, 428, on smell, and Harline and Put, *A Bishop's Tale*, 210–11, on reputation or logic; Geary, *Furta Sacra*, 54, on investigators returning with still other relics. Christian, *Local Religion*, 171, notes that documentation of relics was not common in Spain before the mid-sixteenth century. On emphasizing the virtues of saints, M. P. Carroll, *Madonnas That Maim* (Baltimore, 1992), 34; Finucane, *Miracles and Pilgrims*, chapter 1; Vauchez, *Sainthood*, 49, 372–74, 499–508; J. Pelikan, *The Christian Tradition: A History of the Development of Doctrine. Vol. III. The Growth of Medieval Theology (600–1300)* (Chicago, 1978), 179–81; W. Christian, *Apparitions in Late Medieval and Renaissance Spain* (Princeton, 1981); the virtues of saints were not necessarily for emulation, but for consideration in sainthood, or for pondering by the faithful to move them to piety.

THE VICARIATE'S SUMMONING OF THE TAILORS: BAG, Acta, 1657–1660, April 2, 7, 12, 13, 1660; also the loose testimonies in RAG, Bisdom, B4629. The installation of Van den Bosch in M. Cloet, ed., *Het bisdom Gent* (Gent, 1991), 79–81. The summons to the two house masters, and the chaplain, is mentioned in the tailors' attempt at plea bargain on February 3, 1661, in RAG, B4629, and a short brief in the same file noting that summons were delivered on July 12, 1660, and September 1.

ANNA MARIA'S RESPONSE: New pieces of Fiacre approved by the vicariate and bishop in BAG, Acta, 1657–1660, March 26, 1659, permission for veneration of relic of Fiacre, with letter of authentication from the prioress of the convent of Fontaines-les-Novains in France, and Acta 1660–64, October 24, 1660, approbation of a new relic of Fiacre, from France, where it had been preserved since "time immemorial" in a parish church in the barony of Bouvelinghen. The new edition of Fiacre's life was entitled, *Het wonderlyck ende miraculeus leven vanden glorieusen belyder den H. Fiacrus, in 't Vlaems gheseyt den H. Friael, den welcken van over langhen tijt ende veel jaeren is besocht gheweest inde vermaerde abdye ende clooster van Groenen-Briele tot Ghendt, alwaer verscheyden geapprobeerde Reliquien vanden selven H. sijn rustende, wiens solemnelen feestdagh is comende den 30. Augusti* (Gent, 1661). The edition also notes it was drawn from the legends of the saints by Herbertus Rosweydus, Zacharias Lippello, and a French book "approved by F. Laevinus Meytius, doctor of Theology" in 1598. Hence this was hardly a new edition in content, but only in purpose, prepared expressly to bolster the claims of Groenebriel on the saint.

Whose Fraud Anyway?

CONDEMNATIONS OF GREED: Erasmus was one of the most famous on this point, though hardly alone, in Eire, *Idols*, 44, for instance, or Christian, *Local Religion*, 104, and 247.

TAILORS' GUILD AND ECONOMIC LIFE OF GENT: Most of the material here is drawn from H. Deceulaer, *Pluriforme patronen en een verschillende snit: sociaal-economische, institutionele en culturele transformatie in de kledingsector in Antwerpen, Brussel en Gent, 1585–1800* (Amsterdam, 2001), an enormously helpful and fortuitously timed publication. Also Decavele, *Gent*, 128–29; *Algemene Geschiedenis der Nederlanden*, v. 1 (Haarlem, 1979), 124–58; J. Dambruyne, "De Gentse bouwvakambachten in sociaal-economisch perspectief (1540–1795)," in C. Lis, H. Soly, eds., *Werken volgens de regels: ambachten in Brabant en Vlaanderen, 1500–1800* (Brussels, 1994): 51–66, especially; H. van Werveke, *Gent: Schets van een Sociale Geschiedenis* (Gent, 1947), 7–8; finally M. Cloet, ed., *Itinerarium visitationum Antonii Triest, episcopi gandavensis (1623–1654). De visitatieverslagen van bisschop Triest* (Leuven, 1976), 140, a brief account of his visit to the tailors' chapel in 1629, plus RAG, Bisdom, B2851, his visit of September 6, 1645, K18449, a visitation by a later bishop in 1671, and K18462, a visitation of February 9, 1778.

PINNING DOWN FRAUD: On shrines not necessarily possessing relics of the saints honored there, see Soergel, *Wondrous*, 24. Rules of property suspended, in Geary, *Furta Sacra*, 108–15, Sumption, *Pilgrimage*, 34; an example in AAM, Jezuieten, 16:9, includes a related and common justification from an Italian priest that he stole some relics from Cologne because they would be better respected and venerated in Italy. The problem of simulated sanctity or rivals in sanctity in F. Beer, *Women and Mystical Experience in the Middle Ages* (Woodbridge, 1992), 12, citing the ridicule of Jan Ruysbroek toward Bloemardinne of Brussels, but her followers ridiculed as much the more famous Ruysbroek; also F. Tomizza, *Heavenly Supper* (Chicago, 1991), which includes a more clear-cut case of fraud, yet a case of a woman called "Catherine of the Wounds," in Gent around 1700, suggests a more ambiguous problem—was she deliberately defrauding people or not? Her disciples were as convinced of her holiness as church leaders were convinced of her deceit; this in RAG, Bisdom, R1043/2. See especially on this the very recent A. J. Schutte, *Aspiring Saints: Pretense of Holiness, Inquisition, and Gender in the Republic of Venice, 1618–1750* (Baltimore and London, 2001). Wunderli, *Peasant Fires*, 118, 128 notes people recanting miracles they had claimed, or admitting they had been paid to claim, but were all such recantations done without pressure, from churchmen predisposed to condemn them? This isn't evidence, of course, but a predisposition to support or condemn a wondrous event was common. Guibert of Nogent's quote in Sumption, *Pilgrimage*, 43, Caesarius of Heisterbach's, 86, and Paulinus of Nola's, 212.

TAILORS' LAST DEFENSES AND CONDEMNATIONS: Their September defenses are inferred from a brief written by the ecclesiastical court, on September 18, 1660, in RAG, Bisdom, B4629. More testimony from pilgrims in the same file, as are the tailors' partial confession of wrongdoing and the court's final judgment.

ENDINGS: The argument over the hedge in Vanderhaeghen, *Groenen Briel*, 278, June 27, 1704. That pilgrims were still coming to Groenebriel after 1700 in RAG, Bisdom, B4628/8, a comment by J. Ooms, writing to the bishop; later letters of events in 1793 and 1811 are also in this file.

CHAPTER FOUR

Hiding the Host

The folder on Aldegonde is in AAM, Officialiteit, 10, number 3. This collection has not yet been indexed or inventoried, however, and it's possible that the numbering will change or has changed. The documents are interviews with her on May 31, 1652, June 13–15, and June 25, plus interviews with other witnesses on June 15, 18, 23. The names of the men who conducted the first interview are given: a certain Canon Daniels and a J. Goubault, possibly a minor canon of St. Goedele's, according to P. De Ridder, *Inventaris van het oud archief van de kapittelkerk van Sint-Michiel en Sint-Goedele te Brussel*, 3 vols. (Brussels, 1987–88), no. 902. But the name, or names, of the later interviewers were not recorded; the hand is clearly different from the first interview, however. And it is only probable that there were two interviewers present the second time. Also included in this folder are a few letters from other persons asked for information: a certain Antony van Berchem, in Antwerp, dated July 4, 1652; a Jacques Leentkens, dated October 13, 1652; and a priest from Gent, undated but also late 1652.

The opening scene in the chapel is drawn especially from testimony of Jennie Poisan, Aldegonde's roommate; Elisabeth Peeters, another resident of the House for Penitent Daughters; and the mistresses of the House—Marie de Graff and Anna vande Schreynen. The configuration of the chapel may be only roughly inferred from the documents: clearly the sisters went forward to a window that divided them from the choir, the classic division of convent churches as well. In fact, the documents give me the idea that this chapel was connected to a larger church, and set off from it by a wall, behind which sat the Penitent Daughters.

REFORMING INSTITUTIONS, AND THE STATUS OF ALDEGONDE'S HOUSE: The first interviewers note that Aldegonde appeared before them in the "House for Penitent Daughters"—almost exactly the name of a full-fledged convent in

Brussels, which was also variously called Bethanie, the White Ladies, or the Sisters of Mary Magdalene, in AAM, Kloosters, Bethanie Brussels. At first I assumed that this was where Aldegonde stayed. But upon closer inspection, it was clear that Bethanie did not include at this time the mistresses Marie de Graff or Anna vande Schreynen, either as nuns or lay sisters. Moreover, the documents about Bethanie include no mention of a subsidiary House for Penitent Daughters. Hence I concluded that Aldegonde's place was a separate institution, probably under the supervision of Archbishop Boonen, and part of the growing number and variety of reforming houses for women. R. Foncke, "Uit de rekeningen van Aartsbisschop Boonen's testament—uitvoerders," *De Brabander* 3 (1923): 101–04, suggests Boonen founded this house, on the canal toward Rupel. But M.E. Perry, "Magdalens and Jezebels in Counter-Reformation Spain," in A. J. Cruz and M. E. Perry, eds., *Culture and Control in Counter-Reformation Spain* (Minneapolis, 1992), 133, suggests that some convents for former prostitutes did include separate lay quarters for recent entrants, a practice decried by Rome that insisted that professed nuns were to supervise and teach directly the converting prostitutes. Perhaps something similar existed in Bethanie. More on the new sorts of female reform institutions in S. Cohen, *The Evolution of Women's Asylums Since 1500: From Refuges for Ex-Prostitutes to Shelters for Battered Women* (Oxford, 1992), especially 3–32, 36, 56–79, 81–86, 105–106, 114, 114–116.

On keeping a candle next to the soiled host, see G. J. C. Snoek, *Medieval Piety: From Relics to the Eucharist* (Leiden, 1995), 60, 227.

Abusing the Miracle

DEVELOPMENT AND PRESTIGE OF THE EUCHARIST, INCLUDING AFTER THE REFORMATION: C. M. A. Caspers, *De eucharistische vroomheid en het feest van sacramentsdag in de Nederlanden tijdens de late middeleeuwen* (Leuven, 1992), especially chapter 4; C. Caspers, G. Lukken, G. Rouwhorst, eds., *Bread of Heaven: Customs and Practices Surrounding Holy Communion* (The Hague, 1995); Snoek, *Medieval Piety*, 1, 2, 4, 5, 40, 58, 60, 78, 98, 120, 179, 224, 227, 235, 300, 350; M. Rubin, *Corpus Christi: The Eucharist in Late Medieval Culture* (Cambridge, 1991), 36–46, 81, 113, 291; P. Geary, *Furta Sacra: Thefts of Relics in the Central Middle Ages* (Princeton, 1990), 25; E. Muir, *Ritual in Early Modern Europe* (Cambridge, 1997), 160–64; P. Camporesi, *The Fear of Hell: Images of Damnation and Salvation in Early Modern Europe* (University Park, PA, 1990), 166–70; M. Steven Ydens, *Historie van het H. Sacrament van Mirakelen, Berustende tot Bruessel inde Collegiale kercke van S. Goedele*, (Brussels, 1608), 1, 76, discussed as well in L. Duerloo, W. Thomas, *Albrecht & Isabella, 1598–1621* (Brepols, 1998), 237, A. Pasture, *La Restauration Religieuse aux Pays Bas sous les Archiducs Albert et Isabelle (1596–1633)* (Leuven, 1925), 330, and F. Costerus, *Dialogue oft T'samen-sprekinge over de solemnele processie des H. Sacraments van Mirakelen, jaerlycx te Bruessel ghehouden . . .* (Brussels, 1611), which is especially concerned with refuting Protestant criticisms. Also K. Thomas, *Religion and the Decline of Magic* (New York, 1971), 33; and the

Council of Trent, session 13, chapter 3, as in J. Waterworth, *The Canons and Decrees of the Sacred and Ecumenical Council of Trent* (London, 1848), 76–79, 82–84; M. P. Carroll, *Madonnas that Maim* (Baltimore, 1992), 118.

FREQUENT COMMUNION, ESPECIALLY FOR WOMEN: C. W. Bynum, *Holy Feast and Holy Fast: The Religious Significance of Food to Medieval Women* (Berkeley, 1987), chapters 4–7 especially; Rubin, *Corpus Christi*, 120; and R. Bell, *Holy Anorexia* (Chicago, 1985).

FEAR OF RECEIVING THE HOST UNWORTHILY: Rubin, *Corpus Christi*, and *Gentile Tales: The Narrative Assault on Late Medieval Jews* (New Haven, 1999), 34; Snoek, *Medieval Piety*, 53; J. Grubb, *Provincial Families of the Renaissance: Private and Public Life in the Veneto* (Baltimore, 1996), devotes a chapter to nonreception of the host; D. Sabean, *Power in the Blood* (Cambridge, 1984), chapter 1; L. Burkhart, *The Slippery Earth: Nahua-Christian Moral Dialogue in Sixteenth-Century Mexico* (Tucson, 1980), for this idea in the new world.

USING THE HOST PRIVATELY, OFTEN IN IMITATION OF THE CLERGY: Rubin, *Corpus Christi*, 63, 66, 335–41; *Gentile Tales*, 54, 96; Snoek, *Medieval Piety*, 49, 59, 77, 82, 90, 309, 317, 341, 354, 363, 375, 377; R. Gaston, review of M. Rubin, *Corpus Christi*, in *Journal of Ecclesiastical History* 47/1 (January 1996): 157–59, on the sacramentals, as well as R. Scribner, "Cosmic Order and Daily Life: Sacred and Secular in Pre-Industrial German Society," in K. Von Greyerz, ed., *Religion and Society in Early Modern Europe: 1500–1800* (London, 1984), 23; R. Finucane, *Miracles and Pilgrims: Popular Beliefs in Medieval England* (London, 1977), 198; Thomas, *Decline of Magic*, 33, 34, 41, 181, 255, 267; D. Gentilcore, *From Bishop to Witch* (Manchester, 1992), 102–03; Trent, Session 12; P. Soergel, *Wondrous in His Saints* (Berkeley, 1993), 167; Muir, *Ritual*, 216; AAM, Kloosters, Franciscanen, Generalia, 12, case of Francis Impens, an unauthorized priest-exorcizer, and medieval examples in J. Toussaert, *Le sentiment religieux en Flandre à la fin du Moyen-Age* (Paris, 1963). For various prayer formulas see J. Van Haver, *Nederlandse Incantatieliteratuur: een gecommentarieerd compendium van Nederlandse bezweringsformules* (Gent, 1964), 50, 243–46, 389, 411; G. Rooijakkers, *Rituele repertoires. Volkscultuur in oostelijk Noord-Brabant* (1559–1853) (Nijmegen, 1994), 607; Carroll, *Madonnas that Maim*, 121, 122; AAM, Vicariaat, III, V, Belezingen en exorcismen, a nineteenth-century transcription of a series of cases on magic in Wommersom, from 1592 to 1797.

JEWS AND ALLEGED HOST DESECRATION: Rubin, *Gentile Tales*, 1, 28, 71, 80, 99; Muir, *Ritual*, 215–16; M. Pauli, *Vier Historien van het H. Sacrament van Mirakel, in de Abdije van Hercken-rode in t'landt van Luyck, ten Augustijnen tot Gendt, S. Goedelen tot Brussel, Ten Augustijnen tot Loven* (Antwerp, 1762); Ydens, *Historie van het H. Sacrament van Mirakelen*; Pasture, *Restauration*, 330.

PROTESTANTS AND HOST DESECRATION: Rubin, *Corpus Christi*, 354, 355, plus 319 for actions against the host even before the Reformation, and continued by Protestants.

CATHOLICS AND WITCHES AND HOST DESECRATION: F. Vanhemelryck, *Heksenprocessen in de Nederlanden* (Leuven, 1982), 121; L. Maes, *Vijf eeuwen stedelijk strafrecht. Bijdrage tot de rechts- en cultuurgeschiedenis der Nederlanden* (Antwerp and The Hague, 1947), 207; Rubin, *Gentile Tales*, 34, 68, 71, 83, 125; Pasture, *Restauration*, 53–54, 331; Camporesi, *Fear of Hell*, 125–42; Muir, *Ritual*, 217.

A *Sorry Tale*

The brothel next to the Laken gate in J. De Brouwer, *De kerkelijke rechtspraak en haar evolutie in de bisdommen Antwerpen, Gent en Mechelen tussen 1570 en 1795*, 2 vols. (Tielt, 1971–72), II, 552.

THE IMPORTANCE OF CIRCUMSTANCE AND INTENT IN CONFESSION, AND ITS INFLUENCE ON CANON LAW: J. Delumeau, *L'aveu et le pardon: les difficultés de la confession, XIIIe–XVIIIe* siècles (Paris, 1990), 101–05; J. A. Brundage, *Medieval Canon Law* (New York, 1995), 171; H. C. E. Midelfort, *A History of Madness in Sixteenth-Century Germany* (Stanford, 1999), 190.

DISTANCE AND SIMILARITY BETWEEN CHURCHMEN AND ORDINARY BELIEVERS: See the notes under "The Bishop's Men," in Chapter 2, which discusses this topic from another point of view, but relies on many of the same sources; especially A. Vauchez, *Sainthood in the Later Middle Ages* (Cambridge, 1997), has much to say about the fundamental agreement among all levels of society in regard to the supernatural. Gentilcore, *From Bishop to Witch*, 218, notes that the church tried to lump all magic together, including healing, divination, love magic, spells, treasure hunting, and so forth, for all were ultimately from the devil. The question of magic will be a central feature of Chapter 5.

ALDEGONDE'S NARRATIVE: From the interview of June 13–15.

MAY TREES AND SPINNING BEES AND OTHER YOUTHFUL ACTIVITIES: Rooijakkers, *Rituele repertoires*, 330, 348, 360. "The flowers" in M. Wiesner, *Women and Gender in Early Modern Europe* (Cambridge, 1993), 44.

EAVESDROPPING: J. Sumption, *Pilgrimage: An Image of Medieval Religion* (London, 1975), 12, 13.

SPIRITUAL DAUGHTERS: A good starting point is M. De Vroede, *Kwezels en zusters: de geestelijke dochters in de Zuidelijke Nederlanden, 17de en 18de eeuw* (Brussels, 1994).

SEXUAL ABUSE AND EARLY SEXUAL ACTIVITY: S. Nordgren, "Too Much, Too Soon," Associated Press article, September 11, 1995, citing a study conducted by scholars at the University of Washington.

UNMARRIED POPULATION OF NORTHWESTERN EUROPE: In Wiesner, *Women and Gender*, 62, 100.

PROSTITUTION AND POVERTY: Cohen, *Women's Asylums*, 20, 36; M. Van der Auwera, "Armoede en sociale politiek te Mechelen in de 16e en de 18e eeuw," *Bijdragen tot de Geschiedenis* 59 (1976): 227–48; E. Muylle, "Een stedelijk sociaal patroon: Mechelen circa 1643," *Bijdragen tot de Geschiedenis* 66 (1983): 169–87.

FIGHTING PROSTITUTION AFTER THE REFORMATION: U. Rublack, *The Crimes of Women in Early Modern Germany* (Oxford, 1999); P. Schuster, *Das Frauenhaus: Städtische Bordelle in Deutschland (1350–1600)* (Paderborn, 1992). J. Brundage, "Prostitution in the Medieval Canon Law," *Signs* 1/4 (1976): 835, on medieval precedents for targeting especially the pimps, procurers, and brothel keepers; Cohen, *Women's Asylums*, 18, notes the leading role played by Jesuits in this effort, and, in fact, it was a Jesuit in Mechelen, Pater Grinsel, who arranged a place for Aldegonde in the Hospice of St. Julian, then later in the House for Penitent Daughters in Brussels.

ON CHURCH COURTS AND THE CLERGY: De Brouwer, *Rechtspraak*, I, part 2, chapter 3. Also S. Haliczer, *Sexuality in the Confessional: A Sacrament Profaned* (Oxford, 1996).

THE MEDIEVAL HERITAGE OF PROSTITUTION: Brundage, "Prostitution," 830–40; Cohen, *Women's Asylums*, 15, 43; Rublack, *Crimes*; Schuster, *Das Frauenhaus*; De Brouwer, *Kerkelijke Rechtspraak*, I, 140; S. Altink, *Huizen van Illusies: Bordelen en Prostitutie van Middeleeuwen tot Heden* (Antwerp, 1983), 60, claims that Madrid had eight hundred brothels.

EXECUTIONERS AND BROTHELS: Brundage, "Prostitution," 840.

CONTRACEPTION AND ABORTION: Wiesner, *Women and Gender*, 64, 70, 75, 76; Gentilcore, *From Bishop to Witch*, 149.

The Heart of the Matter

AGE AT FIRST COMMUNION: C. Bruneel, "L'âge de la communion sous l'ancien régime: une direction de recherche," *Revue d'Histoire Ecclésiastique* 71 (1976): 392–401.

IRREVERENT QUESTIONS ABOUT THE HOST: One such warning in J. Evangelista, *Het Eeuwigh Leven, Qui manducat meam Carnem, et bibit meum Sanguinem*, *habet vitam Aeternam* . . . (Leuven, 1644), chapters 4 and 5, where he warns not to think too hard about how this happens but simply follow the church, and that which one doesn't understand only confirms one's valiant faith.

WORRIES ABOUT CONFESSORS: Haliczer, *Sexuality in the Confessional*, but especially Delumeau, *L'aveu et le pardon*, 15, 17, 20–31, 42, 48–49, 101–05.

ANTONETTE: This friend of Aldegonde is mentioned several times; the description of her appearance is from a note on a letter about her; Antony van Berchem, October 13, 1652, cited at the beginning of this chapter.

COUPLERS AND LOVE MAGIC: Gentilcore, *Bishop to Witch*, 210–12; Van Haver, *Nederlandse Incantatieliteratuur*, 395, 396; Muir, *Ritual*, 217; the description of the coupler here from Altink, *Huizen van Illusies*, 57; Thomas, *Decline of Magic*, 34; Camporesi, *Fear of Hell*, 142; M. E. Perry, *Gender and Disorder in Early Modern Seville* (Princeton, 1990), 118, on the handful of cases heard by the Inquisition regarding love-magic, though no use of the host is mentioned specifically.

OTHER MAGIC, AND ROPEDANCERS: Rooijakkers, *Rituele repertoires*, who notes ropedancers among such professional entertainers as acrobats and market singers, all of whom were regularly banned from performing on holy days, near churches or in taverns; Thomas, *Decline of Magic*, section on Magic, for a multitude of similar magical examples, including 181 for "Matthew, Mark, Luke, and John . . ." Other examples from De Brouwer, *Kerkelijke Rechtspraak*, I, 96–97, AAM, Vicariate, III.V. Belezingen en Exorcismen, Van Haver, *Nederlandse Incantatieliteratuur*, 243–46, 411. More on magic in Chapter 5.

The Search for Corroboration

CONFESSION AND PROOF: Brundage, *Canon Law*, 132, 177; R. Wunderli, *Peasant Fires: The Drummer of Niklashausen* (Bloomington, 1992), 133; De Brouwer, *Kerkelijke Rechtspraak*, I, 34, 88, on torture. Gratian's comment about harlots in Brundage, "Prostitution," 843.

INCEST: Appropriate punishments in De Brouwer, *Kerkelijke Rechtspraak*, I, 137–38.

STEPPARENTS: Finucane, *Miracles and Pilgrims*, 110.

INTERVIEWS WITH OTHER WITNESSES: Conducted between June 15 and June 23, 1652, cited at the beginning of this chapter note. The letters sent out by interviewers or the court, about Aldegonde's activities elsewhere, also there.

SILENCE ABOUT THE PAST IN HOUSES OF REFORM: This was a major problem in Bethanie, in Brussels; AAM, Kloosters, Bethanie Brussels, visitations of 1590 to 1650.

ALDEGONDE'S APPEARANCE: Testimony of Mertin Garzias, who believed Aldegonde was about thirty, but looked much older; Aldegonde at this time was only twenty-two!

MAY WITH THE EVIL EYES: Her proper name is Mayken, or Maria, Bisschops; De Brouwer, *Kerkelijke Rechtspraak*, II, 552, identifies a May With the Green Eyes accused of brothel keeping, in 1664, but this is the same woman, for she too is Mayken Bisschops. Obviously there was something striking about her eyes, or De Brouwer transcribed "quaede" (evil) as "groene" (green).

CURSES UPON AND KILLING OF BABIES: J. Friedman, *The Battle of the Frogs and Fairford's Flies* (New York, 1993), 180; or W. L. Braekman, *Spel en Kwel in Vroeger Tijd: Verkenningen van charivari, exorcisme, toverij, spot en spel in Vlaanderen* (Gent, 1992), 118, the example of a witch taking a baby in her arms and breathing on it, among other examples.

The Search for Guilt

INCONCLUSIVE QUALITY OF MANY LEGAL PROCEEDINGS: Brundage, *Canon Law*, 134, but this is also apparent from a perusal through the huge collection of Officialiteit in the AAM.

POSSIBLE PUNISHMENTS: Listed at length in De Brouwer, *Kerkelijke Rechtspraak*, I, 185–262, and the division into major and minor offenses on 89.

SEXUALITY, AND PUNISHMENT OF PROSTITUTION: Brundage, "Prostitution," 825–45, especially 835–36. Vauchez, *Sainthood*, 370, on women and the clerical mind; Wiesner, *Women and Gender*, 46–48; Friedman, *Battle of the Frogs*, 180, 194; Cohen, *Women's Asylums*, 15, 43; Rublack, *Crimes*; and Schuster, *Das Frauenhaus*. De Brouwer, *Kerkelijke Rechtspraak*, I, 140 on prosecution of brothels, and I, 285–86 on growing weariness among courts in the eighteenth century with prosecuting prostitution.

JUDICIAL PROCEEDINGS AND CULPABILITY: The major work here is Midelfort, *A History of Madness*, which includes an entire chapter on the history of the insanity defense; 385 on "flagrant" sin, "terror," and natural contributors to mental illness; 190 on the "interior condition of the heart." Also helpful were M. Goodich, *Violence and Miracle in the Fourteenth Century* (Chicago, 1995), 69; S. Nalle, *Mad for God: Bartolomé Sanchez, The Secret Messiah of Cardente* (Charlottesville, 2001), 52–85, 89–101, 103–07, 125–27, 136, 147, 152, 153–55; R. Kingdon, *Adultery and Divorce in Calvin's Geneva* (Cambridge, 1995), 60–61; B. Gregory, *Salvation at Stake: Christian Martyrdom in Early Modern Europe* (Cambridge, 1999), 77–81.

POSSESSION: D. P. Walker, *Unclean Spirits: Possession and Exorcism in France and England in the Late Sixteenth and Early Seventeenth Centuries* (Philadelphia, 1981).

THE POSSIBILITY OF WITCHCRAFT: For treatment of suspected witches generally, see Thomas, *Decline of Magic*, section on witchcraft; Vanhemelryck, *Heksenprocessen;* L. Maes, "Un procès de sorcellerie en 1642, évalué à la lumière de récentes études européennes et d'après la législation et la théorie du droit du XVIIe siècle," *Handelingen van de Koninklijke Kring van Mechelen* 79 (1975): 243–68, which dates the last trial for witchcraft in Brussels at 1636; but Braekman, *Spel en Kwel*, 116, 206, lists various cases around 1650, and D. Van Ysacker, "Het aandeel van de zuidelijke nederlanden in de europese heksenvervolging (1450–1685)," *Trajecta* 9/4 (2000): 329–49, who notes the last burning in 1685; J. Klaits, *Servants of Satan* (Bloomington, 1985); B. Levack, *The Witch-Hunt in Early Modern Europe* (New York, 1987), G. Rooijakkers, L. Dresen-Coenders, M. Geerdes, eds., *Duivelsbeelden: een cultuurhistorische speurtocht door de Lage Landen* (Baarn, 1994); and especially Midelfort, *A History of Madness*, which devotes much of the chapter on the insanity defense to witchcraft, especially 196–223. The use of torture on July 4, 1652, in the presence of the judge in De Brouwer, *Kerkelijke Rechtspraak*, I, 88; the execution of two defrocked priests in I, xxvii, October 1625 and February 1652. The use of the host as a distinguishing factor in identifying witches in Wiesner, *Women and Gender*, 231, referring to Spain and Italy.

APPROACHES TO INSANITY: Above, plus Midelfort, *A History of Madness*, 183–85, 190, and especially 196–223, the medical influences of Weyer and Zacchia.

PUNISHMENTS FOR THE UNSOUND OF MIND, AND COST: De Brouwer, *Kerkelijke Rechtspraak*, I, 185–262, lists ordinary punishments, all of which might be mitigated if one were deemed only partially responsible. Midelfort, *A History of Madness*, 189, 190, 192, 387. Expenses in the archbishop's own small prison ran to six stivers a day, a weighty expense for a poor family such as Aldegonde's. One fellow was locked up there forever, however, so it was not impossible that she remained there too. The seventy times seven idea is in Cohen, *Women's Asylums*, 36. Bethanie in AAM, Kloosters, Bethanie Brussels, especially the visitations of the archbishop from 1590 on.

MARIE PANTOUFFER: De Brouwer, *Kerkelijke Rechtspraak*, II, 560, notes that she was married to a Spaniard, that her husband was hanged as a horse thief, that she "ran with every man" during Lent of 1651, was friends with the daughter of the executioner of Brussels, and on August 7, 1654 was accused of prostitution again, working in the brothel of Petrus Smets, alias Peter the Piper.

CHAPTER FIVE

Virtually all of the manuscript sources for the Helmont trial are in the AAM, in two specially bound registers, hereafter noted as Helmont I and II, totaling about six hundred recto-verso folios. The documents in each register are generally easily distinguishable, and have been numbered consecutively by a later hand. Hence, I:2, means volume I, document number 2. Many of the documents in registers I and II were published wholly or partially in C. Broeckx, "Notice sur le manuscrit Causa J. B. Helmonitii, déposé aux Archives Archiépiscopales de Malines," *Annales de l'Académie Royale d'Archéologie de Belgique* (1852): 277–327, 341–67; and Broeckx, "Interrogatoires du Docteur J. B. van Helmont, sur le Magnétisme animal," *Annales de l'Académie Royale d'Archéologie de Belgique* (1856): 306–50. Many biographers and historians since have relied on these published sources for their information, but this is not without problems. First, R. Halleux, "Helmontiana," *Mededelingen van de Koninklijke Academie voor Wetenschappen, Letteren en Schone Kunsten* (1983): 33–36, points out that there are numerous errors in the transcriptions, and second, a significant chunk of the documents has not been published. I have consulted both the originals and Broeckx's transcriptions, plus documents not previously published, including the correspondence among the Helmont family, the Council of Brabant, and the diocesan court of Mechelen, the significance of which is discussed further below.

A couple of other loose documents somehow ended up separately in the still uncatalogued boxes of the diocesan court, or "Officialiteit," boxes 14 and 15. These included a copy of his *Eisagoge in artem medicam*, his summary of Paracelsus, written in 1607 and published in 1634, 158 pages long; this work, including marginal notes in Helmont's hand, shows early enthusiasm for Paracelsus, which Helmont amended later.

SCENE OF THE ARREST: Taken from information in Helmont I:2, Isabella van Halmale to the Chancellor of Brabant, May 6, 1634; I:3, Diocesan Court to the Chancellor, May 7, 1634; I:7, Van Halmale to the Judge, July 5, 1634; I:12, Van Halmale to the Diocesan Court, October 24, 1634; I:15, Diocesan Court to Van Halmale.

The Making of an Adept

HELMONT'S BIOGRAPHY AND WORK: The literature grows rapidly, and I list here only those I found most useful, beginning with the numerous works available in English by W. Pagel, *Joan Baptista Van Helmont, Reformer of Science and Medi-*

cine (Cambridge, 1982); "The Spectre of Van Helmont and the Idea of Continuity in the History of Chemistry," in M. Teich and R. Young, eds., *Changing Perspectives in the History of Science: Essays in Honor of Joseph Needham* (London, 1973); "The Position of Harvey and Van Helmont in the History of European Thought," *Journal of the History of Medicine and Allied Sciences* 13 (1958): 186–98; "The Debt of Science and Medicine to a Devout Belief in God. Illustrated by the Work of J. B. van Helmont," *Journal of the Transactions of the Victoria Institute* 74 (1942): 99–115, "Van Helmont's Concept of Disease—To Be or Not to Be? The Influence of Paracelsus," in a variorum collection of Pagel's writings entitled *From Paracelsus to Van Helmont: Studies in Renaissance Medicine and Science* (London, 1986), which also includes "Medieval and Renaissance Contributions to Knowledge of the Brain and Its Functions," "The 'Wild Spirit' (Gas) of John Baptist van Helmont (1579–1644) and Paracelsus," "J.B. van Helmont, De Tempore, and Biological Time," and "The Smiling Spleen." Also important are A. G. Debus, *Man and Nature in the Renaissance* (Cambridge, 1978), 116–31; *The Chemical Philosophy: Paracelsian Science and Medicine in the Sixteenth and Seventeenth Centuries*, 2 vols. (New York, 1977), especially v. 1, 277–92 on the weapon-salve controversy, and the first section of v. 2 on Helmont, including 376, the assessment of Helmont as the most important chemical philosopher of the early seventeenth century; "The Chemical Debates of the Seventeenth Century: The Reaction to Robert Fludd and Jean Baptiste van Helmont," in M. L. Righini Bonelli and W. Shea, eds., *Reason, Experiment, and Mysticism in the Scientific Revolution* (London, 1975), 20–23, 44, especially on the perfection of the imperfect in nature.

Critical in Dutch and French are A. J. J. Van de Velde, "Helmontiana I: 'De Dageraad' van J. V. van Helmont," *Verslagen en Mededelingen van de Koninklijke Vlaamse Academie voor Taal- en Letterkunde* (1929): 453–76; "Helmontiana II" (1929): 715–35; "Helmontiana III" (1929): 857–79; "Helmontiana IV" (1932): 109–22; and "Helmontiana V" (1936): 340–87. These must be supplemented with important recent studies by R. Halleux, "Helmontiana," op. cit., which does a superb job of setting Helmont's ideas in the context of Natural Philosophy and Paracelsianism, "Helmontiana II," *Mededelingen van de Koninklijke Academie voor Wetenschappen, Letteren en Schone Kunsten* (1987): 17–36; "Visages de Van Helmont, depuis Hélène Metzger jusqu'à Walter Pagel," *Corpus* (1988): 35–43; "Gnose et expérience dans la philosophie chimique de Jean-Baptiste Van Helmont," *Bulletin de la Classe des sciences* 65 (1979): 217–27; "Theory and Experiment in the Early Writings of Johan Baptist van Helmont," in D. Batens and J. P. van Bendegem, eds., *Theory and Experiment* (Reidel, 1988): 93–101.

Other studies include P. Nève de Mévergnies, *Jean Baptiste van Helmont, Philosophe par le feu* (Liège, 1935), which basically pokes fun at those trying to make Helmont a genius or, more provincially, Flemish hero, because he is clearly embarrassed by Helmont's mysticism and Natural Philosophy; H. S. Redgrove and I. M. L. Redgrove, *Joannes Baptista Van Helmont* (London, 1922); W. Rommelaere, *Études sur J. B. Van Helmont* (Brussels, 1868), 8–21; W. R. Newman, "The Corpuscular Theory of J. B. Van Helmont and its Medieval Sources," *Vivarium* 31/1 (1993): 161–91; N. E. Emerton, "Creation in the Thought of J. B. Van Helmont and Robert Fludd," in P. Rattansi and A. Clericuzio, eds., *Alchemy and Chemistry in the 16th and 17th Centuries* (Kluwer, 1994): 85–101, shows how these two Natural Philosophers used the Bible differently, though it was equally important to both of them; B. Heinecke, "The Mysticism and Science of Johann Baptista van Helmont (1579–1644)," *Ambix* 42/2 (July 1995): 65–78; A. Browne, "J. B. van Helmont's Attack on Aristotle," *Annals of Science* 36 (1979): 575–91, on Helmont's perhaps unconscious imitation of Aristotelian methods of argument; A. Clericuzio, "From van Helmont to Boyle. A Study of the Transmission of Helmontian Chemical and Medical Theories in Seventeenth-Century England," *British Journal for the History of Science* 26 (1993): 303–34, including the importance of Severinus's influence on Helmont; G. Schamelhout, "Johannes Baptista van Helmont: Medicus hermeticus, philosophus per ignem, 12 Januari 1579–30 December 1644," *Koninklijke Vlaamsche Academie voor Geneeskunde van Belgie—Verhandelingen* VII (Brussels, 1945), 339–57; M. Florkin, "Lectures: Pour salver Van Helmont," *Bulletin de l'Académie Royale de Médecine de Belgique*, VI série, 10 (1945): 355–72; H. De Waele, *J.-B. van Helmont* (Brussels, 1947). I. Kelter, "Moses the Philosopher: Catholic Authors and the Search for a Sacred Philosophy in the Early Modern Era," unpublished paper, American Catholic Historical Association Conference, April 30, 1999, notes that Valerius (1512–78) of the Trilingual College also rejected, on biblical grounds, Plato and Aristotle, showing that such anti-classical sentiments were already in the air in Leuven, despite Helmont's characteristic tone of fighting the battle alone.

Many of these studies include biographical information, but various details of that biography are addressed in "Jan Baptist van Helmont," in *NBW* (Brussels, 1987), vol. 12, cols. 329–37; G. Dez Marez, "L'État Civil de J.-B. van Helmont," *Annales de la Société Royale d'Archéologie de Bruxelles* 21 (1907): 107–23, which is countered by J. Cuvelier, "Rond J. B. van Helmont's Burgelijken Stand" (1930): 101–11; and perhaps finally solved in A. J. J. Van de Velde, "Geboorte en Overlijden van J. B. van Helmont," *Jaarboek—Koninklijke Vlaamse Academie voor Wetenschappen, Letteren en Schone Kunsten* (1943): 131–36.

DREAMING: S. F. Kruger, *Dreaming in the Middle Ages* (Cambridge, 1992); other dreams of Helmont in Redgrove and Redgrove, *Joannes Baptista van Helmont*, 22, 23.

MARTIN DEL RIO: A. Le Roy, "Martin-Antoine Del Rio," *BN*, vol. 5 (Brussels, 1876), cols. 476–91, and his famous *Disquisitionum magicarum libri sex* (1599), and P. G. Maxwell-Stuart, ed., *Martin del Rio: Investigations into Magic* (Manchester, 2000).

NATURAL PHILOSOPHY, PARACELSIANISM, AND THE ATTACKS ON TRADITIONAL SCIENCE AND MEDICINE: B. Easlea, *Witch Hunting, Magic and the New Philosophy: An Introduction to Debates of the Scientific Revolution 1450–1750*

(Atlantic Highlands, NJ, 1980), x, 12, 15, 19, 25, 26, 39, 42, 43, 89, 90–112, 135; W. Pagel, "The Reaction to Aristotle in Seventeenth-Century Biological Thought: Campanella, Van Helmont, Glanvill, Charleton, Harvey, Glisson, Descartes," in *From Paracelsus to Van Helmont*, chapter 4; W. Pagel, "Religious Motives in the Medical Biology of the XVIIth Century," *Bulletin of the History of Medicine* 3 (1935): 213–31; A. R. Hall, *The Scientific Revolution, 1500–1800* (Boston, 1954), 312–26; M. Boas, *The Scientific Renaissance, 1450–1630* (New York, 1962), 183–96; K. Johannisson, "Magic, Science, and Institutionalization in the Seventeenth and Eighteenth Centuries," in I. Merkel and A. G. Debus, eds., *Hermeticism and the Renaissance: Intellectual History and the Occult in Early Modern Europe* (Washington, 1988), 251–60; A. G. Debus and M. T. Walton, eds., *Reading the Book of Nature: The Other Side of the Scientific Revolution* (Kirksville, 1998); A. Debus, *The Chemical Philosophy: Paracelsian Science and Medicine in the Sixteenth and Seventeenth Centuries*, 2 vols. (New York, 1977); A. G. Debus, "The Medico-Chemical World of the Paracelsians," in Teich, Young, eds., *Changing Perspectives in the History of Science;* S. Shapin, *The Scientific Revolution* (Chicago, 1996), 1–3 (disputing the notion of a coherent, self-conscious scientific revolution), 12, 20, 30, 42, 57, 65, 80, 85, 89, 96, 101, 106, 109, 122–23, 136, 165; E. M. Klaaren, *Religious Origins of Modern Science: Belief in Creation in Seventeenth-Century Thought* (Eerdmans, 1977), especially v, 72–74; C. Webster, *The Great Instauration: Science, Medicine and Reform, 1626–1660* (London, 1975), especially 201–02; C. Webster, *From Paracelsus to Newton: Magic and the Making of Modern Science* (Cambridge, 1982), 1–4, 9–11, 17, 57–59, 75, 89, 100; B. Vickers, ed., *Occult and Scientific Mentalities in the Renaissance* (Cambridge, 1984), introduction; W. Eamon, *Science and the Secrets of Nature: Books of Secrets in Medieval and Early Modern Culture* (Princeton, 1994), 4, 5, 9, 39–40, 121, 140–43, 195, 196, 204, 205, 208, 211, 218, 221, 259, 270, 351; L. Daston, K. Park, *Wonders and the Order of Nature, 1150–1750* (New York, 1998), 14–18, 94, 113, 114, 121, 127–28, 142, 160, 162, 170, 172, 218–21, 229, 239; B. Janacek, "Thomas Tymme and Natural Philosophy: Prophecy, Alchemical Theology, and the Book of Nature," *Sixteenth Century Journal*, 30/4 (1999): 987–1007; G. H. Williams, "Paracelsus," in *The Oxford Encyclopedia of the Reformation*, 4 vols. (Oxford, 1996), v. 3, 211–13; C. K. Pullapilly, "Agostino Valier and the Conceptual Basis of the 'Catholic Reformation,' " *Harvard Theological Review* 85/3 (July 1992): 307, on earlier efforts to reconcile Aristotelian thought with the latest intellectual trend, in this case Humanism; H. Kearney, *Science and Change, 1500–1700* (New York, 1971), for a short, useful summary of the different traditions; K. Thomas, *Religion and the Decline of Magic* (New York, 1971), 14, on the practice among Natural Philosophers of consulting old women, herbalists, and "empirics" rather than academic medicine, and an assessment by Thomas Sydenham that the poor were better off not being able to afford traditional physicians; also 269 on John Dee, who used special stones and holy angels "to make intercessions to God to reveal to him the nature of his creation";

H. A. E. Midelfort, *A History of Madness in Sixteenth-Century Germany* (Stanford, 1999), 108, on Paracelsus's characteristic reclusiveness, like Helmont's. "Man's innate knowledge of divinity" from P. Elmer, "Medicine, Religion and the Puritan Revolution," in R. French and A. Wear, eds., *The Medical Revolution of the Seventeenth Century* (Cambridge, 1989), 34. The greater threat of learned magic in Gentilcore, *From Bishop to Witch*, 226, 261.

MORE SPECIFICALLY ON MEDICINE: French and Wear, *The Medical Revolution*, especially P. Elmer, "Medicine, Religion and the Puritan Revolution"; L. Brockliss, C. Jones, *The Medical World of Early Modern France* (Oxford, 1997); N. Siraisi, *Medieval and Early Renaissance Medicine* (Chicago, 1990); M. Lindemann, *Medicine and Society in Early Modern Europe* (Cambridge, 1999), 3–4, 23, 27, 68, 75, 79, 80 (that iatrochemistry in the guise of Christian philosophy—Helmont's system—was not what triumphed, but rather iatrochemistry without the religion), also 104, that the social background of most medical students was usually from the "ranks of the bourgeoisie and families of clerics, physicians, and lawyers," rather than the nobility, whose sons rarely entered the profession, and then only from the lower ranks; H. Binneveld and R. Dekker, eds., *Curing and Insuring. Essays on Illness in Past Times: The Netherlands, Belgium, England and Italy, 16th–20th Centuries* (Hilversum, 1993); D. Amundsen, *Medicine, Society, and Faith in the Ancient and Medieval Worlds* (Hopkins, 1996).

THE SPIRITUAL ASPIRATIONS OF ALCHEMY: D. Harkness, "Shows in the Showstone: A Theater of Alchemy and Apocalypse in the Angel Conversations of John Dee (1527–1608/9)," *Renaissance Quarterly* 49 (1996): 707–37, or K. Thomas, *Religion and the Decline of Magic* (New York, 1971), 269, 270; Seligmann, *Magic, Supernaturalism, and Religion* (New York, 1948), 87, among many examples.

The Long Arm of Magnetism

JOHAN ROBERTI: J. P. Graussem, "Jean Roberti," in *Dictionnaire de Théologie Catholique*, v. 13 (Paris, 1937), 2754–56; J. Vannerus, "Jean Roberti," *BN*, v. 19 (Brussels, 1907), 515–32.

The Magnetic Cure of Wounds: De magnetica vulnerum curatione (Victor Leroy: Paris, 1621). A later English edition was included in a publication called *A Ternary of Paradoxes*, and entitled *The Magnetick Cure of Wounds*, translated by Walter Charleton, Doctor in Physick and Physician to the late King (London, n.d., but perhaps as early as 1649). Like Helmont, Charlton later repudiated his support of the weapon-salve. Quotations in the text are from the English edition, though I have modernized spelling when it promoted clarity.

HOW THE MAGNETIC CURE WAS PUBLISHED: Halleux, "Helmontiana," is the one who attributes publication to the efforts of Jean Gallé. See also Rommelaere,

Études, 28–39, Pagel, *Joan Baptista van Helmont*, 39, Van de Velde, "Helmontiana," I and II, for other accounts of the emergence of *The Magnetic Cure*. Pagel, *Joan Baptista van Helmont*, 13, writes that even Helmont's admirer Robert Boyle specifically noted that his admiration did not extend to *The Magnetic Cure*. Primary sources include Helmont II:20 (Letter to vicariate, October 30, 1630) II:15 and II:30 (interviews); II:32 (letter to Archbishop Boonen, undated, but from contents apparently 1627); II:34 (another letter from Helmont, either to Boonen or another churchman).

THE SPECIAL QUALITIES OF BLOOD: especially P. Camporesi, *Juice of Life: The Symbolic and Magic Significance of Blood* (New York, 1995), 14–22, 28, 38; P. Niebyl, "Galen, Van Helmont, and Bloodletting," in A. G. Debus, ed., *Science, Medicine and Society in the Renaissance*, v. 2. (New York, 1972), 13–23; W. Pagel, "Harvey and Glisson on Irritability with a Note on Van Helmont," in *From Paracelsus to Van Helmont*, chapter 8.

MORE SPECIFICALLY ON MAGNETISM: P. Fara, *Sympathetic Attractions: Magnetic Practices, Beliefs, and Symbolism in Eighteenth-Century England* (Princeton, 1996), 164, 167; R. Darnton, *Mesmerism and the End of the Enlightenment in France* (Harvard, 1968); Camporesi, *Fear of Hell*, 146, for an example of sympathy but not over distance. An example of an earlier contemporary work on magnetism generally is William Gilbert, *De magnete, magneticisque corporibus, et de magno magnete tellure: physiologia nova, plurimis argumentis, et experimentis demonstrata* (London, 1600), published in a modern edition by Culture et Civilisation (Brussels, 1967). Debus, *Man and Nature*, notes as one basis of sympathy the classical Paracelsian idea of the macrocosm-microcosm: "All particular things contain in them a delineation of the whole universe." Helmont eventually rejected that macrocosm-microcosm. An objection to working over distance is summed up nicely in Estes, "Good Witches," 158: "It was a rule of nature that 'every agent worketh upon the patient by touching.' "

WITCHCRAFT AND NATURE: Besides materials above on witchcraft, see L. L. Estes, "Good Witches, Wise Men, Astrologers, and Scientists: William Perkins and the Limits of the European Witch-Hunts," in *Hermeticism and the Renaissance*, 156–61; G. K. Waite, "David Joris en de opkomst van de sceptische traditie jegens de duivel in de vroeg-moderne Nederlanden," in G. Rooijakkers, L. Dresen-Coenders, M. Geerdes, eds., *Duivelsbeelden: een cultuurhistorische speurtocht door de Lage Landen* (Baarn, 1994), 217, noting that most Netherlandish theologians after 1475 held to the traditional Augustinian view that demons could work only through natural means and that the marvels one saw from them were merely illusions, carrying the effect of being supernatural. Helmont agrees with this, and thus contradicts that part of *The Magnetic Cure* . . . which denies the devil can use nature, in Van de Velde, "Helmontiana V," 374.

RELICS: C. Webster, "Paracelsus Confronts the Saints: Miracles, Healing and the Secularization of Magic," *Social History of Medicine* 8/3 (December 1995): 402–21, which notes Paracelsus's belief that all bodies, even dead bodies, possessed curative properties, and especially saintly bodies—this was quite similar to Helmont's belief. From a modern perspective, Wortley, "Three Not-So-Miraculous Miracles," points out that if relics hadn't worked sometimes, "our forebearers would have stopped using them."

APOTHECARIES AND BALMS FROM MUMIES: Camporesi, *Juice of Life*, 21, among other references.

THE DIVINE ROLE OF PHYSICIANS: H. C. Kee, *Miracle in the Early Christian World* (New Haven, 1983), especially chapter 3, reviews the inspiring classical example of Asklepios, at whose shrine pilgrims received dreams and visions to promote their physical cures. Also D. J. Constantelos, "The Interface of Medicine and Religion," in J. T. Chirban, ed., *Health and Faith: Medical, Psychological and Religious Dimensions* (College Park, 1991), which also discusses Asklepios; Debus, *The Chemical Philosophy*, II, 357; Debus, "The Medico-Chemical World of the Paracelsians," 91; also Seligmann, *Magic*, 50.

RIVALRY BETWEEN PHYSICIANS AND CLERGY: W. Frijhoff, "Johan Wier en Jacob Vallick: Medicus tegen pastoor?" in W. de Blécourt, W. Frijhoff, M. Gijswijt-Hofstra, eds., *Grenzen van genezing: Gezondheid, ziekte en genezen in Nederland, zestiende tot begin twintigste eeuw* (Hilversum, 1993), 17–45; C. Caspers, "Duivelbannen of genezen op 'natuurlijke' wijze. De Mechelse aartsbisschoppen en hun medewerkers over exorcismen en geneeskunde, ca 1575–ca. 1800," in De Blécourt, Frijhoff, Gijswijt-Hofstra, eds., *Grenzen van genezing*, 46–66; and in the same volume, H. de Waardt, "Van exorcisten tot doctores medicinae. Geestelijken als gidsen naar genezing in de Republiek, met name in Holland, in de zestiende en de zeventiende eeuw," 88–114; finally, D. Gentilcore, "Contesting Illness in Early Modern Naples: *Miracolati*, Physicians and the Congregation of Rites," *Past & Present* 148 (1995): 117–32; Brockliss, Jones, *The Medical World of Early Modern France*, 86; Amundsen, *Medicine, Society, and Faith*, 7, notes that church fathers were wary of physicians, though not wholly opposed to medicine; French, Wear, eds., *The Medical Revolution*, especially on physicians promoting Natural Philosophy, 16–17, 34.

Interrogations

MORE SPECIFICALLY ON MAGIC AND THE CHURCH: K. Seligmann, *Magic, Supernaturalism, and Religion* (New York, 1948), 1, 38, 50, 79, 81, 83–87, 94–98, 111–16, 206, 207; R. Kieckhefer, *Magic in the Middle Ages* (Cambridge, 1989), 9–14, 45, 56, chapters 5 and 7, 176, 182–85, 191, on the distinction between demonic and natural magic emerging in the thirteenth century among some intellectuals, including churchmen, though many theologians were prepared to fear the worst; D. P. Walker, *Spiritual and Demonic Magic* (London, 1958), 36–40, 75, 76, 83, 90, 145, 178–85, on the church as a source or model of magic for ordinary believers (though it was rare for anyone to state this explicitly), the threat of "natural, non-demonic magic" to the church, and the difficulty of distinguishing between good, natural magic, which someone like Del Rio was willing to concede might exist, and demonic magic, and the example of the banquet; Del Rio also believed that demons were real and numerous, suggesting once again the important link between belief in demons and belief in God, for those such as Helmont who expanded the realm of nature and decreased the importance of demons thereby decreased the importance of God as well; G. Knight, *A History of White Magic* (New York, 1978); V. J. Flint, *The Rise of Magic in Early Medieval Europe* (Princeton, 1991), especially 13, 21 (on magic being a pejorative term by the early Middle Ages already), 33, 67, 87 (on the difficulty of the church's program to kill illicit magic while retaining general belief in supernatural power), 204, 301 (on Augustine's counsel to assess the intent of a thing in determining its origins), 304, 341, 359, 360, 380; D. O'Keefe, *Stolen Lightning: The Social Theory of Magic* (New York, 1982), 122, 210 (on the view of the medieval church as a repository of magic, and that the church "creates or models" magic for society); A. Megged, "Magic, Popular Medicine and Gender in Seventeenth-Century Mexico: The Case of Isabel de Montoya," *Social History* 19/2 (1994): 189–207; Van Haver, *Nederlandse Incantatieliteratuur*, 48 (on the special powers of certain people distinguishing them as magicians, including those born on Good Friday, or a seventh son, and so forth); Clericuzio, "From Van Helmont to Boyle," 308 (on magic to Natural Philosophers as a high knowledge of the "real nature of things").

OBJECTIONS TO THE PRETERNATURAL, AND AGRIPPA VON NETTESHEIM'S DEMONS: Daston, Park, *Wonders*, 127–28; Eamon, *Science and the Secrets of Nature*, 196; also 204 on the intent of Natural Philosophers to reduce superstition. The messiness and collapse of the preternatural in L. Daston, "Marvelous Facts and Miraculous Evidence in Early Modern Europe," *Critical Inquiry* 18 (Autumn 1991): 93–124; 106 on preternatural events being the result not merely of remarkable natural causes, but cunning work of demons.

The Difficulty of Establishing "Nature" or "Supernature": P. Dear, "Miracles, Experiments, and the Ordinary Course of Nature," *Isis* 81 (1990): 663–683; C. S. Anderson, "Divine Governance, Miracles and Laws of Nature in the Early Middle Ages: The 'De Mirabilibus Sacrae Scripturae' " (UCLA Dissertation, 1982); J. Wortley, "Three Not-So-Miraculous Miracles," in S. Campbell, B. Hall, D. Klausner, eds., *Health, Disease and Healing in Medieval Culture* (New York, 1992), 159–68.

THE SPANISH INQUISITION: H. Kamen, *The Spanish Inquisition: A Historical Revision* (New Haven, 1998), is an interesting starting point.

JEAN LEROY: Not much is preserved about him in the AAM, but his basic dates and offices are in the reading room, in a bound manuscript edited later by (ironically) a canon named P. J. van Helmont, "Codex B, Series Praepositorum, decanorum, archidiaconarum, etc.," compiled in 1817, f. 86.

THE BASIC SOURCES FOR 1627: Helmont I:2, Van Halmale to Chancellor of Brabant, May 6, 1634 refers to his being threatened with imprisonment already in 1627 or 1628; so does I:7, July 5, 1634, which states he had been threatened with imprisonment for seven years; II:7 (the condemnation of 1624; II:8 is the same text as the condemnation of 1634, but adds more signatures); II:15 (Helmont's responses in 1627); II:32 (undated letter to Boonen, but from contents 1627); II:27 (note signed by Helmont, promising to appear the next day, September 4; no year is given but the interrogation of 1627 was on this day).

FOR 1630: Helmont I:1 (criminal libellum against Helmont, with his answers); II:3 (the condemnations of 1630); II:16 (Helmont's responses in 1630); II:20 (Helmont to the Vicariate, October 30, 1630, explaining again the genesis of his work); II:21 (letter from Taillart, supporting Helmont, dated November 13, 1624, which Helmont offered as evidence); II:22 (letter from Jean Gallé, January 23, 1618, implying approval for views on magnetism); II:23 (certificate from Joannes van Ophem, a priest in St. Goedele's, and J. van Asseldonck, canon of St. Goedele's, attesting to Helmont's orthodoxy); II:24 (summons to appear in court on October 17, 1630); II:26 (decree by judge to await further judgment of the faculty of theology of Leuven); II:28 (questions put to Helmont in 1630); II:30 (interview of Helmont in 1630); II:34 (Helmont to unnamed, but Broeckx suggests Boonen, and the context makes this probable; this is also the letter in which Helmont explicitly expresses regret for having been so forthcoming in the interrogation of 1627); II:38 (Jean de la Marck to Helmont, May 6, 1618, approving ideas on magnetism); II:39 (Jean de Salme to Helmont, March 1, 1622, implying approval of magnetism but especially poking fun at Jesuits). Many of these are also included in Broeckx, "Notice," and "Interrogatoires." The "libertinage flamboyant" from R. Pintard, *Le Libertinage Érudit* (Paris, 1943), 58.

ABJURATION: Helmont II:4 is a copy of the formula prepared by Schinkelius of the faculty of theology; it's not dated, but is probably 1630, when the theologians offered their judgment of Helmont's 1627 interview.

CASE CLOSED IN 1630: A note at the end of this interrogation, "suspendatur causa in adventum D. Official," led Van de Velde to conclude that the court dropped the whole case at this time, or was prepared to. But this statement suggests to me simply a delay in the proceedings. Better evidence that someone was thinking of dropping the case came in Leroy's 1634 explanation of Helmont's arrest—namely, that Archbishop Boonen had hoped after 1630 that the case would fade into obscurity.

BIT ON POMPONAZZI: from Eamon, *Science and the Secrets of Nature*, 205.

Arrest

BASIC SOURCES, INCLUDING SEIZED ITEMS: Helmont II:10 (God, Father of the Fecundity of the Sexes); II:11 (concerning original sin and a summary of his theological errors compiled by someone else); II:25 (the judge's chronology of events in 1634); II:26 (prosecutor wishes to present additional charges, and Helmont's appearance before the judge to request release); II:29 (the three interviews of 1634); II:31 (signed explanation by Helmont of how the book came to be published); II:33 (another request by Helmont to be released from prison); II:35 (Helmont to Boonen, undated, but based on contents, especially his asking for release, March 5, 1634, the day after the arrest); II:42 *(Eisagoge)*; II:43 (Philadelphus); II:44, 48 (two commentaries by Helmont on Hippocrates); II:47 (Helmont's notes on *Het Begryp van de Duytsche Theologie)*; II:50 (Helmont's summary of current medical knowledge, 176 pages long); II:51 (External Man); some of the writings seized as evidence are not numbered, such as "Mercury Triumphant," French works on critical days and horoscopes; many of the interrogatory sources are also in Broeckx, "Notices" and "Interrogatoires."

PHILADELPHUS: The term is used in such places as "A Dialogue Philosophicall," a summary of Paracelsian thought by Thomas Tymme, in Janacek, "Thomas Tymme."

The Bitter End

EXCHANGES AMONG HELMONT (AND FAMILY), THE DIOCESAN COURT, AND THE COUNCIL OF BRABANT: This is the most important part of the collection not to be used in previous works. See II:41 (Helmont to Boonen, undated, which has nothing to do with the current case but is Helmont intervening with him on behalf of a nun of Grand Bigard; this suggests that Helmont believed he had some respect from the archbishop); I:2 (Halmale to Chancellor, May 4, 1634); I:3 (Diocesan Court to Chancellor, May 22, 1634); I:4 (Halmale to Chancellor, May 23, 1634); I:5 (Halmale to Chancellor, May 27, 1634); I:6 (Diocesan Court to Chancellor and Halmale, May 27, 1634); I:7 (Halmale to Chancellor, July 5, 1634); I:8, 9 (supporting documents for I:7); I:10 (Diocesan Court to Chancellor and Halmale, October 5, 1634); plus I:11 (various attached documents supporting jurisdiction of the Diocesan Court); I:12 (Halmale to Chancellor, October 23, 1634—97 pages long, plus supporting documents); I:15 (Diocesan Court to Chancellor and Halmale, undated, but 135 pages long, and in response to I:12); II:19 and 53 (supporting documents for Diocesan Court, opinion of three lawyers of Brussels that the Diocesan Court has jurisdiction in such cases).

COMPARISONS TO GALILEO: M. Finocchiaro, *The Galileo Affair* (Berkeley, 1989), 13–14, on the importance of politics in the proceedings, especially the recent military victories of Protestants and the Jesuit-Dominican conflict, as well as the nature of canon law, and 33, Galileo's multiple interrogations, sentencing, and imprisonment. Also S. Drake, *Galileo* (Oxford, 1980), 2, on Galileo's intention to help the Church cope with difficult new discoveries, rather than to oppose the Church; and 6–7, on Galileo's contention that he tried to unite scripture and reason, while his foes were the ones to separate them; 78, Galileo, like Helmont, was under arrest when his daughter died, but he lived the rest of his days under the surveillance of the Inquisition, and had a clear sentence pronounced upon him; and 91, Galileo was crushed by the verdict of "vehement suspicion of heresy"; J. Langford, *Galileo, Science, and the Church* (Ann Arbor, 1966); W. R. Shea, "Galileo and the Church," in Lindberg, Numbers, eds., *God and Nature*, 114–35—his discoveries with the telescope were initially hailed in Rome, though he was made to change various things in his book on sunspots, including references to "divine goodness" inspiring him to explain the Copernican system publicly; this he changed to "favorable winds"; he was also required to delete all references to scripture in one explanation of why the heavens were not immutable.

THE TENSION BETWEEN CHRISTIANITY AND SCIENCE: D. C. Lindberg, R. L. Numbers, *God and Nature: Historical Essays on the Encounter Between Christianity and Science* (Berkeley, 1986), including articles by R. S. Westman, "The Copernicans and the Churches," W. R. Shea, "Galileo and the Church," W. B. Ashworth, Jr., "Catholicism and Early Modern Science," and Pintard, *Le Libertinage Érudit*, chapters 1–3, 242, 317, on Guy Patin, Helmont's strong critic.

MIXED SENTIMENTS OF CLERGY IN THESE CONTROVERSIES: Drake, *Galileo*, 4–7, on the mixed sentiments of his clerical judges; 61, some priests sought to prove the Copernican theory from the Bible. Or Sumption, *Pilgrimage*, 273, on the Council of Constance's condemnation of Wyclif, yet many of the same people who condemned him were likewise trying to restrict the cult of the saints which Wyclif had condemned. Or Finucane, *Miracles and Pilgrims*, 54, Roger Bacon, often seen as an early father of science, might in one breath condemn certain wonder tales then in the next tell others which he held as absolutely true.

THE VAGUE ENDING: Helmont II:36, July 7, 1635, from a certain Langenhove, but not clear to whom addressed, mentions that he told the Chancellor (of the Council of Brabant) that which the addressee proposed yesterday: namely, that Helmont had permission to leave his home daily and see some sick person. II:37,

July 8, 1635, Calenus to Boonen, expressing alarm at Langenhove's letter. AAM, Archiepiscopalia, Boonen, 226 (agenda), August 13, 1635, the archbishop promises to Helmont that he may go to Mechelen to visit his sick in-law; and September 10, gives Helmont license to treat the lord of Droogenbosch; also February 4, 1637, Boonen gives documents relating to Helmont's case to an advocate named Cypoets. II:14, March 16, 1636, apparently the Council of Brabant, decreeing that, after the exchanges between the parties, it has decided that the case will be heard after all in the diocesan court. That Helmont couldn't go visit his sick children who eventually died of the plague in II:40, Helmont to Boonen, December 10, 1638, complaining of the damage and sorrows resulting from his arrest and loss of manuscripts, and the impediments of "28 months"—the latter suggests that he was not released immediately from house arrest in March 1636, but several months later. II:1, March 20, 1639, critique by Plempius (of the medical faculty at Leuven) of Erycius Mohy's "Poudre sympathieque," and thus condemning action at a distance; II:2, more criticisms from Leuven from the theology faculty of Leuven, also in 1639; II:5, extract of a letter from Dr. Moreau, of Paris and a Galenist, March 7, 1642, against Helmont's tract on fevers; II:6, extract of a letter from Plempius, April 1642, condemning Helmont's tract on fevers.

BOONEN'S ROLE: Van de Velde, "Helmontiana II," says Boonen protected Helmont; Rommelaere, *Études*, 36, cites Patin crediting Marie de Medici's intervention for Helmont.

END OF HELMONT'S LIFE: Pagel, *Joan Baptista van Helmont*, 32–33, on his continued writings about sympathetic attraction; *NBW,* 1987, and Rommelaere, *Études*, 40–43. The pardon from Boonen in Mévergnies, *Jean Baptiste van Helmont*, 142–43, drawn from Foppens, *Bibliotheca Belgica*, v. I.

HELMONT'S WRITINGS AFTER THE INTERROGATIONS FADED: *Dageraad ofte Nieuwe Opkomst der Geneeskonst, in verborgen grond-regulen der Nature* (Rotterdam, 1660), a posthumous collection of many of his writings, which includes the hope that "My entire wish, purpose and intent is that your incomprehensible name should be sanctified, not because Thou art named the best and Greatest, but because Thou alone art the All." The "Philadelphus" was never published in his lifetime, but in the nineteenth century by C. Broeckx, in *Annales de l'Academis Royale d'Archeologie de Belgique* 25 (1869): 65–138; similarly with the two commentaries on Hippocrates (II:44, 48); the 176-page manuscript summarizing medical knowledge has never been published (II:50); the *Eisagoge* was published in 1634 (II:42), the tract on Fevers in 1642, on Spa in 1624.

THE FORTUNES OF NATURAL PHILOSOPHY AND ESPECIALLY THE TRIUMPH OF MECHANICAL PHILOSOPHY AFTER HELMONT: The bit on Patin from Pintard, *Le Libertinage*, 317. A. G. Debus, "Alchemy in an Age of Reason:

the Chemical Philosophers in Early Eighteenth-Century France," in Merkel, Debus, eds., *Hermeticism and the Renaissance*, 231–250; K. Hutchison, "Supernaturalism and the Mechanical Philosophy," *History of Science* 21 (1983): 297–333; Knight, *A History of White Magic*, 123–25; Knight notes in this regard that just like the Natural Philosophers the mechanical philosophers were not a clear school, and were not wholly opposed to Natural Philosophy—in fact, some individuals, with Isaac Newton surely the most famous, promoted tenets of both, but usually are remembered for the tenets deemed acceptable by later generations, thus mainly the mechanical philosophy; Easlea, *Witch Hunting*, 19–20, notes that the mechanical philosophers did not necessarily agree among themselves, especially regarding Newton's gravity; Estes, "Good Witches," 161, points out how the mechanical philosophy was favored by the Puritan theologian William Perkins because it seemed more acceptable to God, and avoided all the unpredictability and uncertainty and charms of Natural Philosophy. Also P. Harrison, "Newtonian Science, Miracles, and the Laws of Nature," *Journal of the History of Ideas* 56/4 (October 1995): especially 531, 552. Newton's critics of his theory of gravity in Para, *Sympathetic Attractions*, 180; Debus, "The Chemical Debates," 44, on the likely influence of Helmont on Isaac Newton, for Helmont was well known in English circles by this time; Webster, *From Paracelsus to Newton*, 9, notes that Newton's copies of Helmont's books (especially his son, Franciscus Mercurius, who adopted many of the ideas of his father), were heavily annotated; also J. T. Young, *Faith, Medical Alchemy and Natural Philosophy: Johann Moriaen, Reformed Intelligencer, and the Hartlib Circle* (Aldershot, 1998), 186, for another English example of Helmont's influence; and last A. Wear, *Knowledge and Practice in English Medicine, 1550–1680* (Cambridge, 2000), which features extensive discussion of Helmont's ideas in England. Soergel, *Wondrous*, 167, on church leaders considering the laity "morally corrupt, degenerate, filled with superstition." See De Brouwer, *Kerkelijke Rechtspraak*, I, 95, who notes the frequency with which provincial synods railed against superstition, and the church court and vicariate acted against it. Bynum, "Wonder," 5, on wonder seeking its own destruction; Daston, Park, *Wonders*, 218–20, Descartes's comment that there was nothing so strange in nature that his mechanical philosophy could not explain, thus furthering the destruction of wonder. And Daston, "Marvelous Facts and Miraculous Evidence," 121–23, on the social causes of the failure of Natural Philosophy (drawing on S. Shapin, *A Social History of Truth: Civility and Science in Seventeenth-Century England* [Chicago, 1994])—miracles were linked with "rabble-rousing enthusiasts," public order would be at the mercy of "an innumerable company of croaking Enthusiasts," worried some, so that a mechanical worldview was simply safer and more pleasant; Easlea, *Witch Hunting*, 89, makes the same comment, and on 135 notes the "embarrassing social connections" of Natural Philosophy; 108 on Mersenne's anger at Giordano Bruno, for instance, for undermining Christianity with his natural magic, and the Christian basis of the mechanical philosophy; also 112, 123, 127, 135, 137, 139, 140, 150–54, 158, 180, 200, 201, 208, 210, including the quote from

Thomas Sprat. Mersenne further in Debus, *The Chemical Philosophy*, v. 2, 295–96; also W. L. Hine, "Marin Mersenne: Renaissance Naturalism and Renaissance Magic," in Vickers, *Occult and Scientific Mentalities*, 167, 168. Also on Christian roots of mechanical philosophy, Lindberg, Numbers, *God and Nature*, 12, W. B. Ashworth, Jr., "Catholicism and Early Modern Science," in Lindberg, Numbers, 136, 139; Dear, "Miracles," 674, on Mersenne's opposition to naturalism as a result of "his need to maintain the integrity of miracles;" see also A. Funkenstein, *Theology and the Scientific Imagination from the Middle Ages to the Seventeenth Century* (Princeton, 1986).

EPILOGUE

Number of modern shrines in M. Nolan and S. Nolan, *Christian Pilgrimage in Modern Western Europe* (Chapel Hill, 1989), 1–5.

OTHERWORDLY EXPLANATIONS: The miraculous staircase is in Santa Fe in the convent of the Sisters of Loretto, and discussed in C. R. Albach, "Miracle or a Wonder of Construction?" *Consulting Engineer* (December 1965); "Pope Declares Miracle Clears Way for Sainthood: Girl's Cure Is 2nd to Be Attributed to Mother Drexel," *Deseret News* (January 29, 2000), E-8; "Faith and Healing," *Time* (June 24, 1996): 58–68; "Religious Relic Saved from Fire," Associated Press, on the shroud of Turin; *De wonderbare genezing van Pieter de Rudder: Het kanoniek onderzoek, 1907–1908* (Oostakker, 1957), is an impressive case of healing in the nineteenth century. Also R. Harris, *Lourdes: Body and Spirit in the Secular Age* (New York, 1999).

CATHOLIC-PROTESTANT ARGUING: "Religious Sensitivity," *Christianity Today*, explaining the sacking of Sergio von Helder, a bishop of the Protestant Universal church in São Paulo, Brazil, after attacking an image of Our Lady of Aparcedia on live television, hitting and kicking it twenty-two times.

THE STRUGGLE FOR CONTROL OF THE HOLY: "Nun Shuts Area of Visions, Healing," *The Providence Journal*; "Oral and Written Pilgrim Tales from Northeast Brazil," *Journal of Latin American Lore* 9/2 (1983): 191–230; V. Perica, "Mary-Making in Herzegovina: From Apparition to Partition," forthcoming, discussing the problem of Medjugorje; R. Laurentin, "Le retour d'Yvonne-Aimée de Malestroit," *Historama* 21 (1985): 68–72; D. Van Biema, "Modern 'Miracles' Have Strict Rules," *Time* 145/15 (April 10, 1995): 72; J. H. Conway, M. J. Reynolds, R. Andrich, " 'Miracle' or 'Hoax' Reacton: What's Really Happening in Medjugorje," *National Catholic Reporter* 24/17 (February 19, 1988): 9; P. Carlson, L. S. Healy, "Irish Pilgrims Swear Their Statue of the Virgin Shakes, but a Local Priest Remains Unmoved," *People Weekly* 23 (September 10, 1985), 41; "Mary Tree:

Faith in a Knothole," *Salt Lake Tribune* (December 9, 2000), B-1, "Bishop Declares No Miracles: Some Faithful Unconvinced," *Salt Lake Tribune* (September 5, 1992), A-10, and many others.

SCIENCE AND MIRACLES: "Does 'Dark Energy' Pervade Empty Space? Invisible, intangible force may be so powerful that it counteracts gravity and causes stars, galaxies to split apart," *Salt Lake Tribune* (June 24, 1999): A-8; "Scientists Deny Clone Report," Associated Press, March 9, 1997, London; "Research: Spirituality Is Good Medicine," *Daily Herald* (February 3, 2001): C-4; "Prayer Seems Linked to Relieving Illness, but Is It God at Work?" *Salt Lake Tribune* (December 28, 2000): C-2.

ILLUSTRATIONS AND CREDITS

Map, page ix: The Spanish Netherlands After 1629

Prologue, page xii: Kathryn Richey, *The Abbey of Park*

Chapter one, page 10: An Early Chapel at the Jesus Oak. Adaptation of the original, in the first history of the shrine, Bartholomeus Segers, *Den Pelgrim van Sonien-Bosche naer O.L. Vrauw van Iesukens-eyck* (Brussels, 1661)

Map, page 19: Jesus Oak and Environs, Kathryn Richey

Chapter two, page 52: Studio of Peter Paul Rubens (1577–1640), Flemish, *The Virgin Nursing the Christ Child*, oil on panel, Gift of Mrs. Richard A. Hudnut, Utah Museum of Fine Arts, University of Utah, Salt Lake City, Museum #1951.015

Chapter three, page 92: J. Van Vliet, *The Tailor*. Copyright Royal Library Albert I, Brussels (Prentenkabinet).

Map, page 96: The Tailors' Chapel and the Groenebriel, Kathryn Richey

Chapter four, page 126: Dirck van Baburen, (1590/95–1624),

Dutch, *The Procuress*, 1622. Courtesy, Museum of Fine Arts, Boston. Reproduced with permission.

Chapter five, page 178: D. Ryckaert, *Alchemist in His Laboratory*. Royal Museum of Fine Arts, Belgium.

Epilogue, page 240: *Panorama of the Jesus Oak*. Archive of the Abbey of Park.

ACKNOWLEDGMENTS

A summer stipend and fellowship from the National Endowment for the Humanities, a research fellowship from the Katholieke Universiteit Leuven (KUL) in Belgium, and various grants from the History Department, David M. Kennedy Center, and College of Family, Home, and Social Sciences at Brigham Young University supported the research and writing of this book. To all of them my profound thanks.

Prior Swaerte of the Abbey of Park, in Belgium, kindly shared his archives, while Eddy Put generously pointed out to me there the files of the Jesus Oak. Constant Van de Wiel, longtime archivist of the Archdiocese of Mechelen-Brussels, and the current archivist, Alois Jans, offered their usual helpfulness and expertise. Thanks as well to the staffs of the State Archive in Gent, the City Archive of Gent, and various libraries of the KUL.

I owe special thanks to Jan Roegiers, former librarian and current chair of the history department at the KUL, for arranging financial support, office space, and housing; for his hospitality; for organizing such a memorable walk to Scherpenheuvel; and for his willingness to share his unbounded knowledge of early modern religion and culture. His reading of the manuscript saved me from many errors. I must also single out Michel Cloet, now emeritus, who first welcomed me at the university; Eddy Put, who first showed me around Belgian archives, then became a coauthor, close friend, and the strongest influence on my literary conscience; and Herman van der Wee, who offered insightful suggestions on the manuscript, more Belgian hospitality, and much else. In addition, Johan Verberckmoes, Louis Vos, Steven Vanden Broecke, Jeanine Delandtsheer, Werner Thomas, Eddy Stols, and still others at the KUL have long helped me to feel at home there and offered much important advice. Thanks as well in Belgium to Walter Prevenier, formerly of the University of Gent, and my exemplary and tireless walking companions, Rob Brustens, Jeroen Nilis, and Toon Barten, who helped me to understand pilgrimage better.

On this side of the Atlantic, Brad Gregory and Jodi Bilinkoff went beyond the call of duty and friendship in reading the manuscript and offering crucial corrections and suggestions, for which I offer my deepest thanks. The students of History 485, Miracles in European Christianity, also made valuable comments, both on the manuscript and in our more general discussions of miracles—valuable because I developed this book in part for college students. My sister, Kathryn Richey, contributed several illustrations. Megan Armstrong, Tom Brady, Kendall Brown, Sam Cardon, Karen Carter, Jim Fisher, Jeff Jacklin, Kevin Kenner, Theodore Rabb, Claire Schen, Anne Schutte, Jim Tracy, Becky Richards, the late Herbert Rowen, Erika Rummel, and Larissa Taylor also contributed to this book in various ways, from critiquing the manuscript to writing letters of recommendation to aiding with research to arranging talks to providing ideas and inspiration, often over many years. I thank them one and all.

Thanks last to John Ware for playing so well his role as critical but supportive agent, Trace Murphy at Doubleday for being so enthusiastic about the book, and my family for their usual patient support, tangible and otherwise.

INDEX

Page numbers of illustrations appear in italics

I

J

K

L

M

Also by Craig Harline

Conversions

Two Family Stories from the Reformation and Modern America

This powerful work explores the parallel disruption of two families—one in seventeenth-century Holland, the other in America today—when a beloved family member converts to another religion. Despite different settings and outcomes, their situations involve nearly identical dynamics and heart-wrenching choices. Through the author's deeply informed imagination, the experiences of a seventeenth-century European family are transformed into immediately recognizable terms.

Cloth ISBN 978-0-300-16701-6

"A beautiful and moving book. Harline is a master at narrative and at making the most painstaking research look effortless. These two unconnected stories required very different approaches, yet Harline's writing binds them together with an odd, yet arresting symmetry, overflowing with integrity and insight."—Carlos Eire, Yale University

Sunday

\ History of the First Day from 3abylonia to the Super Bowl

'hrough a fascinating blend of stories and analysis, ıistorian Craig Harline examines Sunday—from :s ancient beginnings among the early Christians ɔ brunch and football in America today.

\ delicious study of Sunday. . . . Fine popular ɔcial history."—*Booklist*

Harline . . . adopts a brilliant day-in-the-life trategy to explore the history of the Christian abbath in various cultures and times. . . . An] engaging and wonderfully written popular istory."—*Publishers Weekly*

Paper ISBN 978-0-300-16703-0

'or more information visit:
'aleBooks.com

Yale UNIVERSITY PRESS

Also by Craig Harline

A Bishop's Tale

Mathias Hovius Among His Flock in Seventeenth-Century Flanders

Craig Harline and Eddy Put

This absorbing book takes us back to the busy, colorful world of a Netherlandish Catholic bishop and his flock from 1589–1620. Based upon the recently discovered daybook of Mathias Hovius, the book focuses not only on his life but also on key events and characters of the period. Episodes in the lives of monks, nuns, pilgrims, peasants, saints, and others bring to life the experience of religion during the Counterreformation.

Paper ISBN 978-0-300-09405-3

"Delightful. . . . I know of no other book which conveys so vividly and, in the end, so reliably, the sheer range and rigor of the Northern European Counter-Reformation in its most militant phase. . . . This book deserves the widest possible readership."
—Eamon Duffy, *Commonwealth*

The Burdens of Sister Margaret

Inside a Seventeenth-Century Convent; Abridged Edition

Based on a treasure trove of letters, this fascinating book tells the history of a seventeenth-century nun in a convent in Leuven and how her complaints—of sexual harassment, fears of demonic possession, alliances among the other sisters against her—led to her banishment from the convent on two occasions. Highly acclaimed when it was first published as a revealing look at female religious life in early modern Europe, the book is now available in an abridged paperbound version with a new preface by the author.

"A window to the past. . . . I loved, just loved, this book."
—Carolyn See, *Washington Post*

Paper ISBN 978-0-300-08121-3

"Better-than-fiction social history. . . . This is a glimpse into diaries, letters, hearts, minds, hatreds, and hopes; it will enthrall."—*Christian Century*

For more information visit:
YaleBooks.com

Yale UNIVERSITY PRESS